AF605822

BODIES IN CHINA

Bodies in China

Philosophy, Aesthetics, Gender, and Politics

Eva Kit Wah Man

State University of New York Press

The Chinese University Press

ISBN: State University of New York Press 978-1-4384-6635-4
ISBN: The Chinese University Press 978-962-996-785-7

Published for North America by:
State University of New York Press, Albany, New York
www.sunypress.edu

Published for the rest of the world by:
The Chinese University Press
The Chinese University of Hong Kong
Sha Tin, N.T., Hong Kong
Fax: +852 2603 7355
E-mail: cup@cuhk.edu.hk
Website: www.chineseupress.com

Printed in Hong Kong

Library of Congress Cataloging-in-Publication Data
Man, Eva Kit Wah
Bodies in China: Philosophy, Aesthetics, Gender, and Politics / Eva Kit Wah Man
ISBN: State University of New York Press 978-1-4384-6635-4 (hardcover : alk. paper)

Library of Congress Control Number: 2016954465

10 9 8 7 6 5 4 3 2 1

CONTENTS

III. Body and Gender Matters

ACKNOWLEDGEMENTS

I am most grateful for the support of my family, of my colleagues at the Department of Humanities and Creative Writing of the Hong Kong Baptist University, and for the assistance of Jason Leung, Dr Gladys Chong, and Vicki Low, who have granted me support and eased my worries and pressure in the writing and the editing process of this book, which has taken up my efforts through the last decade. Finally, I sincerely thank Ye Minlei and Joyce Liu, editors of CUP, for their continuous support and encouragement, and the two anonymous reviewers for their great comments and detailed advice, which have led me to new knowledge horizons. More importantly, they have demonstrated to me what an academic community should be in terms of its professional ethics.

Eva Kit Wah Man

INTRODUCTION

This anthology assembles my research and writings of the past two decades on traditional and current global issues related to Chinese female bodies and gendered bodies in general. The texts and subjects in the book act as cross-references among the chapters, in terms of their materials, sources, and theoretical frameworks. It illustrates several core philosophical issues that overlap, but which are important grounds for comparative research and dialogue among Chinese philosophies, feminist studies, and cross-cultural thoughts around the subject. The interdisciplinary approach also integrates philosophical enquiries with contextual studies throughout the book, which echoes the main agenda of feminist philosophy. As implied in the title, the issues of body are related to philosophical enquiries, aesthetic representation, and gender politics that are simultaneously historical and contextual.

This book discusses new conceptual models that feminist scholars are seriously investigating that might displace dualism and emancipate notions of the body from Cartesian mechanistic models and metaphors. In this light, the various chapter themes of the book review traditional and contemporary alternatives. In the fields of gender, body, and aesthetics, comparative studies that bring in both Western feminist philosophical perspectives and Chinese philosophical discourses deserve much attention. This book seeks to address the meaningful revelations that come about via comparative study and case studies.

Most Western philosophical paradigms are based directly or indirectly on the binary oppositions of rational-irrational, subject-object, nature-culture, form-matter, mind-body, active-passive, and presence-absence that ancient Greek philosophers like Aristotle hinted at, and, above all, on the implications of these binaries on issues of gender, body, and mind. They attribute these oppositions to the establishment of the masculine and rational culture in the West. Philosophical debates and criticisms on these paradigms have hardly looked beyond the West; therefore, in this book, I want to reflect on Chinese philosophy in the above discussions. Some of the questions I seek to address include: Does Confucianism rule out the capacity of women as moral subjects and hence as aesthetic subjects? Do forms of Chinese philosophy in some ways contribute or correspond to the patriarchal Confucian culture? In terms of patriarchal values, the situation in Chinese philosophy is similar to and at the same time different from that of the West. This book explicates these differences via case studies under historical and cultural contexts. It explores whether Chinese philosophy is able to provide sources or frames of reference for the development of alternative perspectives sought by Western feminist scholars.

I also aim to address, demonstrate, and offer perspectives that may provide alternative models in some of the key debates on gender, body, and aesthetics. The findings revealed in these case studies tell of paradigm shifts and fundamental differences, making the dialogue between Chinese philosophy and Western feminist philosophy immensely interesting and tricky. The overall objective of this book project is to engage Chinese philosophy as a critical intervention for reframing the existing scholarship on gender issues and aesthetics.

I found a lot of wisdom in a range of feminist philosophies of the body—also limitations. The discourses begin with Plato, who proposed dualisms of form-matter and of mind-body, and who asserted that the body interferes with, and is a danger to, the operations of reason. Plato believed that man is a spiritual or non-corporeal being trapped in the body, the *soma*. His discourse on the *hypodoche* is considered as one on materiality, that when nature receives form as a sensible object, *her* proper function is to receive, take, accept, welcome, include, and even comprehend. *She* has no proper shape and is not a body. The receptacle principle, which applies universally, is then associated with the female, which is constructed as a nonthematizable materiality, but which never resembles either the formative principle or what it creates. This element of sensuous and passionate corporeality enables philosophers to maintain the essential "neutrality" of the mind while allowing individual and sexual differences.

I purposely divide my writing into three sections in this book. The first section, "Body Discourses in Chinese Philosophy," contains philosophical discussion on body and mind. I bring in theoretical and philosophical discussion of Western traditions such as those of Plato, Descartes, and Kant to examine their views on body and mind and how the Chinese philosophical ideas offered by Confucians and Daoists provide alternative body ontologies for critical feminist practices.

The second section, "Body Aesthetics and Art," reviews female aesthetic representations in classical traditional Chinese works ranging from *The Book of Songs*, women's embroidery, sexuality and suggested ways of kissing, and contemporary body art as represented by the controversial body artist He Chengyao. These chapters demonstrate the intertwining relationships among body, sexuality, aesthetics, and ascribed gendered roles in social environments. Here, my writing widely discusses, with concrete examples, concepts of *yin*, *yang*, and *qi* in scholarly studies of the body, gendered roles, art, and aesthetics. I particularly add in this section the environmental aesthetics developed by Arnold Berleant and compare it to a Chinese garden. The discussion takes the bodily experience of the subject and the interaction between the subject and her environment as a core part of the aesthetic experience. The Deweyan model is revisited for comparative purposes.

The third section, "Body and Gender Matters," aims to unfold the changing perceptions of femininity from imperial to contemporary China. The first two case studies touch on female body ideals in the literary fantasies of the late Ming, in the iron girls of Communist China, and in the Olympics hoopla of the Beijing Olympics in 2008. These case studies are compiled in two parts, making a developmental perspective possible. This section also includes a psychoanalytic perspective, bearing the agenda that mind and body are interactively related. The case study is about the first application, by Pan Guangdan in the 1920s, of Freudian psychoanalysis to the female literatus Feng Xiaoqing 馮小青 (1595–1612). The discussion then extends to the relations among mental illness, bodily weakness, and physical sickness. The section also discusses Hong Kong women's fashion in the 1960s after the political riots of 1967 and under strong British colonial rule. It tells once again true stories of the ways that women's bodies were shaped by colonial politics. Finally, the subject of sex and emotion in the development of the ethical discourse on Chinese female sex workers from the late Qing to the present day is discussed, which looks at body and gender matters in a topic that has seldom been examined. This section discusses the global economy, which has great impacts on notions of female beauty today. Regardless of the multicultural and historical factors in its formation and construction processes, the global economy brings homogenizing tendencies in women's fashion and standards of appearance. But contestation over contemporary female beauty within the turbulent modern history of China deserves consideration in all its particularities, including in the policies and regulations posed by the state, treating the female body as an apparatus.

I use certain methodologies throughout this anthology to draw coherent themes from among all the case studies. In Chapter 1, "Contemporary Feminist Body Theories and Mencius' Ideas of Body and Mind," I touch on basic Confucian body discourses that are well articulated in Mencius' ideas of the body and mind and refer to the fact that numerous feminist philosophers and biologists have been trying to destabilize the notion of "biological sex." The return to biological essentialism is strongly contested, since "physical experiences" do not make gender, but rather the specific social regulatory ideals by which female bodies are trained and formed do.

In this chapter, I first examine the Western philosophical concepts of corporeality, starting with Plato and Descartes. I then discuss how the works of Spinoza and Merleau-Ponty may offer understandings of body and mind that challenge the Cartesian body-mind dualism. Yet, as informed by Elizabeth Grosz's critique, new concepts of corporeality that go beyond the regime of dualism still need to be developed. In view of this, I propose looking at Confucian philosophy, especially Mencius' ideas of body and mind, to see if it can offer a form of ontology and metaphysics that complements the effort of Western feminist philosophers. This is followed by a comparative analysis of both philosophical traditions. I conclude by arguing that Mencius' ideas of mind and body can initiate a radical rethinking of the connection among reason, body, and ethical-political issues that enables feminists to develop alternative models of corporeality.

In investigating if Mencius' ideas constitute a body ontology useful for critical feminist practices, the answer is mixed, as it is difficult to tell whether Mencius' body is gendered. But if we examine his work in its historical and cultural contexts, taking the Confucian patriarchal society into account, the sage or "great man" or "superior man" would appear to refer to men only. Since women in the Confucian tradition are viewed as feeble in terms of their moral capabilities, it is said that they need to be educated and controlled, otherwise they might upset the patriarchal social order. Female bodies are dangerous and threatening since they can be seductive, leading men to excessive sexual desire or socially deviant behavior; however, women's behavior can be beneficial to men under Confucian regulation, or if they act according to the instructions of the Daoist theories of sexuality. In translations of and commentaries on Mencius, his usage of "man" and "he" to indicate the human is a hint that Mencius' body is gendered as a male body. Second, ideologically speaking, the identification of women with materiality that feminists have pointed out to be feminine-oriented may also be detected in Mencius' work. The small components that Mencius refers to could be interpreted as the material and ontological bases—that is, the "female" side—of human existence. They are aligned with the "receiving" principle, waiting passively for the form-giving process and for moral imperatives—both activities supervised by the mind. The Western binary of passion-reason seems to correspond to that of vital force-moral will in Mencius, also in that the former should follow the latter in order to attain a harmonious humanity.

Despite the associations we make within the social, historical, and ideological contexts of Mencius, the binary structure is the main question that remains. Are Mencius' ideas of the body the same as the mind-body binary of which Western feminists are critical? The Confucian cosmological model cannot be said to be the same, yet the texts seem to have separated vital force and will, *ming* 命 and *xing* 性, emphasizing in every respect the superiority of the latter over the former. The chapter finally turns to *I-Ching*, the basic text on Confucian cosmology, and to the notions of *yin* and *yang*. The revelation is that the *yin* (the female principle-force-aspect, representing the receptive and the potential) and the *yang* (the male principle-force-aspect, representing the creative and the actual), as well as the difference and differentiation of things that are aligned with the interaction of the two, do not exhibit any real opposition or antagonism in Chinese philosophy. They are only opposite insofar as they are complementary. There is neither tension nor hostility between these terms.

I quote Cheng Chung-ying saying that, according to the Chinese cosmological paradigm illustrated in *I-Ching*, the world is a process of change and development, moving toward unity and a state of holistic harmonization. The appearance of discrepancy, imperfection, conflict, contradiction, or struggle is seen as a manifestation of the incomplete sub-processes of the interaction of polarities. Conflicts can be avoided if one strives to conform to human nature (*xing*) by cultivating one's understanding and by adjusting one's action properly. This adjustment is a process of harmonization. To conclude, according to the metaphysics of harmony and conflict in the *I-Ching*, antagonism calls for a moral and practical transformation of humans. One wonders whether we can hope and relax when we consider the Chinese patriarchal suppression of women, accepting this condition as an artificial, contextual, and political practice that Confucian spirituality and moral philosophy can help to transcend? Western feminists might find the *yin-yang* polarity useful, including the mutual generative and destructive modes described in the *I-Ching*, with their contrary and complementary qualities. At least, the principles of holistic unity and organic balance are meaningful ideas distinct from the mechanical-atomistic model of which feminists are critical. It is in these senses that Mencius' ideas of mind and body may initiate a radical rethinking of the connections among reason, the body, and ethical-political issues.

The discussion in this book also touches on aesthetics from time to time, which helps a great deal in laying the ground of the comparative study of body matters. In Chapter 2, "Chinese Philosophy and the Suggestion of a Matriarchal Aesthetics," which deals with the critique of binary oppositions in Western philosophy, I introduce a model of matriarchal aesthetics, as suggested by Heide Göttner-Abendroth, and discuss it in the light of Chinese philosophy. Göttner-Abendroth sets out principles of a matriarchal aesthetics that might provide us with a recent paradigm of feminist aesthetics. The chapter summarizes the principles of matriarchal art, which is in the form of magic and diversity in unity. It is like mythology, which exists as a fundamental category of human understanding. It argues that the universal, objective nature of the structure of matriarchal art mentioned prevents the identification from becoming subjective sentimentality, for it cannot be objectified but is a complex, whole process. The interesting thing is that matriarchal art involves the physical and mental possibilities of communicating with Nature by means of symbolic acts. We should learn to adapt ourselves to Nature, which includes our bodies and our immediate environment. The joy and delight thereby released may be traced back to the harmonious correlation of a change in Nature with a spiritual change in ourselves, a new form of living.

It is under these aspects that matriarchal aesthetics is raised as a useful comparison with Chinese aesthetics. Despite the notion that systematic aesthetics is absent from traditional Confucian and Daoist philosophies, contemporary neo-Confucian scholars such as Mou Zongsan and Tang Junyi have reconstructed theories of human primal experience according to traditional Confucianism and Daoism, which allude to aesthetic experience. In one of his last writings, the translation and critique of Kant's *Critique of Judgement*, Mou presents and recommends the theory of Daoist intellectual intuition, which is aesthetics in nature. First, he points out that the subjective principle of Daoism is *wu wei* (no action), which refers to the effort of the human mind to transcend all kinds of human epistemological functions and move towards the realm of the metaphysical Dao. Daoist philosophy promotes the annulments of human activity and knowledge to recover the presentation of Nature in itself, which has been hidden and distorted by human understanding, perception, and conception. According to Daoism, to know is to not-know, to be wise is to be ignorant; only so-called fools are able to grasp the truth of Nature. Tang Junyi introduces his "host and guest" relation to describe the relationship between things and the mind in the human primal experience, in contrast with the subject-and-object relation in Western theories of knowledge, in which subjects dominate and objects subordinate. According to Tang, the objectification of the mind takes place only after the primal experience, which he describes as "the totality of intuition." His understanding of the experience is actually quite similar to that of Mou.

My suggestion is that, while we can find many similarities between the principles of a matriarchal aesthetics and those of Chinese philosophy, there are points of comparison that we should consider. One of these is that aesthetic experience in both takes place as a fundamental, principal process that provides a "pre-existing inner structure" prior to the objectification process. It demands that our body and mind should adapt to Nature, which includes our immediate environment, leading to the harmonious correlation of change in Nature with spiritual change in ourselves.

The comparison of feminist aesthetics with Chinese aesthetics shows that this area of cross-cultural philosophical dialogue might present scholars working in aesthetics, Western or Chinese, with promising directions for further research. One area that clearly needs more exploration is the comparison (metaphysical and experiential) of the myth/ritual complexes of archaic peoples, to which the feminist paradigm refers, with what we find in Daoist texts. More importantly, this investigation does not deny that there are patriarchal forms and institutions in the Chinese tradition but begins to look at that tradition for resources that might deconstruct the patriarchy.

There is a recent call to reclaim the body and reposition its locus and nature of identity in Western circles of academic and artistic expression. Body theories and body art have become topics of attention in addition to relevant philosophical discussions. Chapter 3 looks at the issue from a comparative perspective, focusing on representative cases in Chinese and Western portrait painting. It first discusses Francis Bacon's work on human bodies, identifying the latter's philosophical and psychological locus. It then outlines the Confucian discourses of the body and related metaphysical grounds, and their revelations for traditional Chinese portrait painting. A Chinese portrait such as that of Gu Kaizhi is introduced and compared with that illustrated by Bacon. In the comparison, the following questions are addressed: How are body discourses related to different bodily expressions? In what ways do Confucian ideas of the body shed light on the recent discussion on reclaiming the body in the West? Are the dichotomies of mind and body resolved in the Confucian tradition? Can active engagement via the process of reworking artwork create new possibilities of bodily expression?

Most human expressions in Gu's work are restrained and delicate; there are few extremes of either emotion or gesture, and the figures seem to combine humanness with a certain ethereal quality. The depiction of human subjects is characterized by its naiveté and its humanistic spirit. This chapter, based on the main theoretical ground of the book, recaps Mencius' theory that the mind is the noblest and greatest component of the body. It is more than simply physical because of its moral consciousness or innate knowledge of goodness. This explains why Gu's portraiture emphasizes the subject's head and face, particularly the eye or pupil, which he believes can speak for the subject's soul or spirit. In comparison, Bacon's subjects are associated with "exhilarated despair," sexuality, and violence, seeming to violate the moral norms of his times. His figures show the "shattering of the subject" or the replacement of a unified self by a fragmented self, which has been read as "loss of self" with psychoanalytic implications. Gu's subjects assert a moral self in his delicate and linear style. The works of Bacon and Gu belong to different cultures in different times, yet can we go further and ask how the recovery of the body in contemporary Western discourse can learn from Confucian theories of the body?

Confucians discuss the body as something ontological and natural, as do some theories in the Western tradition. However, contemporary discourses stress that the difference does not have to do with biological "facts," so much as with the manner in which culture marks bodies and creates the specific conditions in which they live and recreate themselves. The marking is within the operation of various forms of power relations through languages or signifying practices. Chapter 3 revisits Moira Gatens's observation, that what is crucial in our current context is the thorough interrogation of the means by which bodies become invested with difference. The revelation of this study, through traditional and cultural review, is on the model of construction whereby the social acts on the natural, as well as the claim that there is no reference to a pure body that is not at the same time a further formation of the body.

In Section Two, the book focuses on traditional and contemporary Chinese exemplary studies, which includes female body representations in *The Book of Songs*, traditional Chinese embroidery, discourses of kissing, contemporary female body art, and Chinese gardens. Chapter 4 examines the pre-Qin Confucian text of *The Book of Songs* as an important source for the early discussion of feminine ideals in Chinese women's history. It first reviews the discussion on feminine ideals by referring to representative cases or stories described in the source. It then classifies the kinds and modalities of female bodily ideals involved in the songs' gendered narratives, social and political representations, and common human qualities. The chapter seeks to investigate the relations of these recommended ideals with situation ethics; gendered notions of "inner" and "outer beauty"; "love and marriage"; and eros and sexuality. It summarizes the multiple modalities of female bodily ideals suggested in this early literary source.

Among the lines of the songs, we can see that female beauty (*meiren*) in classical Chinese referred to the femaleness, skin color, and erotic qualities of a woman, which include bodily beauty, limb shape, make up, color of dress, and so on, appealing to all the senses. Yet it is the vitality of the body that counts, and also sexual sensations, especially heterosexual ones. These sensations are grounded on male desire, fantasies, and devotion through the notion of beauty, which later departed from physiological and sexual considerations and went into further cultural and normative constraints. The reading interestingly reveals that one should not put moral discourse over the daring emotional and erotic expressions in the ancient text. They are there to be explored and act as valuable sources for the discussion of Chinese female ideals. I suggest that they form the map of a lost female horizon.

Chapter 5 examines women's handicraft, which has shaped Chinese women's physical and emotional life through history. I chose embroidery as a subject of study as it is often associated with and identified as a feminine practice in the history of China. I examine how the practice of embroidery enabled women to be subjects of artistic expression and helped construct their social identities and value systems. The chapter begins with a brief historical development of women's embroidery in China, followed by an examination of the intertwining relationship between this form of handicraft and women's lives. The creation of embroidery represented and fulfilled the Confucian gender and hierarchical roles of women as wives, mothers, and teachers of daughters. The chapter then discusses the extent to which embroidery was a medium of expression and how its creation gave women value as talented subjects. I argue that embroidery as women's art is equivalent to reputable elite male cultural practices like painting, calligraphy, and composition in imperial China. Yet different meanings emerge in contemporary China regarding women's embroidery skills, which have been revived as new forms of production.

The popularity of the work of fashion designer Vivienne Tam is my favorite example of how Chinese embroidery has become a sought-after fashion symbol. I argue that, by creatively developing new aesthetic styles, the self-Orientalizing technique of fashion designers nowadays succeeds in battling the negative stereotypes commonly associated with the Oriental Other. Tam's East-meets-West design incorporates exotic, traditional, and mysterious Chinese elements with new and modern edges, but it is also gendered. She often mixes brocade and embroidery with experimental, modern elements like leather and fake fur, producing what she describes as an "eccentric approach to Orientalism" and femininity. On the one hand, the Orient itself is an Other passively being gazed at by the West. On the other hand, now the Orient gazes back. Tam's fashion work brings out a new femininity in traditional Chinese women's embroidery work, which does not only create a successful market space, but also reconstructs cultural and gender expressions in terms of aesthetics. It is a notable contemporary attempt to show traditional ornamental art in the making, the political and commercial meanings of which are more than female creativity and physical constraints.

Yet besides literary depiction and handicraft, body matters manifest even more explicitly in norms of sexuality. I therefore explore the subject of kissing in China in Chapter 6, a theme that has not been commonly investigated. Kissing in different cultural contexts may signify respect, social ritual, friendship, romantic feeling, passionate love, sexual temptation, and momentary or eternal happiness. Kissing in China, however, has been taken specifically as a form of sexual behavior. Traditionally, the act was restricted to the private space of the bedchamber, which explains why eighteenth- and nineteenth-century Western visitors to China left no record of the Chinese kissing each other in public. I point out that, for a long time in China, there was no specific word in Chinese for kissing; very few public discussions relate it to the art of the bedchamber. In sum, Chapter 6 examines kissing in China as a form of eroticism by deploying traditional points of view and by examining its depiction in the late Qing under Western influence, as well as describing it in its contemporary social context.

To continue the exploration of the body in arts and aesthetics, I choose the body work of Chinese female artist He Chengyao as a case study in Chapter 7. There is a political agenda under the contemporary Chinese context in her extreme bodily art work and performances. I focus on the artist's works of the early 2000s, during which she produced more than twenty works of body art with reference to real family histories and national political traumas in contemporary China. My approach is based on both cultural and cross-cultural perspectives, which aim to demonstrate the artistic function and political agenda of the extreme expression of pain and of the emotional "scars" in these works. This is a subject of gender and art; I also contrast the female body in He's work with those in the beauty industries of the contemporary Chinese economic context. The brief survey of body art in China here echoes Amelia Jones's reading that body art is one of the most dramatic and radical types of culture production. It is certain that the extreme expression of the work of He has incorporated Socialist, family, and gender peculiarities in subversive and accusational gestures. The boldness, roughness, and violence perpetrated on the female body are demonstrations of body politics; the juxtaposition of the bodies of He's mother and her son pose significant readings of political history. The liberation of Chinese bodies and their public showing in the artist's work refer to notions of freedom and captivity.

Chapter 8 is a philosophical reflection on and a comparative study of Arnold Berleant's recent work on nature and habitation in Chinese gardens. It reviews Berleant's notes on the subject and object relation, bodily reaction, and the aesthetic experience that evolves in the environment of a Chinese garden. His reading of Nature and physical habitation in a Chinese garden is examined, and compared with the related comprehension of contemporary Confucian scholar Tang Junyi. In his influential work, *The Spiritual Values of Chinese Culture*, Tang proposes a metaphysical manifestation in the design of traditional Chinese architecture and gardens, and in the interactive relation between man and Nature. The comparative notes in the chapter expand the reading of Berleant, suggested by Tang's bodily notions of "hiding," "cultivating," "resting," and "wandering" in a Chinese garden. Parallel correspondences between the two readings invite comparative aesthetic and critical responses.

Berleant claims that Daoism is key to understanding the Chinese scholar's garden, that its philosophy functions as a pervasive perceptual presence and cognitive undertone. He also considers the Chinese garden as a landscape that represents the Daoist idea of *wu wei* (no action), mentioned previously and a key theme throughout this book. Tang relates the Daoist idea of wandering the ground to the aesthetics of the gardens, as it integrates the physical freedom of the body with the metaphysical transcendence of the mind. I use my visit to Geyuan Garden in Yangzhou as a case study that demonstrates perfectly Berleant's observation and shows that all of the elements and parts of the garden are designed to blend gently together to show the harmonious forces of Nature. In his words, to experience landscape aesthetics is "to (let the body) follow the Dao of Nature, getting oneself in tune with the underlying rhythms of the seasons, the plants, the very universe, so that there was no discrepancy between inner being and outer reality." I could see a lot of correspondences between Berleant's landscape aesthetics and Chinese aesthetics, which supplement and enrich each other in different languages.

In Section Three, I research Chinese female body aesthetics, and relate politics to the development of ideals of female beauty (*meiren*) in China in two historical parts in chapters 9 and 10, where I address the following two overlapping issues: first, how can the related discourses and developments can be understood within the particular historical and cultural context in China and how can it be related to various factors such as economic and political situations? Second, with man as the speaking subject in the Chinese patriarchal system, how do male imaginations (especially those represented by the literati) construct the ideals and the aesthetic qualities of women's bodies as the projection of their wishes or regrets and also as the production of the various forms of their fantasies?

I discuss the first issue in Chapter 9, where I introduce the philosophical discussion of female beauty in the Chinese tradition. I then follow with a contextual study of the development and construction of feminine ideals in the courtesan culture of late imperial China. I illustrate how the notion of female beauty is redefined and represented by male literati under certain political and economic changes in China. In Chapter 10, I discuss the second issue by extending the study to the contemporary notion of female beauty in Communist China, which has departed from tradition to follow the capitalist and cosmopolitan West.

The global economy obviously has had a homogenizing impact on the notion of female beauty today, regardless of multicultural and historical factors. But when the issue of contemporary female beauty in China is brought up, its contestation within the turbulent modern history of China deserves serious consideration, together with the policies and regulations imposed by the state. I suggest in Chapter 10 certain factors that have been constant in the contemporary discourses of Chinese female beauty. It correlates the discourses of female beauty in twentieth-century China to the three cultural phases set by historians: the "enlightening period" from 1919 to 1949; the "degradation period" from 1949 to 1978; and the "awakening period" from 1978 to 2000. The chapter looks at the discourses on female beauty and the built-in political burdens and social implications of these phases, discussing how they have been developed through related cultural, political, and economic discourses. The writing collects resulting historical images of Chinese women and studies their representations. The discussion covers, for contrast and reflection, the *jianmei* women of the 1930s, the "iron ladies" of the Socialist regime, and the "Olympic girls" during the 2008 Beijing Games.

The study concludes with a review of the making of the "Olympics girls." The 2008 Summer Olympic Games held in Beijing produced new forms of female beauty. These female students dream of being Olympics volunteers, frequenting English-language training centers, gyms, and beauty parlors. Tough stories of these young girls are reported in the media, referring to the embodiment of a new self that is not only historically and culturally specific, but also tailor-made as a form of national pride. I conclude that, while the "Olympic girl" is another process of normalization in the history of China, one may query the origins of the ideas and the reasons she has become the standard of female beauty representing China today. It is obvious that certain representations of bodies have been appropriated and incorporated from tradition, yet they have also been seriously reduced to and designed for the international and global imaginations of "Chinese beauties." The making of Olympic girls can also be read as an updated "domestication of cosmopolitanism." Through tailor-made female bodily construction, this new development is negotiating for a place in the world, loaded with desires for a global recognition of wealth, resources, and the pride of the state.

Psychoanalysis and women's psychopathology in feudal China is a vital issue aligned with the subject of this section. Chapter 11 introduces, analyzes, and reviews the first application in China of psychoanalysis, in the case study of a female literatus of the fifteenth century. The study was conducted in 1922 by Pan Guangdan 潘光旦 (1899–1967) on the writer Feng Xiaoqing. It first describes Pan's diagnosis of the woman's mental illness and his appropriation of the concepts of psychoanalysis, which was new to China at the time. It further discusses Sigmund Freud's psychoanalytical model and the theory of narcissism, as understood by Pan, and reviews the application of that understanding to the historical context of China in the 1920s, an era in which Western modernization was seen as a model for national progress. It then turns to an examination of Pan's observations on the living situation of women in feudal China, and the implications for sex education in his own era. It concludes with a reassessment of Pan's views in light of recent feminist critiques, particularly criticism of Freud's narcissistic theory and psychoanalysis as a whole, and views on related gender issues in contemporary feminist psychotherapy.

The more important finding is the psychopathological situation of numerous late Qing women literati. Their mental state, as a result of creating and living in the repressive feudal, patriarchal social situation and structure, is found to be pathological. They are also often diagnosed with tuberculosis and other respiratory diseases. Pan's psychoanalytical reading is that these diseases are the result of sexual repression, resulting in mental imbalance and physical weakness. Pan's meticulous case study of Xiaoqing was the first of its kind in China; it paved the way for gender studies, women's histories, and reflections on the sexual history and psychology of women in China.

As in many Western countries, the 1960s in Hong Kong was a restless period during which tremendous political, economic, and cultural changes occurred. The dominance of fashion in women's lives calls for more attention than the usual feminist questions concerning consumerism and the subordination of women, as fashion should also be regarded as a locus of struggle for identity. Searching for a new female identity via fashion in the 1960s in Hong Kong, which led the modernist trend in East Asia during that era, may be read as a response to the friction between the Eastern colonized and the Western colonizer, between the traditional and the modern, and between the backwardness of China and the advancement of Hong Kong, in both political and cultural dimensions. Chapter 12 conducts a parallel reading of Hong Kong women's fashion and the social and political tensions of the city in the 1960s, when women's fashion attempted to integrate all the various prevailing forces by eclectically combining traditional Chinese styles with current Western trends, and while women remained rather conservative in their ways of thinking. Life before and during the 1960s in Hong Kong is examined and the ways of women dressing and fashion languages are reviewed and compared with the European vogue of the time. Women in the British colony projected their self-images and fantasies onto fashion models, who from time to time appeared fast, carefree, naughty, sharp, discriminating, balanced, easygoing, sophisticated, coquettish, serious, ingenuous, and so on.

While the majority of women in the city were housewives, students, factory workers, and social and family dependents, they gradually began to receive better education and job opportunities and to gain financial independence. They enjoyed more social activities and therefore demanded fashions to express their new identities. Roland Barthes suggests the multiplication of persons in a single being is considered by fashion as an index of power.[1] This may be considered as one of the reasons for the popularity of fashion in Hong Kong in the1960s, a time when women in the colony were building their power via bodily representation, while fashion ceased in Communist China and little was developed in Taiwan and other overseas Chinese communities. The analysis in this chapter refers to Homi K. Bhabha's insight, that in the postcolonial period women can utilize their peripheral position to challenge ideologies in the center. It demonstrates that fashion facilitated this challenge in 1960s Hong Kong as it threatened the feudal Chinese constraints on women by liberating their bodies via fashionable dress; presented the idea of deviating from a backward Communist China by portraying modern Western designs; and held a submissive attitude towards the British government by choosing rebellious ways of dress and gesture in the colonial city.

The last chapter of the book, Chapter 13, explores exchanges of sex and emotion between Chinese female sex workers and clients in Hong Kong and related developments in the cosmopolitan context. It refers to discourses found in oral history and scattered written notes among the handbooks of sex workers in late Qing China. These rare sources review the intimate relationship among prostitution agents in recent Chinese history, as well as the legends and folk stories that act as educational codes of behavior and attitude held toward customers. Most of the instructions are around issues of care and abandonment based on Confucian moral ideas. These pictures are different from the depiction of the relationships between prostitutes and their customers in Hong Kong cinema, which are associated mainly with supply and demand, violence and power, demonstrating direct commercial exchanges in a consumer society. This chapter reviews the traditional discussion on *qing* 情 (emotion) and *yi* 義 (righteousness), and the notion of *li* 禮 (propriety) in prostitution in China. The Confucian discourses reveal notions of sex and emotion that go beyond the customer and client relationship, echoing famous examples in Chinese literature and folklore as well as scenes in early Chinese cinema at the turn of the twentieth century. It is interesting to see the changes undergone in the representation of these complicated relationships in Hong Kong cinema from the 1970s onward, which play on sadistic elements in the rapid growth of the capitalistic society. I also refer to the recent documentaries on sex workers in Hong Kong. The investigation is interdisciplinary in its approach; it reads the subject from philosophical, historical, literary, cinematic studies, and postcolonial perspectives and contributes to a subject seldom studied, relating Chinese bodies to emotion, mind, and values.

Section I

BODY DISCOURSES IN CHINESE PHILOSOPHY

1

CONTEMPORARY FEMINIST BODY THEORIES AND MENCIUS' IDEAS OF BODY AND MIND

Contemporary Feminist Reading of the "Ontological" Body

Feminist philosophers and biologists have been trying to destabilize the notion of "biological sex." For example, Judith Butler famously argues that the body positioned as prior to the sign is always "posited" or "signified" as "prior" and "precedes" its own action. If this is so, then there should not be a mimetic or representational status of language or signs that follow bodies—as the body is only signified as prior to signification.[1] The positing process also constitutes and conditions the "materiality" of the body. She states that what enables this positing is a problematic gendered matrix that ontologizes and fixes the "irreducible" materiality into a bunch of taken-for-granted discourses on sex and sexuality.[2]

We can sketch at least a few ways in which these discourses are conducted. First, as Irigaray argues, in as much as a distinction between form and matter is offered within phallogocentrism, there is an exclusion of the "female." Within the masculine-female (form-matter) binary, the masculine in fact occupies both poles, and the female is not an intelligible term. Irigaray further argues that the "female" is articulated through a further materiality acting as the impossible necessity that enables any ontology.[3] Second, aside from philosophy, the binding, forming, and deforming of gendered bodies through social prohibitions and the so-called cultural intelligibility criteria of sex also constitute and regulate the fields of bodies. According to Moira Gatens, the body politic uses the human body as its image, model, or metaphor. The body politic uses one type of body (male) to signify various items: diverse bodies; the opposition of the "self" to others; and many forms of oppressive ideologies. Now all human bodies are part of these systems of exchange, identification, and mimesis.[4] In addition, medical discourses have so far maintained the hegemony of heteropolarity by mapping differences onto bodies that illustrate gender, thereby eliding Foucault's suggestion of sociopolitical construction of bodies under particular kinds of needs and desires.[5]

Gatens concludes that the recent question is: how does culture construct the body so that it is understood as a biological given?[6] The history of the representation of anatomical differences between man and woman is independent of the actual structure of organs or of what was known about them. Ideologies determined how bodies were seen and which differences would matter.[7] Therefore, a re-evaluation of the importance of the body is conducted in wider arenas, not merely within feminist social theory, but in terms of the analysis of class, culture, and consumption.

Cultural Construction of Female Bodily Existence

How does the above increase our understanding of how the female body is constructed? The return to biological essentialism is strongly contested, since "physical experiences" do not make someone a woman, but rather the specific social regulatory ideals by which female bodies are trained and formed. We can at least include in our consideration the categories of economy, politics, heterosexuality, philosophy, and subject-and-object relations. Economically, Judith Butler points out, the female must be the subordinate term in the binary opposition of masculine-female for that economy to operate.[8] Politically, women are constructed as incapable of performing military service and therefore incapable of defending the political body from attack. This is sufficient to exclude them from active citizenship. The neutral body assumed by the liberal state is implicitly a masculine body.[9] The worst social operation is to treat a woman's speech and her behavior as hysterical (rooted in the Greek word *hystera*, meaning uterus), thereby confining women to the biological. Philosophically, Moira Gatens argues that traditional philosophical conceptions of corporeality are counterproductive to the attempt to construct an autonomous conception of women's bodies. In our culture, every woman is normatively defined as the opposite and complement of man.[10]

It is interesting to read the philosophical metaphors for women's bodies proposed by contemporary philosophers. Iris Young has summarized Simon de Beauvoir's account of woman's existence in the world as a tension between immanence and transcendence.[11] Influenced by Merleau-Ponty's account of the "normal" relationship between human bodies and their environment in actions, Young states that bodily action in the world is commonly distinguished by three features: "ambiguous transcendence," "inhibited intentionality," and "discontinuous unity." Young suggests that women often "live" their bodies in "ambiguous transcendence": transcendence in the sense that the lived body continuously calls forth capacities applied to the world that women used to refrain from using. Female bodily existence is an "inhibited intentionality" that simultaneously reaches toward a projected end with an "I can" and withholds its full bodily commitment to that end in a self-imposed "I cannot." "Discontinuous unity" is inspired by Merleau-Ponty's suggestion that in the enactment of intentions, the body is not an object in itself, but for women, there is a sense that the body is indeed a "subject" as well as an "object." The female body is the object of the gaze of others and an object frequently experienced as limited and limiting. Young said it is important to recognize the specific and historically changing forms of restrictions that have been placed on the women's movement, including such things as restrictive clothing and constricting conventions about female deportment and demeanor. She said that these modalities do not remain constant but are culturally variable, subject to changing circumstances and lifestyle. These restrictions have even acted as a guide to (and prescription for) women's mental health; the very pursuit of the physical standards imposed may actually cause depression, low self-esteem, eating disorders, and, generally, poor mental health.[12]

Traditional Western Philosophies Re-examined

In this first chapter, I am interested in the traditional philosophical conceptions of corporeality that Gatens has cited. Feminist scholars usually begin with Plato, who proposed the dualisms of form-matter and mind-body, and who asserted that the body interferes with, and is a danger to, the operations of reason. He claimed that the word for body (*soma*) was introduced by Orphic priests, who believed that man is a spiritual or noncorporeal being trapped in the body, the *soma*. His discourse on the *hypodoche* is considered as one on materiality, that when nature receives form as a sensible object, "her" proper function is to receive, take, accept, welcome, include, and even comprehend. "She" has no proper shape and is not a body. The receptacle principle, which applies universally, is then associated with the female, which is constructed as a non-thematizable materiality, but which never resembles either the formative principle or what it creates. Hence, as the receptacle, the female is a nonliving, shapeless non-thing, which cannot even be named, leading to the prohibition of the female body as a human form.[13]

The consequent social implications to both women and corporeality are thus often negative, and function conceptually to undergird culturally valued terms such as reason, civilization, and progress. In Gatens's analysis, many philosophers have seen the soul or mind as sexually neutral; the apparent differences among minds are generally seen to be due to the influence of the passions of the body. This element of sensuous and passionate corporeality enables philosophers to maintain the essential neutrality of the mind while allowing for individual and sexual differences. The most superior minds are said to suffer least from the intrusions of the body.[14] Gatens further points out that this dualist notion of the body involves an implicit alignment between women and irrationality. The ideal conception of the rational is, in other words, articulated in direct opposition to qualities typical of the female.[15]

René Descartes is another philosopher of which many feminists are critical. He distinguishes two kinds of substances, a thinking substance (*res cogitans*, mind) and an extended substance (*res extensa*, body), believing that the latter is governed by physical laws and ontological exigencies, while the mind has no place in the natural world. These distinctions have placed the mind in a position of hierarchical superiority over and above nature, including the nature of the body. The critical questions of feminists about Cartesianism include: How can something that inhabits space affect or be affected by something that is non-spatial? How can consciousness ensure the body's movements, its receptivity to conceptual demands and requirements? How can the body inform the mind of its needs and wishes? How is bilateral communication possible?[16] Cartesianism is also criticized as a form of reductionism, denying any interaction between mind and body, instead focusing on the actions of either one of the binary terms at the expense of the other.

Feminist scholars identify at least three lines of investigation of the body in contemporary thought that may be regarded as legacies of the Cartesian view, which treat the body as primarily an object: in the natural sciences, particularly for the life sciences, biology, and medicine; as an instrument or a machine at the disposal of consciousness or allocating an animating, willful subjectivity; and as a vehicle of expression of private thoughts and feelings, that is, as fundamentally passive and transparent.[17] Another consequence of Cartesian dualism is that the male-female opposition has been closely allied with that of mind-body. The conventional reading is that the mind is equivalent to the masculine, and the body to the feminine, excluding women as possible subjects of knowledge. By implication, women's bodies are presumed to be incapable of men's achievements, being weaker, more prone to (hormonal) irregularities, intrusions, and unpredictabilities.[18]

Towards An Open-Ended Ontology

Recently, feminist scholars have seriously sought a new conceptual model that can displace Cartesian dualism and that can emancipate notions of the body from Cartesian mechanistic models and metaphors. In this light, we review traditional and contemporary alternatives.

Some suggest as an alternative the writings of Baruch Spinoza, whose monism is a revision of Cartesian dualism. In Spinoza, there is a multivalent ontology that has been neglected in Anglo-American philosophy.[19] For Spinoza, matter and mind emerge from one underlying process—or *substantia*—that is materially grounded in extension but is also absolute and infinite, and at the same time has mental attributes. Mind and body emerge from—and belong to—the same substance. One reading of Spinoza's monism is that the body is not part of passive nature ruled by an active mind but rather that the body is the inseparable terrain of human action. In contrast to the philosophical traditions mentioned, the mind is constituted by the affirmation of the actual existence of the body, which enables the activity of reason. Activity should be understood as participation in a situation that, instead of being dominated by the mind, depends on the body's character, manner, and context. Feminists recognize Spinoza's account of the body as a process. The body's meaning and capabilities will vary according to its context; its limits and possibilities can be revealed only by its ongoing interactions with its environment.[20]

As Gatens suggests, the implication of Spinoza's model is that—in contrast to the essentialist position—its non-mechanical and non-dichotomized view of nature and culture could acknowledge the cultural and historical specificity of bodies. What Spinoza contributes to feminist politics is that sexual difference does not necessarily mean gender difference; gender differences (behavioral and affective) are different patterns of relationality in a nature that is transformative and constituted by modes of power relations. The role of mother or wife thus refers to a historically specific body that recreates itself in a reduced sphere of activity and social conditions.[21]

Besides Spinoza, feminists also turn to phenomenological reflection on the body, especially to the idea that a subject is not separated from the world or the mind from body, matter, and space. Merleau-Ponty's theory of body is their favorite: the subject is a "being-to-the-world." Merleau-Ponty begins with a fundamental presumption that is different from the Cartesian dualism of mind and body: that the two are necessarily interrelated, and that consciousness and nature are related, as are interiority and exteriority. The body and the modes of sensual perception that occur through it affirm the necessary connections of consciousness, because it is incarnated and always grounded on corporeal and sensory relations. Feminist scholars recognize in Merleau-Ponty the notion that the body is both object for others and a lived reality for the subject. At the same time, it is "sense-bestowing" and "form-giving," providing structure, organization, and ground within which objects are to be situated, against which the body-subject is positioned, and by which meaning is generated. Thus, the primary origins of human action reside not in thought but in movement and motility. The inspiring notion is that consciousness is in the first place not a matter of "thinking" but rather of capability. The most fundamental and essential ability is the fact that body inhabits space and that the objects in it and the possible movements of the body are integrated in an overall orientation toward action in the world. According to Merleau-Ponty, the life of consciousness is subvented by an "intentional arc" based on the body as a nexus of lived and related meanings. He concluded by giving an ontological priority to certain kinds of immediate bodily movements and actions. This attracts feminist politics as a meaningful alternative to Cartesian dualism.

The body has remained a conceptual blind spot in both mainstream Western philosophical thought and contemporary feminist theories.

To summarize our discussion, the human subject has long been regarded as composed by several related binaries: mind and body, sense and sensibility, outside and inside, self and other, depth and surface, reality and appearance, mechanism and vitalism, transcendence and immanence, temporality and spatiality, psychology and physiology, form and matter, and so on. This binary thinking hierarchizes and ranks two polarized terms so that one becomes privileged, while the other is suppressed, subordinated, and negated. The body is typically regarded as passive and reproductive, but largely unproductive. The situation is more complicated when the body is associated with the "female." It has even been proposed that it is in the West and in our time that the female body has been constructed not only as a lack or absence, but as a formlessness that engulfs all form, a disorder that threatens all order.[22] Though there are claims that what needs to be changed are attitudes, beliefs, and values rather than the body itself, Elizabeth Grosz points out that culture itself can only assume meaning and value in terms of its own other(s).[23] This explains why there is a refusal to transgress the mind-body binary by proposing its substitution by monism or by a non-contradictory and non-hierarchized relation between the binarized terms.

It is not clear whether the holistic or monistic positions suggested can really resolve the mind-body problem. Grosz has concisely summarized the feminist questions: By which techniques and presumptions is a non-binary understanding of the body possible? What, ideally, could a feminist philosophy of the body avoid, and what must it take into consideration? Which criteria and goals should govern a feminist theoretical approach to concepts of the body? The answers would certainly avoid the division of the subject into mutually exclusive categories of mind and body. But what is more interesting, Grosz suggests, is to remain suspicious of the holism and unity implied by monism. Since the notion of corporeality and the ways in which materiality can be thought are still under the constraints of our culture, new concepts of corporeality that go beyond the regime of dualism should be developed. The new notions from her recent reflections are those that view human materiality as continuous with organic and inorganic matter, where physical and linguistic materialities interact and make possible a materialism beyond a mechanical physicalism, and that then will reorient physics itself.[24] This new model must show some sort of internal or constitutive articulation, or even disarticulation, between the biological and the psychological, the inside and the outside of the body, while avoiding a reductionism of mind to brain.[25] Merleau-Ponty's notion of the flesh is thus regarded as inspiring, acting as the elementary, precommunicative ontological domain out of which both subject and object mutually interact and develop.

Finally, the new conceptual categories should also comprehend difference. When applied to cultural impositions, these categories should represent and comprehend bodies as a multiple field of possible body "types," young and old, black and white, male and female, animal and human, inanimate and animate—no one of which (*pace*, the male) may stand in for or represent the others. To conclude, we must emphasize that there are alternative ontologies and modes of metaphysics, though these may not have been stressed in the history of the West, but, as Christine Battersby suggests, would be more useful for rethinking female identities.[26]

Mencius' Ideas of Body and Mind Revisited

Could Confucian philosophy be one of the alternative ontologies and metaphysics that feminist philosophers should deploy? I want to focus on Mencius' ideas, since his work discloses material crucial to an understanding of a theory of the body in the pre-Qing Confucian tradition. A few citations and readings are listed below for further discussion.[27]

> (Mencius:) Men have these Four Beginnings just as they have their four limbs. Having these Four Beginnings, but saying that they cannot develop them is to destroy themselves. When they say that their ruler cannot develop them, they are destroying their ruler. If anyone with these Four Beginnings in him knows how to give them the fullest extension and development, the result will be like fire beginning to burn or a spring beginning to shoot forth. When they are fully developed, they will be sufficient to protect all people within the four seas (the world). If they are not developed, they will not be sufficient even to serve one's parents. (2A: 6)

These "Four Beginnings" can be interpreted as innate moral qualities.[28] Mencius' basic argument is that human nature is inherently good in the sense that humans have an innate knowledge of goodness—which Mencius calls *liangzhi*—and an inclination to act according to it. Cheng Chung-ying, a contemporary Confucian thinker, said that this innate knowledge is related to the human being's potential for achieving harmony within herself and also with other people and objects in the world. The problem is how one can preserve the nature and innate sense of right and good and extend it to cover every phase of one's life and activity.[29] The "Four Beginnings" are the four fundamental feelings and sentiments that are forms of moral knowledge, the *liangzhi*. These are feelings and sentiments of compassion, shame, modesty, or reverence, including the distinction between right and wrong. These feelings and sentiments are natural and universal; they can be immediately accessed when a person is situated in proper circumstances. These feelings and sentiments can produce the virtues of benevolence, righteousness, propriety, and wisdom respectively, and the inclination to act accordingly when the moral subject interacts with others. Mencius considered *liangzhi* the ontological foundation of virtues, but it needs to be nurtured and preserved. In other words, these four fundamental moral sentiments are simply potentials for moral action in the development of a person into a whole human being in harmony with all of humankind.[30]

> (Mencius:) It is all right to say that what is not attained in the mind is not to be sought in the vital force, but it is not all right to say that what is not attained in words is not to be sought in the mind. The will is the leader of the vital force, and the vital force pervades and animates the body. The will is the highest; the vital force comes next. Therefore, I say, "Hold the will firm and never do violence to the vital force." . . . If the will is concentrated, the vital force [will follow it] and become active. If the vital force is concentrated, the will [will follow it] and become active. For instance, here is a case of a man falling or running. It is his vital force that is active, and yet it causes his mind to be active too. Ch'ou asked, "May I venture to ask, sir, in what you are strong?" Mencius replied, "I understand words. And I am skillful in nourishing my strong, moving power." "May I ask what is meant by the strong, moving power?" "It is difficult to describe. As power, it is exceedingly great and exceedingly strong. If nourished by uprightness and not injured, it will fill up all between heaven and earth. As power, righteousness and the Way accompany it. Without them, it will be devoid of nourishment. It is produced by the accumulation of righteous deeds

> but is not obtained by incidental acts of righteousness. When one's conduct is not satisfactory to his own mind, then one will be devoid of nourishment." (2A: 2)

> (Mencius): With proper nourishment and care, everything grows, whereas without proper nourishment and care, everything decays. Confucius said, "Hold it fast and you preserve it. Let it go and you lose it. It comes in and goes out at no definite time and without anyone knowing its direction." He was talking about the human mind. (6A: 8)

Vital force refers to bodily substance, matter, and desire; the Chinese word for it is *qi*. We should point out that *qi* is different from will (the moral mind), but both are interrelated in the sense that the moral mind should govern *qi* or virtue will fail, and this is a crucial point for humanity. *Qi* is different from the "strong, moving power," which in Chinese is the *hao ran zhi qi*. In the latter, *qi* is guided by righteousness (*yi*) in the fullest sense and has been compared to "flood breath." Cheng said that in *hao ran zhi qi*, *yi* is the ontological foundation of bodily action. Through one's self-conscientious effort to act according to moral principles, *yi* will naturally lead to the ontological extension of oneself and will transform the world into a universe of significance integral to the individual self.[31]

Yangqi (nourishing the vital force) and *jiyi* (the accumulation of righteous deeds) mean that the moralization of the bodily *qi* has to be conducted from time to time, and the capacity has to be preserved. *Yangqi*'s cumulative effect leads to *hao ran zhi qi*. The bodily *qi* that lacks moral nourishment will not only be easily weakened but will also subvert the moral self when it is violent.

> (Mencius:) There is not a part of the body that a man does not love. And because there is no part of the body that he does not love, there is not a part of it that he does not nourish. Because there is not an inch of his skin that he does not love, there is not an inch of his skin that he does not nourish. To determine whether his nourishing is good or not, there is no other way except to see the choice he makes for himself. Now, some parts of the body are noble and some are ignoble; some great and some small. We must not allow the ignoble to injure the noble, or the smaller to injure the greater. Those who nourish the

> smaller parts will become small men. Those who nourish the greater parts will become great men. (6A: 14)
>
> (Mencius:) Those who follow the greater qualities in their nature become men and those who follow the smaller qualities in their nature become small men. When our senses of sight and hearing are used without thought and are thereby obscured by material things, the material things act on the material senses and lead them astray. That is all. The function of the mind is to think. If we think, we will get them (the principles of things). If we do not think, we will not get them. This is what Heaven has given to us. If we first build up the nobler part of our nature, then the inferior part cannot overcome it. It is simply this that makes a man great. (6A: 15)
>
> (Mencius:) The five kinds of grain are considered good plants, but if they are not ripe, they are worse than poor grains. So the value of humanity depends on its being brought to maturity. (6A: 19)

Critical commentary of the above citations has disclosed a moral metaphysics in Mencius. The sentence "this [the mind] is what Heaven has given to us" signifies a person's relation to the ontological ground *tian* (heaven). The Confucian Heaven is the transcendental ground of everything in Nature (including human beings) whose essential characteristics are endowed by Heaven as the moral mind. Contemporary neo-Confucian Mou Zongsan described the relation between Heaven and the human mind as a "distanced interaction." Thus, the mind is the noblest and the greatest component of the body; it is more than simply physical because of its moral consciousness or innate knowledge of goodness. The smaller components are the physical ones that have basic functions like hearing and vision. The physical needs or desires of the smaller components have to be subordinated to the control of the "thinking greatest-component," which constitutes the center of moral principles and will. As we have said, moral knowledge and its capabilities need to be developed and preserved in order to transform the human subject into a "great person" or sage.

Cheng, also a contemporary Confucian interpreter, said both moral psychology and moral metaphysics (involved in this transformation) provide a basis for understanding what a person should do—through moral practices—in one's personal life and in one's social intercourse with others. According to traditional Confucianism, this process is the central and ultimate concern of human activity.[32]

> (Mencius:) When Heaven is about to confer a great responsibility on any man, it will exercise his mind with suffering, subject his sinews and bones to hard work, expose his body to hunger, put him to poverty, place obstacles in the paths of his deeds, so as to stimulate his mind, harden his nature, and improve wherever he is incompetent. (6B: 15)

This citation demonstrates the significant exercise of the mind in dominating and repressing the smaller components of the body—though this involves suffering. For it is only through the stimulation of the mind and the hardening of the body that a person is able to fulfill the great responsibility bestowed by Heaven. In humanity, the vital point is not to lose control of one's mind or let the mind lose its focus for moral education and knowledge. This process includes a series of exercising principles that Mencius mentioned elsewhere. Cheng summarized these principles as "not forgetting" (*wu wang)* the nature of the human mind and "not helping to nurture" (*wu zhu zhang)* the distraction of moral will caused by the physical desires of the smaller components of the body. These principles contribute to the already mentioned nourishment of the great flood of *qi* (*hao ran zhi qi*), which, as Cheng correctly points out, is not contrived and artificial, but is based on righteousness.[33]

> (Mencius:) It is due to our nature that our mouths desire sweet taste, that our eyes desire beautiful colors, that our ears desire pleasant sounds, that our noses desire fragrant odors, and that our four limbs desire ease and comfort. But there is also fate (*ming*) [whether these desires are satisfied or not]. The superior man does not say they are man's nature [and insist on satisfying them]. The virtue of humanity in the relationship between father and son, the virtue of righteousness in the relationship between ruler and minister, the virtue of propriety in the relationship between guest and host, the virtue of wisdom in the worthy, and the sage in regard to the Way of Heaven—these are [endowed in people in various degrees] according to fate. But there is also man's nature (*xing*). The superior man does not (refrain from practicing them and) say they are matters of fate. (7B: 24)

> (Mencius:) Form and color [our body] are nature endowed by Heaven. It is only the sage who can put his physical form into full use. (7A: 38)

Cheng's concise reading of "structure" (*ming*) and "nature" (*xing*) may help us understand the famous session (7B: 24) in which Mencius said that both mind and *xing* mingle within the individual being, representing and fulfilling the different functions that constitute being human. *Xing* is able to fulfill the person in terms of achieving identification with Heaven (*tian*), which provides nature to humans and enables them to achieve greatness; whereas *ming* is able to fulfill the person in terms of interaction with others. *Ming* is not a deterrent to one's virtue, but is sometimes an occasion for fulfillment, since it is the fate of life, and so life itself is seen as the giving of *ming*, which includes the nature of those small bodily components. Mencius said that one needs to receive fate the right way, that is, to avoid what is undesirable and fulfill what is desirable.[34] Undesirable things include dangerous situations that can cost life; desirable things include moral deeds or virtues. This is what Mencius meant by saying "the sage who can put his physical form into full use." Therefore, the "superior person" will devote herself to the actualization of the human *xing* and will not simply sit there and resign everything to fate.

Feminist Reflections on Mencius' Ideas of Body and Mind

What does the above discussion of Mencius' ideas of the body disclose? Can these ideas constitute an alternative body ontology that is useful for critical feminist practices? If we go through Mencius' answers to questions posed by feminists, our response to the last question is both *yes* and *no*. First, it is difficult to tell whether Mencius' body is gendered, but if we examine his work in its historical and cultural contexts, taking the Confucian patriarchal society into account, the sage or "great man" or "superior man" would refer to men only. Since women in the Confucian tradition are viewed as feeble in terms of their moral capabilities, they need to be educated and controlled; otherwise they will upset the patriarchal social order. Female bodies are dangerous and threatening since they can be seductive, leading men to excessive sexual desire or socially deviant behavior; but women's behavior can be beneficial to men under traditional Confucian regulations, or if they act according to the instructions of traditional Daoist theories of sexuality. Translations and commentaries on Mencius' usage of "man" and "he" to indicate human is a hint that Mencius' body is gendered as male. Second, ideologically speaking, the identification of women with materiality that feminists have pointed out can also be detected in Mencius' work. A vital force pervades and animates the body, assembles the small components, which are the material senses governed by the mind, or the greatest component. The small components could be interpreted as the material and ontological bases—that is, the "female" side—of human existence. These small components are also where the "receiving" principle is, waiting passively for the form-giving process and for moral imperatives—both activities supervised by the mind. Vital force can become violent and resistant, which is simply what Western feminists have pointed out in Western philosophical theories about female bodies, which are believed to engulf all forms and threaten order. The Western binary of passion-reason seems to correspond to that of vital force–moral will in *Mencius*, including in that the former should follow the latter in order to attain a harmonious humanity.

In spite of the associations we make above within the social, historical, and ideological contexts of *Mencius*, the binary structure is the main question that remains. Are Mencius' ideas of the body the same as the mind-body binary of which Western feminists are critical? The pre-Qing Confucian cosmological model cannot said to be the same as the Western, although the texts seem to have separated the small and greatest components, vital force and will (and related notions of the female and mastering order), *ming* and *xing*, emphasizing in every respect the superiority of the latter terms over the former. To explain this, we need to turn to *I-Ching* (the spelling used in this book), the basic text of Chinese cosmology, especially the problem related to *yin* and *yang*, since it pertains to the subject of gender. It should be stressed that the discussion here does not mean to reduce the complexity and multiplicity of the *yin-yang* concept to what is found in the *I Ching*, with the understanding that there are various formulations of the *yin-yang* relationship. In the *I-Ching*:

> One *yin* and one *yang* is called Dao [the way]. What we inherit from [the Dao] is good. What forms things in nature [*xing*] . . . Being full of being is the great deed; being fresh and novel every day is called

> luxuriant virtue. To produce life is called change. To form forms [*xing*] is called *qian* [the creative principle]. To follow up [the *qian*] is called *kun* [the receptive principle]. To exhaust numbers in order to know the future is called derivation. To comprehend change is called conducting an affair. The unpredictability of the changes [due to the interchange of *yin* and *yang*] is called the divine. . . . Thus *Yi* has the great ultimate, which generates the two norms. Two norms generate four forms. Four forms generate eight trigrams.[35]

Cheng explicates that, in the *I-Ching*, there are always two opposite but complementary forces in the process of change. These are the *yin*, also referred to as the female principle-force-aspect, representing the receptive and the potential, and the *yang*, the male principle-force-aspect, representing the creative and the actual. Difference and differentiation of things are manifestations of the interaction of *yin* and *yang*, like the vital force and the moral mind. These general polarities are also exemplified by cold-hot, hard-soft, rest-movement, high-low, but they do not exhibit any real opposition or antagonism; they are only opposite insofar as they are complementary. There is neither tension nor hostility between these terms. According to the *I-Ching*, the world is a process of change and development, moving toward unity and a state of holistic harmonization. The appearance of discrepancy, imperfection, conflict, contradiction, or struggle is seen as the manifestation of incomplete sub-processes of the interaction of polarities. Moreover, conflict is only a matter of a person's inability to conform to reality and to appreciate the intricacies of change. Conflict can be avoided if one strives to conform to nature (*xing* in the human sense) by cultivating one's understanding and adjusting one's action properly. This adjustment is a process of harmonization. To conclude, according to the metaphysics of harmony and conflict in the *I-Ching*, antagonism calls for a moral and practical transformation of humans.[36] With this belief, we can hope that when we consider the Chinese patriarchal suppression of women, we may consider this condition as an artificial, contextual, and political practice that Confucian spirituality and moral philosophy can help to transcend.

With an understanding of the *I-Ching*, including the Chinese model of causality that this essay can only mention but is unable to discuss fully, we could say that Mencius' ideas of the body belong to a metaphysics that is close to Spinoza's but cannot be matched by that of Merleau-Ponty. Spinoza's model stands out from other Western models with its notion of *substantia* that is absolute and infinite, but also materially grounded. This ultimate substance acts as the ground of both mind and body, with its non-mechanical, non-binary, and non-essentialistic nature that enables the body to become a process interacting with its situated context. However, Mencius' Heaven refers to the Confucian principle of holistic unity, in which all things are one under the Dao or Heaven, which is not materially grounded but the transcendental and ultimate principle, the oneness that gives rise to multiple things. Risings from this oneness are mind and body, which interact with each other. But another Chinese text, the *Doctrine of the Mean,* said that it is only the (moral) nature of the mind that is endowed by, and corresponds directly to, the nature of Heaven. Therefore, in the Confucian tradition, it is not actual bodily existence that enables the activity of (moral) reason, as Spinoza implies; nor do the body and its schema have any ontological priority with the "flesh" as the metaphysical ground, as Merleau-Ponty suggests.

The final question remains: With the superior status of the mind, can Mencius' ideas of the body act as a useful model for feminists concerned with the origin of (female) bodily suppression? The usefulness might lie in the pre-Qing Confucian cosmological belief underlining the Mencius' work: that all things and processes in the world move toward balance and harmony, even if there are changes and transformations. Feminists might also find the *yin-yang* polarity useful, including the mutual generative and destructive modes described in the *I-Ching*, with their contrary and complementary qualities.[37] Thus, the superior relation of the mind over the body is simply a symbolic and dynamic phase moving toward (human) harmony. The principles of holistic unity and organic balance are meaningful ideas distinct from the mechanical-atomistic model of which feminists are critical. These principles are also basically indicative of the concrete experiences of life, history, and time.[38] It is in these senses that Mencius' ideas of mind and body can initiate a radical rethinking of the connections among reason, the body, and ethical-political issues.

2

CHINESE PHILOSOPHY AND THE SUGGESTION OF A MATRIARCHAL AESTHETICS

This chapter explores the metaphysical and experiential differences between the types of myth/ritual complexes of archaic peoples to which the feminist paradigm referred and what we find in the Daoist texts. As throughout this book, the discussion here points out that cross-cultural philosophical dialogue might present scholars working in aesthetics, Western or Chinese, with promising directions for further research. The study in this chapter does not deny that there are patriarchal forms and institutions in the Chinese tradition, but begins to look at that tradition for resources related to bodily experiences that might deconstruct that patriarchy and provide us with some new directions in the consideration of cross-cultural aesthetics.

Feminist Critique of Kant's Aesthetics

It is no surprise that Kant's philosophy has been a favorite subject of criticism by feminist scholars. In part, this has to do with the nature of his philosophy and, in part, with his open statements on the roles of women. I will try to illustrate this by laying out some of the critical analysis by feminists of the two main notions in Kant's aesthetics—taste and the sublime.

Feminist aestheticians like Korsmeyer and Hilde Hein believe that there are significant connections between Kant's views on women and his theory of taste.[1] While Kant took the prevailing eighteenth-century view that the female sex is naturally inferior in rational and moral capacities and that they are creatures of inclination, concerned mainly with outer appearance, his notion of taste has similar characteristics:

> To show taste in our conduct is very different from expressing our moral way of thinking. For this contains a command and gives rise to a need, whereas moral taste only plays with the objects of liking without committing itself to any of them.[2]

It is further pointed out by feminist scholars that Kant's notions of taste and women are both systematically contrasted with and ultimately subordinated to individual morality and masculinity, respectively.[3] Both of them need to be disciplined in order to do good to culture as they are rooted in sensibilities that are basically not trustworthy. According to Kant, the validity of aesthetic judgments or judgments of taste depends upon the harmonious relationship between the understanding and the imagination. Imagination combines the manifold of intuition while understanding provides the unity of the concept uniting the presentations. As Kant said, "Understanding alone gives the law."[4] Feminist readings of the relation of imagination to understanding in judgments of taste have claimed it to be analogous to that of a wife to her husband in a marriage. Both are domesticated by a masculine understanding.[5]

A masculinist orientation has also been detected in Kant's notion of the sublime. The experience of the sublime is an inner response to an outer occasion that provides us with a perspective on our "elevated destiny" or paradoxical psychological effects of epic and tragic poetry. According to Kant, the condition of the sublime is the obedience of imagination to a kind of law that utilizes nature as a schema for representing the ideas of reason. The experience of Kant's sublime is said to be characterized in overtly masculine terms like *powerful*, *active*, *threatening*, *dominating*, *masterful*, and so on, which are regarded as universal norms for the character and judgment of all human beings.[6] Feminist aestheticians point out that, with Kant's reading of the feeble nature of women, they are less capable of having the experience of the sublime and of developing the crucial human aesthetic, rational, and moral dimensions therein. In his 1764 article, "Observations on the Feeling of the Beautiful and Sublime,"[7] Kant said,

> The virtue of a woman is a beautiful virtue. That of the male sex should be a noble virtue. Women will avoid the wicked not because it is unright, but because it is ugly; and virtuous actions mean to them such as are morally beautiful. Nothing of duty, nothing of compulsion, nothing of obligation![8]

The rejection of this kind of feminine aesthetic attitiude is further promoted by Kant's aesthetics in his later work, *The Critique of Judgment* (1790), in which he says that real aesthetic judgment should be "disinterested." The aesthetic subject should abstract himself from all kinds of practical values, desires, and emotions and concentrate on the contemplation of the forms of objects. Obviously, Kant's women lack this kind of capacity. When it comes to his notion of the sublime, which involves psychic disturbance, by contrast, and a transcendence of terror, again, only moral man is exclusively qualified. According to Kant, only educated men are able to cope with the passive faculty of intuition related to objects by exerting regulation of moral law of the subjects.

Feminist scholars claim that the exclusion of women from human aesthetic and moral qualities can be traced back to Kant's distinction of form and matter. In Kant's philosophy, moral and aesthetic judgments are concerned only with form (the good a priori) and not with matter (chaotic empirical "stuff"). This in effect reestablished the ancient Greek links between form and maleness and matter and femaleness. Feminists are suspicious of such a division.[9] Feminist critics have suggested that non-Kantian transcendental arguments are possible and that we should consider aesthetic arguments that neither appeal illicitly to external grounds, nor insist on the uniqueness of the conceptual schemes.[10] Feminist aestheticians are yearning for alternatives and new languages in aesthetics in which the abovementioned division is no longer valid. New language is necessary as it is claimed that the common vocabularies as well as those used by the institutions of art, epistemologies, and critical discourses are all preformed in masculine ways and that radical changes in aesthetic discourse are necessary.[11]

Such feminist criticism is part of a much broader contemporary criticism, which has challenged in fundamental ways the model of

Western traditional philosophy. Gender is one of those fundamental categories. Along with Derrida's concepts of phallo-centrism and logo-centrism and Foucault's historical analysis of sexuality and the relation of knowledge to power, we find feminist concepts such as de Beauvoir's reading of man's capacity for transcendence, Kristeva's semiotics, Irigaray's critique of the subject and object relation in the history of Western philosophy. They are all concerned directly or indirectly with the binary oppositions of rational-irrational, subject-object, nature-culture, form-matter, mind-body, active-passive, presence-absence, and so on, and their implications for issues of gender. They attribute these oppositions to the establishment of masculine and rational culture in the West. Their philosophical criticism invites our reflection on Chinese philosophy as well.

Questions related to the above discussion include: Can Chinese philosophy provide us with a resource or at least a frame of reference for the development of an alternative aesthetics along the lines sought by Western feminist scholars? I would like to deal with the question in this chapter by introducing a model of matriarchal aesthetics suggested by a Western feminist scholar, and to discuss it in the light of two contemporary neo-Confucian philosophers who have suggested similar models related to aesthetic experience.

The Suggestion of A Matriarchal Aesthetics

Based on art forms found in the work, which already have matriarchal features, Heide Göttner-Abendroth has set out nine principles of a matriarchal aesthetics. I believe that these are abstracted from arts practiced in matriarchal societies. Matriarchal aesthetics acts as a great resource and foundation for recent paradigms formulated in feminist aesthetics.[12] Here I summarize these principles in the following paragraphs.

Matriarchal art is in the form of magic, in the sense that magic intrudes into reality by means of symbols and has the effect of changing reality. According to the ancient wisdom of magic, it was necessary to communicate with nature via symbols in order to make people understood, to make it clear to nature that it should stand by its intention. It is believed that communication with nature could help the fragmented, specialized, stereotyped individual of today to regain her/his totality.

Matriarchal art is diversity in unity. Unlike patriarchal aesthetics (for example, Kant's), the unity is not dogmatic and the diversity not subjective. Diversity in unity refers to a way of thinking that was inherent in the structure of old matriarchal mythology and was the basis of the beliefs of all early complex cultures. This way of thinking was repressed by the patriarchal forms of thought that followed.

Matriarchal art transcends the traditional mode of communication, which consists of author-text-reader. It is not limited to a product or a text but a process, which gives a pre-existing inner structure, like the ritual of dance, in which people participate collectively to create the external expression, so all are simultaneously authors, text, and spectators. Matriarchal art, like mythology, exists as a fundamental category of human understanding, not in the meaning of Kant, but in a more ancient meaning from which all later artistic artifacts of the imagination developed. The arbitrary chain of associations of the imagination emphasized by patriarchal aesthetics is only its very late and degenerated aspect. It is said that matriarchal art follows its own rules through bodily experience.

In matriarchal art, there is no division between emotion and thought. It is said that the universal, objective nature of the structure of matriarchal art mentioned prevents the identification from becoming subjective sentimentality, the theorizing from becoming abstract arbitrariness, and the action from becoming mere catharsis. These statements obviously can be referred to Kant's aesthetic judgment and his notion of the sublime. It is also said that matriarchal art welds together feeling, thinking, and doing in the form of the concrete mythological image and, in this totality, releases true ecstasy in the participants. The true ecstasy unites the intellect, emotions, and bodily action in a climax where no one power is limited by another. They are expressed simultaneously, each to its utmost capacity. Ecstatic moments are described as "the chords of the harmony of the spheres played on the fragile instrument that is man and woman (bodies)." Only by entering the process can one experience it.

As it is a dynamic process characterized by ecstasy, matriarchal art cannot be evaluated and interpreted by outsiders, for it cannot be objectified and therefore is coherent without being dogmatic as it does not prescribe meanings. However, it has a positive impact on reality. Because matriarchal art cannot be objectified, it cannot be subdivided into genres. Thus, the division between art and non-art and between art and life are all redundant. It is a complex whole process, which takes place on many levels; the isolation of any single element is inappropriate.

It is said that, with matriarchal art, the erotic is the dominant force replacing discipline. Its primary principle is the continuation of life as a cycle of rebirths and not inhuman ideals. It brings about social changes, which override the divisions in the aesthetic sphere and return to art its original public role, bringing about the aestheticization of the whole of society.

Finally, matriarchal art is not art in the sense of patriarchal aesthetics that is fictional, which is based in the fundamental dualisms mentioned above. Rather, matriarchal art seeks to shape life and change life; it is itself energy and drives towards the aestheticization of society.

As matriarchal art involves the possibility of communicating with nature by means of symbolic acts, it is demanded that we should learn to adapt ourselves to nature, which includes our bodies and our immediate environment. It is stressed that the joy and delight thereby released can be traced back to the harmonious correlation of a change in nature with a spiritual change in ourselves that is a new form of living.

We can see that such a matriarchal paradigm accentuates nature's unity with human beings as opposed to nature's exploitation and utilization by men; it also emphasizes the harmony of the individual's capacities as opposed to their fragmented specialization. I want to suggest that each of these is already implied in traditional Chinese philosophy. As our focus is aesthetics, I would like to compare this paradigm with aspects of Daoist and Confucian aesthetics in order to see if there are fundamental similarities and differences and thus to place these models in critical dialogue with one another, towards exploring how they might learn from each other.

The Aesthetic Experience in Traditional Chinese Philosophies and Matriarchal Art

Despite the saying that systematic aesthetics is absent from traditional Confucian and Daoist philosophies, contemporary neo-Confucian scholars Mou Zongsan (referred to in Chapter 1) and Tang Junyi, his contemporary, have reconstructed theories of human primal experience according to pre-Qing Confucianism and Daoism, which allude to aesthetic experience.

In one of his latest writings, his translation and commentary on Kant's *Critique of Judgement*, Mou presents and recommends the Daoist theory of intellectual intuition, which is aesthetic in nature. First, he points out the subjective principle of Daoism as *wu wei* (no-action) suggested in *Laozi*, which refers to the effort of the human mind to transcend all kinds of human epistemological functions and move towards the realm of a more metaphysical Dao. *Laozi* promotes the annulments of human activity and knowledge to recover the presentation of nature in itself, which has been hidden and distorted by human understanding, perception, and conception. According to *Laozi*, to know is to not know, to be wise is to be ignorant, only the so-called fools are able to grasp the truth of nature.

Mou Zongsan further explicated the notion of *xuan zhi* 玄智 as a form of intellectual intuition. According to Mou's interpretation, in the realm of the Dao when the human mind has stopped knowing and travels with *qi*, it would, together with other things, present itself in its original nature. These are not "phenomena" in the Kantian sense of epistemology, but the original nature of things the presentation of which can only be resumed after the abolition of the dominant scheme of subject-object relation exerted by the knowing subject.

It is said that the state of intellectual intuition of the mind in the Daoist sense stated above is the "calmness of mind" described by Zhuangzi's *xinzhai* 心齋:

> Do not be the master of knowledge (to manipulate things). Personally realize the infinite to the highest degree and travel in the realm of which there is no sign. Exercise fully what you have received from Nature without any subjective viewpoint. In one word, be absolutely vacuous [*xu* 虛]. The mind of the perfect man is like a mirror. It does not lean forward or backward in its response to things. It responds to things but conceals nothing of its own. Therefore it is able to deal with things without injury to (its reality).[13]

In the "calmness of mind," there are no differentiations of mind and body, form and matter, or subject and object but the emergence of all things (including the minds) in themselves. They are juxtaposed with each other without being known. Mou calls the static "negative and static form of birth," which is basically disinterested, non-intentional and non-regulative; it is therefore aesthetic in nature. His elaboration of the state is as follows:

> The state of mind of *xinzhai* is the termination, tranquility, emptiness, and nothingness that follow the abolition of the quest and dependency on learning and knowing. The *wu wei* of the above necessarily implies a certain kind of creativity whose form is so special that it can be named as negative creativity . . . that in the light of the tranquil state . . . things present themselves in the way that they are . . . not as an object, but as an ideal state . . . and this is the static intellectual intuition.[14]

In the transcendental realm of the Dao, a thing is not an object but an "ideal state," a form in itself, appreciation of which is only capable with the Daoist wisdom, that is, the "intellectual intuition" or "the principle of no form" (無相原則), in which the sense of beauty and aesthetic pleasure, which is the real form of freedom, springs up in tranquility. Achievement of this state requires the effort of transcendence of all human epistemological constraints or judgments that Kant's aesthetics prescribes, and engagement in the metaphysical realm of the Dao. This explains the criteria and aesthetic categories in Daoist aesthetics, for example, Laozi's *qi* 氣, *wei* 味, *miao* 妙, and *xu* 虛, which refer to the activities and characters of the realm, and are applied in the evaluation of Chinese arts.

It should be noted that, according to the contemporary reading of Mou Zongsan and Tang Junyi, human primal experience of a similar nature is also implied in the Confucian theory of the mind, which they read out of traditional Confucian texts from pre-Qing to the Song. Mou names it the Confucian "intellectual intuition." In his influential reading, the human mind also transcends the subject and object relation and is engaged with Nature. Nature fills the human mind with its attributes of benevolence and creativity, and enables things to actualize themselves under the light of the mind that copes with things. Mou emphasizes that the intuition involves his so-called principle of ontological actualization, in contrast with the principle of cognitive presentation" in the Western epistemological sense, in which things are perceived as objects.[15] The deeper the engagement of the human mind with Nature or Heaven, the more the mind will function, which initiates fuller actualization of things under its light; and the more beautiful the form, the greater the potential to lead one to stronger aesthetic emotion. This helps us to understand both the moral and aesthetic categories central to Confucian philosophy, such as harmony, vividness, and so on.

Tang Junyi introduces his so-called host and guest relation, on the other hand, to describe the relationship between things and the mind in the human primal experience, in contrast with the subject and object relation in Western theories of knowledge in which subjects dominate and objects subordinate. According to Tang, objectification of the mind takes place only after the primal experience, which he describes as "the totality of intuition" (his understanding of the experience is very similar to that of Mou). Hence comes the division of subject and object. Functions and activities of the mind (including artistic ones) then begin to exert their influences and judgments onto the perceived matters.[16]

Again, my suggestion is that we can find many similarities between the principles of a matriarchal aesthetics as outlined above and those of traditional Chinese philosophy. Points of comparison that we might pursue further include the following. Both emphasize communication with nature in gaining a form of human totality. Both refer to a unifying way of thinking, contrasting with "patriarchal aesthetics," which is regarded as dogmatic and subjective. The aesthetic experience of both take place in a fundamental, principal process, which gives a "pre-existing inner structure" prior to the objectification process, in which the relation of the object of art (the text), the author, and the audience is formed. Both models involve a form of inner ecstasy or erotic force that is the origin of the intellect, emotions, and actions; the primary principle of matriarchal art is claimed to be the continuation of life as a cycle of rebirths, which resembles the circulation of life (*qi*) in Daoism and the principle of creativity of Heaven in Confucianism.

One can see that matriarchal aesthetics' desire to bring about the aestheticization of society is analogous to Confucianism's concern with the moral growth of the individual and society. Matriarchal art as energy itself, is a drive towards the aestheticization of society and the ability to shape life and change life. It also coincides with the Daoist and Confucian aesthetic experience, where the human mind is elevated to a transcendental level and produces a dramatically different life experience. Both models demand that we should adapt ourselves to nature, which includes our bodies and our immediate environment. This reminds us of the famous Daoist analogy, the joy and delight of the butcher Ding in

Zhuangzi's work, which leads to the harmonious correlation of a change in nature with a spiritual change in ourselves.

The comparison of a suggested model of feminist aesthetics with Chinese aesthetics outlined above obviously needs more detailed research than is presented here. However, even this brief study shows that this area of cross-cultural philosophical dialogue might present scholars working in the field of aesthetics, Western or Chinese, with promising directions for further research. One area that clearly needs more exploration is of the differences (metaphysical and experiential) between the types of myth/ritual complexes of archaic peoples to which the feminist paradigm referred and that in pre-Qing Confucian and Daoist texts.

3

RECLAIMING THE BODY: FRANCIS BACON'S FUGITIVE BODIES AND CONFUCIAN AESTHETICS ON BODILY EXPRESSION

The Case of Francis Bacon: Fugitive Bodies

Whenever I look at the distorted bodies in Francis Bacon's figure paintings, I take a breath and try to enjoy the bodies by thinking of the comments of one of his critics, Andrew Brighton. Brighton suggested the following questions when looking at a Bacon painting: What ideas and values does our view of the work oblige us to have and defend? Why has it been celebrated, condemned, or ignored by critics, historians, and institutions?[1] This thinking has initiated my interest in comparing the discussions held on body portraiture of the very intriguing Bacon and of the Chinese tradition. It is not only because representation is a fundamental issue in bodily discourses, and that comparative study on the subject should be very revealing as this book project believes, but one may also find thinking related to the more foundational question of the link between subject and object, when object refers to body most of the time.

I would like to start from the radical attempts that Francis Bacon made in his representation of the body, and contrast them with Confucian body aesthetics as followed by Gu Kaizhi, a master of portraiture in Chinese art history. The study here wishes to implement comparison before pondering whether one is better than the other, to explore whether the problems of the mind and body split in Bacon's case are resolved in the Confucian tradition, and to ask how the recovery of the body in contemporary Western discourse can learn from Confucian theories of the body. Maybe only the answer to this question is positive: can we propose that active engagement through the process of reworking the body of art is able to create other possible expressions of the body?

"Exhilarated Despair," Sexuality, and Violence

Supposedly, when Bacon attained major public recognition at the end of World War II, despair was in fashion. Art critics and editors announced at the time that the modern movement's struggle happened "between men, betrayed by science, bereft of religion, deserted by the pleasant imaginings of humanism against the blind fate. It was closing time in the gardens of the West and an artist would be judged only by the resonance of his solitude or the quality of his despair."[2]

Bacon's early paintings have been seen as reflecting the war itself and in particular the images of concentration camps that emerged as the Allies liberated Europe in the latter part of 1944. *Three Figures at the Base of a Crucifixion* was one of his works completed in 1944 before the pictures of the camps were released.[3] This painting was supposedly one of the resources for Bacon's visual articulation of a culture of pessimism, but in fact it formed the context and not the pretext of his rhetoric of despair. Bacon himself confirmed in an interview that his paintings were concerned with his own kind of psyche, which he described as "exhilarated despair."

It is natural for people to take Bacon's personal history into account when looking at his work. Bacon was born in Dublin in 1909 to English parents at the time when Ireland was in the violent process of becoming independent from Britain, and his family was under threat of attack during his childhood. This experience is described as crucial to the reception of Bacon's paintings, linked both to his masochistic homosexuality and to the violence and pessimism attributed to his work. The fact that in the late 1920s Bacon lived briefly in Berlin, a city that accepted his sexuality, might well have provided him courage in asserting his particular form of sexuality, which he made the core of his paintings.[4] We might agree with critics that Bacon seeks to "come immediately onto the nervous system," to "unlock the valves of feeling and therefore return the onlooker to life more violently," and that his works are convulsive and physiological.

Loss of Self

Bacon's bodies also impress people as "fugitive" as well as expressing "exhilarated despair," masochistic sexuality, and violence.[5] As Ernst van Alphen suggested, Bacon's bodies hinder any attempt to derive from them a sense of existence, identity, or solidity, but these are also the reasons that bodies may well be central to an aesthetic and philosophical understanding of his paintings.[6] Van Alphen further suggested that Bacon's representation of the body is partly affiliated with, and partly opposed to, current Western philosophies. In these philosophies, the body is what others see but what the subject does not. The subject becomes dependent on the other in a way that ultimately makes the body the focus of a power struggle with far-reaching ramifications.

What does this point indicate when we look at Bacon's images? It means that we see bodies as a series of fragments dangling on the string of the inner sensation of self, and lacking the wholeness that the self-other relationship would produce. Van Alphen specifically refers to this lack in *Self Portrait* (1969), in which faces are fragmented in such a way that we cannot decide whether formless elements belong to the faces of subjects or not.

Subject and non-subject thus become one flat visual field constructed on contiguity, making it impossible to speak of a subject or self. Van Alphen said that this is the way Bacon represents the inner experience of self, which ends by deconstructing the idea of self according to the self-other binary.[7] Further readings based on this assumption help engage the ambiguities and complexities of Bacon's bodies. For example, Bacon always avoids putting more than one figure on the same canvas because such togetherness would suggest the becoming of a self through the other. His work would rather fragment the subject or close out the possibility of a unified self.

Critics have also pointed out that the lack of a visual relationship between self and other can explain the isolation of Bacon's subjects in terms of the space that surrounds them. There are elements in his paintings that isolate the subject in space: the boxes, platforms, cage structures, and so on. Many critics have seen these as means of short-circuiting the development of an action or a relationship; for example, in *Head IV* (1949).[8]

How about those works of Bacon that involve desire between two parties? One interesting interpretation of the play of desire in Bacon is that the self may become indistinguishable from the other, and the outer body of the subject would then disintegrate, becoming no more than an aspect of the body of the other. In *Two Figures in the Grass* (1954), the two naked men meld. Their bodies are blurred and fragmented. One critic argued that the sexual desire of the two men may destroy the distance between them and fragment their selves. It was also suggested that love-making was an assault on the self's boundaries and, according to Bacon, sexual desire leading to loss of self, showing sexual relations as essentially masochistic.[9]

In addition to the loss of self, another question that has been raised about Bacon's bodies is: How can the fragmented experience of self be preferable to the experience of the self as whole? In Bacon's paintings, there is no space in which the body can be framed or embedded according to the conceptual categories of the interior and the exterior. One example is *Painting* (1978), in which a naked figure tries to lock (or unlock) the door with his foot. The extremely artificial posture seems to express the danger and anxiety involved in this simple act. It remains unclear whether the danger is caused by something inside or outside, or by the act of drawing a line between inside and outside. Another example, *Self Portrait* (1970), repeats this effect, as van Alphen clearly described: the viewer focuses first on Bacon's head, which seems to be a straightforward view of the artist. When the viewer looks at the sides of the painting, however, it becomes apparent that he or she has been looking at a painting of a painting of Francis Bacon. Yet the lower side of the painting appears to be a painting of Francis Bacon in front of a painting. We can see that Bacon seems to consistently deny the possibility that subjects can be defined by the space that surrounds them; he provides no representation of subjects within a meaningful world, hinting that this is paradoxically the only way that the idea of self can be felt and kept alive, instead of being defined by others or by the surrounding space.[10]

Freudian Concepts of the Mind and the Body

What kinds of Western thought or philosophies contributed to Bacon's rebellious body of work? We can trace the way back to the Greek binaries of mind and body, subject and object, essence and appearance, inside and outside, and so on; and relatively recently to Freud and

Nietzsche. Bacon loved to read—and was strongly influenced by—Freud and Nietzsche. Freud's essay "The Economic Problem of Masochism," available in English translation in 1924, sketched what he called "moral masochism" when he argued that the child translates a sense of guilt into a wish for parental punishment, a wish expressed in fantasies of beatings by the father and of having "a passive (feminine) sexual relation to him." Freud's essay is crucial in interpreting Bacon's work.[11] Yet we need to pay attention to the psychoanalytic conceptions of the body. Elizabeth Grosz has said that although psychoanalysis is largely concerned with the analysis and interpretation of psychic activities, and the psyche in Western tradition is generally allied with the mind and opposed to the body, Freud and a number of other psychoanalysts have devoted considerable attention to the body's role in psychic life.[12]

But Freud is not that far from Western philosophies. It is known that he remained committed to a form of psycho-physical dualism inherited from Cartesian philosophy, in which chemical and neurological processes are neither causes nor effects of psychological processes, but are somehow correlated with them. Freud's biological body is overlaid with psychic and social significance accounts; that is, Freud talked about a socially, historically, and culturally sexed body that displaces what was once mythically known as the natural body. Yet he also claimed that the ego must be considered a "bodily ego," a "surface projection" of the libidinal body.

Grosz is correct in her reading that, for Freud, the ego is an internalized image of the meaning that the body has for the subject, and also for others in the social world and for culture as a whole. The ego is described as a shared and/or individualized fantasy of the body's form and modes of operation. And also, one's psychic life history is written on and worn by the body. Oral, anal, and phallic drives are not biologically determined stages of human development (this would reduce the drive to a form of instinct), but are the result of processes of libidinal intensification that correlate with the acquisition of various meanings for various body components. Thus emerged the belief that psychoanalytic theory has enabled feminists and other counter-hegemonic groups to reclaim the body from the realms of immanence and biology, in order to see it as a psycho-social product, open to transformations in meaning and functioning, capable of being contested and re-signified.[13] We can, as well, understand Bacon's bodies from all these perspectives.

Nietzsche's Notions and Influences

Bacon also read Nietzsche seriously. He echoed Nietzsche's existential argument that after the death of God man must create himself, despite having a sense of the self and existence as being without value or meaning. Bacon's work demonstrates the effort in redefining oneself and reclaiming oneself from its relations with others.

It is necessary to review Nietzsche's thoughts on the mind and the body, to see his alternative position in the recent history of Western thought, and to track his influences on Bacon's figuration of bodies. In *Thus Spoke Zarathustra*, Nietzsche destroyed the mind-body dichotomy through the notion of "self":

> What the sense feels, what the spirit perceives, is never an end in itself . . . behind them lies the Self . . . Behind your thoughts and feelings . . . stands a mighty commander, an unknown sage—he is called Self. He lives in your body; he is your body. (Z.I.4)[14]

For Nietzsche, soul or mind is "only a word for something about the body" and human beings are "simply bodies, and nothing else." In *The Gay Science*, Nietzsche read philosophy as a misunderstanding of the body and emphasized the decisions of individuals:

> The popular medical formulation of morality . . . "virtue is the health of the soul," would have to be changed to become useful, at least to read, "your virtue is the health of your soul." For there is no health as such, and all attempts to define such a thing that way have been wretched failures. Even the determination of what is healthy for your body depends on your goal, your horizon, your energies, your impulses, your errors and above all on the ideals and phantasms of your soul . . . Only then would the time have come to reflect on the health and illness of the soul, and to find the peculiar virtue of each man in the health of his soul. In one person, of course, this health could look like its opposite in another person. Finally, the great question would still remain whether we can really dispense with illness—even for the sake of our virtue—and whether our thirst for knowledge and self-knowledge in particular does not require the sick soul as much as the healthy, and whether, in brief, the will to health alone is

> not a prejudice, cowardice, and perhaps a bit of very subtle barbarism and backwardness. (3. 120)[15]

We can now see Nietzsche's phantom on Bacon's bodies, and also the influences of his notion of Dionysian man, as outlined in *Twilight of the Idols*:

> It is impossible for Dionysian man not to understand any suggestion of whatever kind, he ignores no signal from the emotions, he possesses to the highest degree the instinct for understanding and divining, just as he possesses the art of communication to the highest degree. He enters into every skin, into every emotion: he is continually transforming himself . . . (*Twilight of the Idols*. 9. 10)[16]

> . . . one first has to convince the *body*. The strict maintenance of a significant and select demeanour, an obligation to live only among men who do not 'let themselves go', completely suffices for becoming significant . . . It is decisive for the fortune of nations and of mankind that one should inaugurate culture in the *right place—not* in the 'soul' (as has been the fateful superstition of priests and quasi-priests): the right place is the body, demeanour, diet, physiology: the *rest* follows. . . . *Twilight of the Idols* 9. 47)[17]

While others in the Western tradition see the subject as part of the world, and one who needs the perspectives of others in order to feel part of the world one inhabits, Bacon's bodies choose instead to escape from and deform these perspectives.[18]

In this way and in the concern of sexuality, Bacon's artistic choice echoes the effort of some feminist scholars. To take Judith Butler as an example, one finds in her writings a disruption of the continuity between sexed anatomy and gender and sexuality, which privileges the sexed anatomy as the origin of a singular, sexual identity, that is, heterosexuality. The way to disrupt it is to demonstrate that bodies are not the prepared site or space for a pre-existing performance, nor the raw material over which the social or cultural mask is hung, but brought into being through the performance itself. Butler asserts that there is no body that pre-exists discourse, and therefore, no sexuality that is natural to bodies.[19]

Bacon's bodies also remind us that the body is not an originating point nor yet a terminus; it is the result or an effect. Some philosophical writings now hint that the body does have the status of a realm of underlying truth, and try to recover it from medicine or sociology by making it vivid again. The works of Bacon's contemporaries (Jacques Lacan, Merleau-Ponty, and others) theorize that a body is not properly a human body, a human subject, or individual, unless it has an image of itself as a discrete entity, or as a gestalt.[20] This enables the orientation of one's body in space, and in relation to other bodies, that provides a perspective on the world and that is assumed in the constitution of the signifying subject.[21]

Distinct from all these notions, Bacon's bodies are reconstituted in new forms, which is outstanding with respect to the normative bodies and its related histories in his culture. It would be interesting to look at an alternative in another tradition or historical discourse. Since this alternative should not be read by way of a parallel comparison but rather through cultural differences related to the theories of the body we have discussed, I feel comfortable to introduce the artistic principles of Gu Kaizhi, who was famous for his portraits in traditional China.

The Case of Gu Kaizhi and the Principles of Chinese Figure Painting

Gu Kaizhi 顧愷之 (c. 344–406) is famous for his portraits; he captured not merely the appearance but the very spirit of his subject. His teachings have been followed for a long time and have become the main school of Chinese portraiture. Here is a summary of the features of his artistic practice.[22] The linear, articulated, and calligraphic line is combined with broken interior ink washes to produce a richly integrated texture. The brushwork is delicate with little modulation. The main figures provide formal structure, supported by an environment that plays on human interaction, confrontations, and encounters, in the development of which the artist effectively uses pictorial concepts of emptiness and fullness, always suggesting a slowly unfolding activity. Most human expressions are restrained and delicate; there are few extremes of either emotion or gesture, and the figures seem to combine humanness and a certain ethereal quality.[23] The depiction of human subjects is related to its naiveté, its air of grace, its restraint, and its humanistic spirit.

Confucian thoughts about body and mind are reflected in Gu's theories of painting, stated in his own writings and records of his followers. His theories incorporated Confucian thoughts. The first principle of painting portraits is to grasp the particular spiritual rhythm of the subject, the so-called *qian xiang miao de* 遷想妙得, which has to be attained through good imagination. The excellent manifestation of the spirit of the subject is enabled through form. Gu emphasizes the subject's head and face, particularly the eye or pupil of the subject, which he believes can speak for the subject's soul or spirit. He reminds people of the importance of depicting how subjects relate to their environments in portraits. Things an artist needs to care about include the personality of the subjects (especially historical or legendary figures), their social class, and the subject's relation to other characters in the painting. Things of equal importance are the reactions the subject expresses, the social constraints or rituals that affect the subject's bodily behaviors, the positions or places where the subject and other characters are situated, and, finally, the related setting or environment. In order to achieve the realistic effects of the above principles, Gu suggests that artists should make the effort to observe, study, analyze, and understand. Only through one's hard study can one grasp the essence of the subject and related artistic transformations. Gu admits that it is easier to paint animals than landscapes, but painting humans is the most difficult.

One should not miss the moral implications of Gu's theories, for his discussion of spiritual rhythm mainly refers to the moral qualities of his subjects, and those of the artist as well, which enable one to grasp and understand what is important. As an example, *The Fairy of the Lo River* 《洛神賦圖》, an illustration after the time of Gu Kaizhi, preserves the archaic style of his time and demonstrates these principles.[24] In the scene, a fairy bids farewell to the young scholar who had fallen in love with her, wishing for his good fortune and future, and sails away in her magic boat. The flying sleeves of the clothing and the setting of willow trees are said to have grasped the spiritual rhythms of the characters, in praise of love and the virtues of sacrifice.[25]

Another example is one of Gu's very few surviving famous paintings, *The Admonitions of the Instructress to the Court Ladies*

《女史箴圖》, which tells Confucian stories in praise of four groups of famous virtuous women of antiquity.[26] This painting shows the emperor gazing doubtfully at a concubine seated in her sofa bed. The text accompanying the illustrations echo the woman's saying, "If the words that you utter are good, all men for a thousand leagues around will make response to you. But if you depart from this principle, even your bedfellow will distrust you."[27] The figures, the setting, and the postures and spiritual expressions of the subjects are all executed in Gu's best effort and are illustrated according to his suggested principles in recounting folk legend, which is also a Confucian educational text for women. We should note that Confucian teachings greatly influenced Gu's principles, in particular the Confucian theories of mind and body, which should be discussed for the purposes of this chapter.

Confucian Theories of the Body

I recall three theories of the body that are found in early Confucian school in pre-Qin dynasty before 2 BC. They are: Mencius' relational theory of the body and the mind, Xunzi's 荀子 social theory of the body, and the ancient natural theory of the body as represented by Yangzhu 楊朱. All these theories imply the inseparable relation of body and mind. No body is without the implication of the mind and no mind is without its embodiment. When each Confucian theory emphasizes a certain aspect, the conclusive contemporary connotation is that the body is a compound of one's conscious, physical, social, and cultural dimensions. These theories are influenced by two traditions: the Confucian one of rituals—that human body is always ritualized or socialized—and the traditional ancient natural theory of the vital force (*qi*).

I would like to focus on Mencius' (371–289 BC) ideas of the body and mind, as his work not only discloses materials crucial to an understanding of a theory of the body in the Confucian tradition but is itself also a representative discourse. Here one could refer to Chapter 1 of this book for some citations and readings that are also revealing of the implications of Chinese figure paintings.

> Every human being possesses these four beginnings just as he possesses four limbs. Anyone possessing these four and claiming that

he cannot do what they require is selling himself short. If he claims that his prince cannot do what they require, he is selling his prince short. Since, in general, the four beginnings exist within us, it remains only to learn how to enlarge them and bring them to a fullness. This may be compared to the first flicker of a fire, or the first trickle of a spring. (Mencius 2A: 6)[28]

The "Four Beginnings" (四端) are the four fundamental feelings and sentiments that constitute forms of moral knowledge, so-called *liangzhi* (良知). These are feelings and sentiments of compassion, shame, modesty, or reverence, and include the distinction between right and wrong. These feelings and sentiments are believed to be natural, and can be immediately accessed when a person is situated in proper circumstances. The feelings and sentiments can produce virtues of benevolence, righteousness, propriety, and wisdom respectively, and the inclination to act accordingly when the moral subject interacts with others. Mencius considered *liangzhi* the ontological foundation of virtues, and its relation to the body is that it needs to be nurtured and preserved. He said:

"Do not seek in your heart for what you do not find in your words. Do not seek in your Vitality for what you do not find in your heart." The second of these statements I find to be all right; the first, I disapprove. For will is commander over the vitality, while vitality is what fills our persons. Will is of the highest importance; Vitality stands second. That is why it is said, "There is no disorder in the vitality where will is maintained" . . . "If the will is unified, it becomes a motor for the vitality. If the vitality is the unified one, it becomes motor for the will . . . " (Mencius 2A: 2)[29]

Vital force refers to bodily substance, matter and desire; the Chinese word is *qi*. We should point out that *qi* is different from will (the moral mind), but both are interrelated in the sense that the moral mind should govern *qi*, or virtue will fail, and this is a crucial point for humanity. *Qi* is different from the "strong, moving power," which in Chinese is the *haoran zhi qi* 浩然之氣. In the latter, *qi* is guided by righteousness (*yi*) in the fullest sense and has been compared to "flood breath." It is believed that in *haoran zhi qi, yi* is the ontological foundation of bodily action.

Through one's self-conscientious effort to act according to moral principles, *yi* will naturally lead to the ontological extension of oneself and will transform the world into a universe of significance integral to the individual self. The bodily *qi* that lacks moral nourishment will not only easily weaken but will also subvert the moral self when violent. Mencius again:

> There is not an inch of his skin that he does not love, so there is not an inch of it that he does not take care of. Its good and bad parts are derived from no other source than the man himself. In the body there are both honored and despised parts, big and small parts. One does not harm the big with the small; and one does not harm the honored with the despised. The one who takes care of the small parts first is a petty man; he who takes care of the big parts first is big man. (Mencius 6A: 14)[30]

> By following one's bigness one becomes a big man; by following one's pettiness one becomes a petty man . . . Since the senses of hearing and sight do not think, they become obscured by things; they are beguiled by the contact occurring between things. The sense of heart-and-mind, however, thinks. If there is thinking, that sense is achieved; but without thinking it is not achieved. It is something given to us by Sky. If it is first established in bigness, pettiness will not be able to snatch it away. And such an individual will become simply a big man. (Mencius 6A: 15)[31]

We note that the mind is the noblest and greatest component of the body, and it is more than simply physical because of its moral consciousness or innate knowledge of goodness. Smaller components are the physical ones that have basic functions like hearing and vision. Physical needs or desires of the smaller components have to be subordinated to the control of the "thinking greatest-component," which constitutes the center of moral principles and will. As mentioned, moral knowledge and its capabilities need to be developed and preserved in order to transform the human subject into a "great person" or sage. According to the traditional Confucian school, what a person should do—through moral practice—in one's personal life and in one's social intercourse with others is the central and ultimate concern of human activity. The famous saying of Mencius demonstrates the significant exercise of the mind in dominating and repressing the smaller components of the body as follows:

> Therefore, when sky is going to confer great responsibility upon an individual, his heart-and-mind and his determination must first be made to suffer, his sinews and bones must know toil, the skin of his body must show the ravages of hunger, his person must be reduced to the last extremity, all his undertakings must be upset. In this way his heart-and-mind are touched, his nature is provided with endurance, and aid is provided for his incapacities . . . (Mencius 6B: 15)[32]

This idea of repression, practices, or transformation results in an important Confucian idea present in traditional Chinese figure painting, which believes that one's virtues or moral mind would finally manifest and transform one's appearances, "in one's face, back and four limbs, without saying." (Mencius 7A). The following is another conclusion:

> The desirable is called approved; and to contain within oneself is to inspire confidence. When filled fully with both of these, one is called handsome. When filled fully with them to the point of being glorious, one is called great. When out of greatness one produces changes in the world, one is called a sage. What remains unknown despite the fact that one is a sage is called divine . . . (Mencius 7B: 25)[33]

The interpretation is that a sage or a beautiful man full of spirit in figure painting is one who genuinely practices moral virtues, whose appearance is in contrast to a "small man."

Some Comparative Considerations

The works of Bacon and Gu belong to different cultures in different times. Though the interpretations in this chapter should not be seen as a direct comparison, the contrast between the artistic works of these two great portrait masters is notable. While Bacon's subjects are associated with "exhilarated despair," sexuality, and violence that seem to violate the moral norms of his times, Gu's subjects celebrate Confucian virtues, and his works are regarded as tools of moral education. The theme of

Bacon's figures is the "shattering of the subject" or the replacement of a unified self by a fragmented self, which has been read as "loss of self" with psychoanalytic implications. Gu's subjects are not elusive or anything subconscious; rather, they assert a moral self from the figures and through the viewers, and first of all from the artist himself. The contrast is also represented artistically by Bacon's blurred and rough brushes, and Gu's delicate and linear style. There is no visual or reciprocal relationship among Bacon's subjects, and he intentionally avoids any story-telling among his subjects. The bodies of his figures always merge and are hardly differentiated from one another. Gu is famous for emphasizing the pupil of a subject's eye; he believed that it manifested the rhythm of one's spirit. There is often mutual gazing: that between the emperor and his good lady, or the fairy and the scholar she loves, for example, is filled with compassion and moral expectation. There is no absolute distinction between the inside and the outside in Bacon's space, as critics point out, nor is it defined by a surrounding space. Gu's space is consciously both natural and social. He grasps the exactitude of natural environment and also takes into account the subject's social position in related social space.

Moreover, Bacon's loss of self implies a real self behind the scenes, whose subjectivity is marked by artistic choices or forms. This self, according to Nietzsche, is a bodily self beyond the so-called mind and spirit, which are socially and culturally constructed. Gu's self is basically a moral constituted being of the will, the mind, and the body: the moral will and mind cultivates the body and the body, in turn, nurtures the will and the mind through progressive practices.

Confucians discuss their theories of the body as something ontological and natural, as do some theories in the Western tradition. However, contemporary discourses stress that the difference does not have to do with biological "facts," so much as with the manner in which culture marks bodies and creates specific conditions in which they live and recreate themselves. The marking is enabled through discourses that cannot be deemed "outside" or apart from various forms of power relations operated through languages or signifying practices. As Moira Gatens said, what is crucial in our current context is the thorough interrogation of the means by which bodies become invested with differences, which are then taken to be fundamental ontological differences.[34] Judith Butler's point is also noteworthy, that a bodily norm is assumed, appropriated, and taken on as not undergone by a subject, but rather that the subject is formed by virtue of having gone through such a process of assumption.[35]

These sorts of contemporary rethinking call into question the model of construction whereby the social acts on the natural and invests it with its parameters and meanings. The reflection applies to both the Western and Eastern discourses discussed in this chapter, where the natural relinquishes itself as the natural. As claimed, there is no reference to a pure body that is not at the same time a further formation of the body, when the practice of signification, of demarcating, and of delimiting are inevitable.[36]

Section II

BODY AESTHETICS AND ART

4

DISCOURSES ON FEMALE BODILY AESTHETICS AND THEIR EARLY REVELATIONS IN *THE BOOK OF SONGS*

The famous ancient Chinese literary work, *The Book of Songs*, selected more than 300 musical pieces and poems of nobles and laymen from the period of West Zhou (eleventh century BC) to the late Warring States period (sixth century BC). The work contains folksongs, songs of the nobility, ritual hymns, and ballads about significant events in the history of the Zhou people. The work is recognized as a significant creative record reflecting the wars, lives, and large range of social changes as well as literary developments of those periods in China.

There are numerous pieces in *The Airs of the States* (*Guo Feng* 國風) depicting male and female images of the time; a large number focused on women of various kinds. These records or creative images have been important sources not only for the study of the rites, creativity, and related humanistic thought of the pre-Qin period, but also for the aesthetics and ideals of people, men and women. While ethical cultivation had always been the tool of tradition, initiated from a personal level, one can find in these songs discourses on female ideals in emotional and spontaneous ways as well as in the moral constraints imposed during the Zhou patriarchal era. That was an era when myths faded, monarchies strengthened, and feudal and ritual practices dominated. The female beauties described in the book were also the refraction and projection of the supreme aesthetic ideals of the time.

There have been debates on whether the edition was by Confucius, who would have chosen from more than 3,000 pieces collected at the king of Zhou's request, and what the Han commentaries added to these works. I share the following conclusions with scholars Stephen Owen, Haun Saussy, and Arthur Waley.[1]

Most of the songs seemed to have reached their present versions shortly before the anthology was assembled, probably around 600 BC. The anthology belonged to the Zhou court and the courts of the feudal states into which the Zhou kingdom had disintegrated. They were produced in a world in which people could speak about not only their desires but also the fulfillment of those desires, and joy and pain could be spoken about with honesty. The songs embraced the voices of common people, women and lovers, and those from all walks of life outside the heroic ethos. The book also contributed a lot to Chinese myths and legends of the Zhou as the ideal polity. They later played a central role in the great Confucian project of education and self-cultivation. As in a Confucius saying that the book acted as a paradigm of the moral heart: "There are three hundred Songs and one phrase covers them all: 'No straying from the path'" (Analects 2:2). The songs also specified relations across social classes.[2]

Controversies arose when many of the songs seemed not to conform to certain aspects of Confucian morality; they were then reinterpreted by the Traditionalists and by the Han and Song commentators so as to be in accord with their presumed moral perfection. Critics claimed that the implication of moral import represented the parameters for an understanding of the text close to their own time.[3] When *The Book of Songs* became a standard of the Confucian scholastic curriculum and responded to the moral and social conditions of the age, it had a double function: it was at once a live record and boldly expressive literary text, as well as a Confucian classic that articulated moral and political positions. This chapter uses the title *The Book of Songs* of Arthur Waley's translated version, where the *songs* imply more primal and expressive material. While this study broadly refers to commentaries to allow a larger spectrum of readings, it basically agrees with Haun Saussy's admiration of the songs and delegates the "moral effusions" and "political significations" when appropriate.[4] Here I agree with Waley that these songs emerged from different performance contexts and melded with the formal demands of the genre, such as prosody and rhyme. The songs were produced within the sociopolitical framework of the time, and had leaped from performance environments of primary orality to those of secondary orality, and then on to more fixed texts, beginning in the late Warring States period, betraying more complex political and social origins.[5] It later became the norm that the songs "serve as a rhetoric or source of usable phrases," and they were quoted with re-contextualized meanings until they became a classic and came close to attaining the status of doctrine.[6]

I also agree with the observation that the Mao commentaries (150 BC) introduce self-referential moral-political stories to the "scandalous nature" of the poems and defused it, while Zhu Xi's comments in the Song dynasty (960–1260) encouraged a direct engagement with the poems and called upon the power of the subjective mind, urging people not to give too much attention to those negative examples. I sympathize with Zhu Xi's reading, which was distant from the moralizing maneuvers of the ancient prefaces.[7] I read the songs under the dialectical tension and dualistic thoughts between the Mao commentaries context that Waley described as moral-political order and elite culture with its "Small Prefaces" and the elaboration, and that of Zhu Xi, whose preface to the anthology emphasized that they were songs of village lanes and they were what men and women sang to each other, expressing their feelings (*qing*) in words.[8] Finally, I agree with its Great Preface that poetry is the product of earnest thoughts and it expresses the intention of their authors and their inner lives.[9] As Waley said, they read to feel the emotions and to know the authors who wrote about those emotions, and this is the true literary legacy of *The Book of Songs*.[10]

Female Bodily Ideals and Their Modalities

Besides the mother goddesses of the myths and the legends of the pre-dynastic Zhou and Shang-Yin periods mentioned in *The Major Odes* and *The Hymns*, the more vivid female images in *The Book of Songs* were the young ladies portrayed in *The Airs of the States* and *The Minor Odes*. They came from different regions and were related to various customs and traditions, manifesting a range of temperaments, physical attributes, and manners. They were also of different classes, including nobles, courtesans, young brides-to-be, middle-aged women, fishing women, laborers, silk workers, weavers, and farmers. These women probably sang and danced well; their excellent performance and expression contributed to a repertoire of songs and poetry. The works performed, as the neo-Confucian Zhu Xi recommended, were products of the Zhou civilization, setting a contrast to the dark age of Shang-Yin and promoting the cultural quality and standard of the time.

A large range of adjectives related to beauty and praise of femininity were projected onto female historical characters and figures of the songs. Examples are the famous phrase "the modest, retiring, virtuous young lady" (窈窕淑女), in "The Ospreys Cry" (關雎) in the *South of Zhou,* which refers to queens and court ladies who cause their suitors to think about them while awake and asleep (輾轉反側); and the words "beauty" (美) "lovely" (姝), and "handsome" (孌) in "Of Fair Girls" (靜女) in *The Airs of Bei* (邶風), which may refer to the lady of the duke of Qi, as the commentaries suggest. Other innovative phrases were "clear are her eyes; fine is her forehead" (子之清揚，揚且之顏) in "Companion of Her Lord till Death" (君子偕老) in *The Airs of Yong* (鄘風), designating various appealing physical features.

Metaphors of nature were used to describe female beauty. Favorite metaphors included the sun and the moon in the East (for example, "Sun in the East" 東方之日 , in *The Airs of Qi* 齊風), gems (for example, "Bamboo Rod" 竹竿 in *The Airs of Wei* 衛風 and "In the Wilds is a Dead Doe" 野有死麇, in *The South of Shao* 召南) and flowers (for example, peach blossoms in "Peach-tree" 桃夭, in *The South of Zhou* 周南 ; the flower of the ephemeral hedge-tree in "There Was a Girl with Us in the Carriage" 有女同車, in *The Airs of Zheng* 鄭風) depicting the color, the brightness, and the freshness of young female bodies. In the poem "A Splendid Woman" (碩人), in *The Airs of Wei*, one finds metaphors applied to female bodily parts: the blades of the young white-grass represent her fingers; congealed ointment her skin; a tree-grub her neck; melon seeds her teeth; a cicada her forehead; and [the antenna of] the silkworm moth her eyebrow, and so on; in others, clouds represent black hair in masses (for example, "Companion of Her Lord till Death" in *The Airs of Yong*. These metaphors expressed more than physical appeal, for they represented cleanliness, tidiness, health, and inner beauty.

Tidiness was essential, as manifested in the elaborate hair dress with cross pins. In the same song, in the lines "her black hair in masses like clouds, no false locks does she descend to / There are her ear-plugs of jade, her comb-pin of ivory," the gems and jades signify the multiple values of wealth, class, fine taste, good fortune, and personal virtue. While the metaphors applied to both gentlemen and ladies, the women who wore these gems showed the inner qualities of loyalty, purity, and perseverance, as depicted in "Small War-Chariot" (小戎), in *The Airs of Qin* (秦風).

Some interesting points to note about female physical appeal. There is praise of majestic physical size, for example, in "A Splendid Woman" (碩人), in *The Airs of Wei*,[11] "Swamp Shore" (澤陂), in *The Airs of Chen* (陳風),[12] and "Axle-Pin of a Coach" (車舝), in *The Minor Odes* (小雅).[13] These large ladies are accompanied by strong horses and situated in various natural and artificial settings (rivers, marshes, suburbs, a carriage). They are nobles with elegant dress and elaborate accessories, which represent their wealth and power. The songs clearly describe their bodily parts (fingers, skin, neck, teeth, forehead, eyebrows, eyes) and even their relaxing manners, suggesting good health and strength. One could see them and smell them and hear them clearly when perceiving the works. One could also feel that they are proud of their good-sized physiques, filled with feminine qualities and human vitality.

The aesthetic judgments might be read as practical considerations. Size is related to productivity, wealth, health, strength, and power and it could reflect the group imagination of a peasant society. An example is the song "Pepper Plant" (椒聊), in *The Airs of Tang* (唐風),[14] which celebrated productivity and associated it with beings of majestic size. Besides the court ladies and the nobles, there were other female characters in the songs who were laborers working diligently, sewing and picking things and suggesting good physique (for example, "The Seven Month" 七月 , in *The Airs of Bin* 豳風 and "In the Ten-Acre Field" 十畝之間 , in *The Airs of Wey* 魏風). These healthy characters were expected to have strong offspring as well, which was a common social anticipation in peasant society (as in "Locusts" 螽斯, in *The South of Zhou*). These considerations may explain why large ladies were rated over small ones in these songs.

The character for "beauty" in Chinese (美) depicts a big goat that provides food and is clearly imbued with the meaning of utility in an ancient farming society. Beauty is good and beneficial, serving basic needs like goods, food, and clothes. This illustrates that the notion of "beauty" is cultural and contextual. Beauty to the Chinese is therefore not necessarily gender-specific. Waley's translated version of "Swamp Shore" in *The Airs of Chen* does not refer to a majestic lady but a man. It is believed that the term *majestic* was applied to both men and women as a physical ideal of the era.

There is praise of whiteness. White is the favorite and ideal female bodily color in *The Book of Songs*. White designated the color of female teeth, forehead, fingers, and hands, as depicted in the phrases "hands white as rush-down, skin like lard, neck long and white as the tree-grub, teeth like melon seeds" (手如柔荑，膚如凝脂) in the song "A Splendid Woman" in *The Airs of Wei*. Dress was always in white, light, and pure colors. The color represented refined aesthetic quality similar to the praise of whiteness in today's cosmetics. It was also loaded with value, designating purity, loyalty, and chastity.

Yet slenderness was also praised. Certain parts of the female body were praised for slenderness. The phrases "the delicate fingers of a bride" (摻摻女手) in "Fiber Shoes" (葛屨) in *The Airs of Wey* and "her fingers were like the blades of the young white-grass" (手如柔荑) in "A Splendid Woman" in *The Airs of Wei* are examples. Entering the Warring States period, the slenderness and curvy movements of female bodies were applauded, illustrating certain changes. Songs like "Moon Rising" (月出) in *The Airs of Chen* and "There Was a Girl with Us in the Carriage" in *The Airs of Zheng* captured vividly the ways of the maturing body. There are also phrases hinting at slim waistlines, like "moving at ease" (好人提提) in "Fiber Shoes." This change in the appreciation of size suggests changes in economic growth and also in modes of production.

In the praises of beauty in the songs, one sees both colorful and elaborate dress codes and natural attributes. Green and red were used for ritual celebrations, white for all purposes and elegant effects. Colors and dress codes demonstrated distinct social occasions and identities. Yet besides being a social language, colors acted also as expressive tools. A good example is the lady in splendid green and yellow in "The Green Coat" (綠衣), in *The Airs of Bei*. Here, Waley's translated version specifically portrays a male and female dialogue, in which the lady had purposely made a coat for her lover that is green on the outside and lined with yellow on the inside. The coat was sewn as a reminder of her devotion, which was just like the bright and eye-catching colors and were effective in keeping the heart of her lover. Another example is in "Outside the Eastern Gate" (出其東門), in *The Airs of Zheng*, where a lady dressed in a white jacket, a grayish-green scarf, and a skirt dyed in red from the madder plant. The colors in the white base obviously made her most admirable and unforgettable. One can associate the purity of white and gray with beauty, elegance, and simplicity, which represented sophistication, in particular of women.

The ways in which a woman carried herself were depicted in *The Book of Songs*, with emphasis placed on smiling, lying, and moving postures. The four-word phrases describing these postures were both vivid and poetic; they reminded readers of the portraits of Chinese beauties (*meiren hua*) from which these songs inherited notions about appearance and then in turn acted as an influence, forming circular effects. These poetic depictions were plentiful, contributing to the long and abundant history of Chinese female imagery. Some representative examples refer to tidiness in hair dressing, an important theme in the *meiren hua*.

One should also note the special movements and postures depicted in these songs. In addition to the famous phrase praising "the modest, retiring, virtuous and young lady" in "The Ospreys Cry" of *The South of Zhou* are those found in "Moon Rising" in *The Airs of Chen*. The tenderness, gracefulness, gentle softness, and "the delicate yielding" successfully depict the attraction and tangible imagination of a female body. Special terms were used to describe beauty in these songs, like "my lovely one" (佼人) in "Moon Rising," "beauty" (粲者) in "Fast Bundled," in *The Airs of Tang*, and "a clever woman tearing down a city" (傾城) in "High Regard,"[15] in *The Major Odes* and so on.

There are unattainable women in the songs. The beauties were those who could not be accessed or possessed. There are songs that express the despair of men who were obsessed by the women they adored but found them to be inaccessible. These men could only miss these women, praise them, think about them all the time, sigh and suffer. Commentators attributed these feelings to a metaphorical sense of patriotism, boldly stating that the beauties were mother-states and that the authors missed them as people do in exile, dreaming of a happy ending or loving reunion. Examples of these include the famous piece of "The Ospreys Cry," "The Han is Broad" (漢廣) of *South of Zhou*,[16] and "Hollow Mound" (宛丘) of *The Airs of Chen*. The misery and anguish of the pining men projected quiet and cool images of the inaccessible beauties, who could easily destroy a man's heart. These depictions also made the women both illusory and eternal, within the poetic and aesthetic realm of imaginary settings.

Despite the fact that about a quarter of the songs in the anthology expressed scenes of marriage, demonstrating a sexual division of labor in the patriarchal Zhou period and immediately after, there are still intriguingly explicit sexual suggestions made around female characters. The Zhou period was a society in which polygamy was popular, forced marriages and wife abandonment were quite common, and sons were preferred over daughters, as reflected in many of these songs. Yet, there were also flirtatious scenes that depicted sexy and charming young women looking for love and courtship, as vividly illustrated in the famous "The Ospreys Cry," which indicated related longing, and in the sexual symbols of juicy peaches in the "Peach-tree" in *The South of Zhou*. More explicit examples may be found in *The Airs of Zheng* and the "The Lady Says" (女曰雞鳴),[17] where the woman proposes dressing and undressing for her man; "In the Wilds is a Dead Doe," in *The South of Shao*, where a young girl with sexual longings and acts is mentioned; and "Sun in the East" in *The Airs of Qi*, which portrayed the voluntary sexual act of a woman.

These songs suggest a space of sexual pleasure, where anxious, yet active and open attitudes prevailed among women in the context of social propriety. The women were beautiful in their daring passion and expressiveness, even before *The Airs of Zheng* and other songs related to the theme were critiqued and commented on. But instead of a direct deviation from increasing Confucian control, there seemed to be an undercurrent in which women tried to keep safe while searching for a balance. The song "I Beg You, Zhong Zi" (將仲子), in *The Airs of Zheng* is one example where the lady expresses her fear while declaring her love.[18]

One should also note the common association of women with water in Chinese poetry, which appears in some representative works of *The Book of Songs*. Statistics show that twenty-eight songs in *The Airs of States* contain such an association, with water in the background of scenes where women are singing ("Gird Your Loins" 褰裳 , in *The Airs of Zheng*,[19] lamenting ("Valley Wind" 谷風 , in *The Airs of Bei*),[20] laboring ("Gathering White Aster" 采蘩, in *The South of Shao*),[21] or flirting ("The Zhen and Wei" 溱 洧 in *The Airs of Zheng*).[22] Water was either a direct aesthetic object associated with women or it acted as an analogy, creating and enhancing the necessary atmospheric effects. The most popular example is "Rush Leaves" (蒹葭) in *The Airs of Qin*,[23] in which the adoring person stood by the stream, kicking off "beauty by the autumn water" (秋水伊人), referring to the aesthetic distance necessary for male fantasy or imagining beauty.

The use of water as a metaphor in *The Book of Songs* is an early literary illustration of the primary and primal relationship of water and femininity, as it represented the origin of life and vitality, the nurturing function of which related to the lyrical effect of femininity; a living essential that maintains and gives life, that is, a reminder of female fertility; elements of femininity as the cosmological principle of *yin*, referring to the potentiality of creation; the qualities of "softness," "tenderness," and "fluidity." This notion is inspirational and the association contributed a poetic and aesthetic picture of women by water; it represented ritual constraints where water or a river acts as a barrier to a relationship or as a physical and social distance that one cannot cross; and lastly, it was a setting for the joy and sadness of female characters. While water was the main metaphor, the natural setting of swamps, plants, and peach trees dominated most of the feminine space in the songs and promoted a beautifying effect and fairytale-like atmosphere.

Male Bodily Ideals: A Comparative Reading

The men praised in the songs and who are adored by women tend to be clichés. A representative example is "Shu is Away in the Hunting-Fields" (叔于田), in *The Airs of Zheng*,[24] in which Shu represents the male ideals, being admirable, kind, good, and martial. The key is a strong body that can ride, shoot, and play excellently and morally with courage. "Hey-ho" (猗嗟), in *Airs of Qi*, articulates in exclamatory sounds and rhythms the vivid male ideal of a magnificent bowman and dancer who cannot be mistaken as a wicked person. Majestic male bodies were praised for their quick and active attacks and responses. Qualities of strength, courage, and skills were valued over the gentleness of women.

But the men were more like peacocks, playing the evolutionary game of selection according to sex. These men were admired for their powerful looks and imperial demeanor. Martial strength was emphasized, in the wearing of decorative animal skins, such as the lamb's fur and leopard's cuff in "Furs of Lamb's Wool" (羔裘), in *The Airs of Zheng*,[25] and the tiger-like look and strong reins in "So Grand" (簡兮), in *The Airs of Bei*.[26] While women were set beside water and streams, these adored men were depicted among hunting animals, presenting a fierce rather than aesthetic picture. Their majesty was about muscles and body development, physical exercise, health, and combat power. They also displayed heroic gestures, striving for a balanced walking postures and proper presentation, as vividly described in the phrase "with step grave and slow" (委蛇委蛇) in "Young Lamb" (羔羊), *The South of Shao*.[27] One should note that the male heroic air also implied moral strength; their behavior proper and in control, even humorous, like those described in "Little Bay of the Qi" (淇奥), in *The Airs of Wei*.[28]

The other domain different from the women in the songs and in reverse were the colors of clothes. This domain showed that *The Book of Songs* reflected the situation before the gender construction of the increasing Confucian and political maneuvers of the era. Red, green, and yellow are the colors of male peacocks; these colors displayed their attractiveness based on an elaborate identity, shown sometimes as an individual and sometimes as a group. Proof may be found in the songs "The Seventh Month," in *The Airs of Bin*, when the women make big red cloths for men;[29] "Gathering Beans" (采菽) in *The Minor Odes*, where the men wear red greaves on their legs, demonstrating capacity;[30] and when soldiers dress in red and green with their weapons, as depicted in "The Closed Temple" (閟宫) of *The Hymns of Lu* (魯頌), in the seventh century.[31] The color green appears twelve times in the *Book*; six of them refer to male dress, acting as a proud color. Yellow was another favorite color for both men and women. The adorable male in the song "Knight of the City" (都人士) in *The Minor Odes* shows off his yellow fox fur under the crowd's gaze.[32] These proud men dress like a rainbow trout, they wear splendid accessories, jewels, and gems, demonstrating a taste for more elaborate dress than women, who regard their own beauty as wrapped in white and fading colors.

It is interesting to compare these two representative portrayals of the genders' dress codes. The first one is "Minnow-Net" (九罭), in *The Airs of Bin*, in praise of a man whose dress is embroidered with patterns of the dragon, mountain, cock, fire, tiger, weed, and rice, as explicated by Zhu Xi in his commentary. The other is the song "A Splendid Woman" in *The Airs of Wei* introduced earlier, where one finds common everyday plants working as metaphors for female bodily parts. The difference is an interesting demonstration that shows a certain representation of gender and beauty before a later development that showed its reverse: that is, the "peacock theory," in which women were colorfully and elaborately dressed, and the look of males was cool and simple, associated with moral purity and strength.

Mind and Body Coherence

While Greek goddesses were noted for their beauty, some of them remained wicked without condemnation. But this is not the case with the female characters of the songs, where the beauties are juxtaposed with their virtues and merits. The coherence of a moral mind and graceful body has always been the theme and standard, mirroring the classical postulate of inner and outer beauty. Physical exquisiteness was measured and checked against inner temperaments, while inner perfection overshadowed outer appearance and enhanced external splendor.

There are songs loaded with moral acclaim and criticism, either enhancing or downgrading the attractiveness of the female characters. A well-quoted example is the sarcastic comment on the unmatched gorgeousness and lack of chastity by a commentator on Lady Wei in the song "Companion of Her Lord till Death" in *The Airs of Yong*, which points to an inner and outer incoherence. The song depicted her elaborate hairstyle, wearing of jewels, and dress, juxtaposed with her gifted physical and facial composure, suggestive of nobility. The picture is indeed a grand one of a first lady who should have all credit. Yet people who knew her lack of chastity and faithfulness perceived an irony instead of the aesthetic scene so delicately described in the song.

On the other hand, loyalty and passion succeeded in enhancing the merits and hence the attractiveness of the subjects. This was well illustrated in the song "My Lord is on Service" (君子于役), in *The Airs of the Royal Domain* (王風), which provides a detailed sketch of the thoughts of a woman longing for her husband day and night. He is in the service; she is rewarded for her love and genuine concern for his well-being. This makes her charming enough to be remembered, even if nothing is written about her appearance.

Another form of coherence exemplifies female magnificence in the form of boldness, independence, and striving for justice and fairness. The well-discussed example is the song "A Simple Peasant" (氓) in *The Airs of Wei*, a touching story self-narrated by a woman who gives detailed accounts of the history of her marriage: the moment of their first encounter, the proposal, then the anticipation, despair, and suffering thereafter. She tries hard to maintain the relationship until she realizes that it was time to end it. This self-awareness and decisiveness makes her outstanding against numerous women of the time who would have chosen to stay in the relationship. While the lamentations in those songs of abandoned women suffering in all kinds of marital constrictions under the patriarchy earn only mercy and sympathy from others, this female character against the odds and constraints of loyalty imposed on her as a woman merited recognition for her self-awakening and determination. There appears to be no dichotomy of mind and body in culture in the early eras; this applies also to female beauty.

Sources for Aesthetic Representation: Visual Illustrations

There is a long tradition in China of representing women within a feminine environment. *The Book of Songs* exerted a great influence on female portraits in China, especially those *meiren hua* of later development. The feminine space in more recent centuries was replete with details of decorative items and architectural layouts, with particular kinds of buildings, paths, railings, decorative objects, painting, and calligraphy; but the trees, flowers, plants, rocks, and personal attributes like clothes and ornaments, makeup, facial and bodily features; and finally tableaux of female activities were portrayals that echo those in some of the songs.[33]

Art critics suggest the concept of feminine space as a totalized entity; beauty was essentially the sum of all the visible forms one expected to find in her space. One identified a woman as a beauty not by recognizing her face but by surveying her courtyard, clothes, her companions, and her idealized expressions and gestures. The appearance of Chinese beauties was epitomized by traditional literati in classical texts as a woman with star-bright eyes, willow-leaf eyebrows, cloud-like hair, and snow-white bosom, which were the signifiers described and recorded as early as in the songs.

One can find similar depictions in *The Manual of Beautiful Women*, by Xu Zhen, around the mid-seventeenth century, which was a popular text that Chinese art critics refer to when discussing female beauty, as with those in the songs. In Wu Hung's faithful translation of the ten-part iconography, namely physical appearance, style, skills, activities, dwelling, seasons and moments, adornment, auxiliary objects, food, and special interests, the prototypes and principles were in the songs. The following list includes the similarities as described in the manual:[34]

> *Physical appearance:* Cicada forehead; apricot lips; rhinoceros-horn teeth; creamy breasts; eyebrows like faraway mountains; glances like waves of autumn water; lotus-petal face; cloud-like hair; feet like bamboo shoots carved in jade; fingers like white shoots of grass; willow waist; delicate steps as though walking on lotus blossoms.
>
> *Style:* Leaving her footsteps on green moss; leaning against a railing while waiting for moonrise; glancing back before departure; throwing out an artful, captivating smile; having just finished singing and becoming fatigued from dancing.
>
> *Skills:* Whereas women in seventeenth-century China were playing the lute; embroidering; weaving brocade; comprehending musical pitches and rhymes; swinging and playing the "double six" game; the women in the songs, as discussed above, were either doing hard laborers' work, sewing, and picking in the field, or the wealthier ones were singing and longing for their men. Yet one must say the female activities in the later portraits were more idealized and imaginary than realistic, in which the women were taking care of orchids, catching butterflies, fashioning clothes, and so on.
>
> *Seasons and moments:* Feminine space became more artificial than that portrayed in the songs; like a bright moon over a painted pleasure-boat; snow reflected on a pearled curtain; silver candles above a tortoise-shell banquet table; more natural scenes like fragrant plants in the setting sun and raindrops pelting banana leaves remind people of the background in the songs.

Adornment: Embroidered skirts; raw silk sleeveless dresses; hairpins; jade pendants; "love birds" belt; gem earrings and "phoenix" head ornaments.

Sexual Suggestions: Expressions of this kind became more repressed and calculated in later developments, while basic gestures remained the same as in the songs, like leaning drunkenly on her lover's shoulder; laughing seductively; secretly exchanging glances, showing slight jealousy, and so on.

These female portraits satisfied both the physical desires and spiritual demands of their times. But some of the main variations that developed were vulnerability, passivity, excessive refinement, and melancholic expression, as illustrated in the stereotypes of the beautiful characters in later eras.[35] In late imperial times, these were read as images of a lost and subordinated country waiting for the power of a new foreign ruler. Yet the feminine ideals represented in the Zhou period, though advancing into the chaotic era of the Warring States, remained expressive, bold, tough, and strong. Women lamented for love, but they were not vulnerable or passive. They took rites into consideration but were determined at the same time, and even when their deeds were right or wrong according to the commentaries, they illustrated vivid characters in their variety. Moreover, when the doubts of female authors are taken into account, the beauties in the songs were not enclosed in an isolated space as those depicted in the *meiren hua*; they were not only ideal lovers of men but also idealized female beauties in the eyes of both genders.

Conclusion: The Lost Horizon?

Female beauty (*meiren*) in classical Chinese referred to femininity, skin color and erotic qualities, bodily beauty, shapely limbs, gentleness of behavior, dress and make up, and so on. In addition to visual appeal, there is the sense of touch, smell, and also the sound of her voice. It is the vitality of the body that counted, and the sensuous qualities that were conceived by the integration of all our senses. One found these touch ups in *The Book of Songs* vibrantly described via the contents, rhythms and the texts in later forms.

According to most classical writings, a woman's beauty also had to be judged through sexual sensation, more often heterosexual ones; that is, the qualities of a *meiren* lay in the passionate eye of male lovers or admirers. The beauty of the goddess and *meiren* in classical myths and stories was basically grounded on male desire, fantasies, and devotion, though the notion of beauty later departed from physiological and sexual considerations and became subject to further cultural and normative constraints. However, arguably, the images of *meiren* were not only the projections of male fantasy but also the internalized values and self-identifications of women of the time.

Zhu Xi regarded the first five pieces of *Airs of Bei* as the works of Lady Zhuang Jiang (莊姜) of Wei (752 BC–) for reasons of historical and biographical correspondence. He himself attributed fifty-four poems to various women authors, including Tai-si, Lady Zhuang Jiang, Lady Qi Huan Gong (齊桓公夫人), Lady Xu Mu (許穆夫人), and other courtesans and noble ladies. Their works comprised nearly one-third of *The Airs of the States*. These compositions showed the virtues of the mind and the practices of these ladies, fulfilling the functions of the *feng* (airs), giving instructions that aimed to transform people through their moving and touching stories and the demonstration of their moral dispositions.[36] The virtues set forth by the ladies in the *South of Zhou* and the *South of Shao* were highly recommended in the *Little Preface*, for example.[37]

But one should not place these moral discourses above the daring emotional and erotic expressions that were embedded in these ancient songs. They are there to be explored, which should act as valuable sources for the discussion of the Chinese female ideals. The songs recorded the vitality, the intuitiveness, the spontaneity, the joy, the passion, and the variety. They form the map of a lost female horizon. In this sense, contemporary readings of female beauty—young skin, slim bodies plus the postures portrayed in present-day cosmetic and fashion industries—are not elements that were praised in the lost horizon of the songs. The values loaded in the discourse of female beauty in the *Songs* go beyond Confucian codes. The female ideals are genuinely fascinating, unprompted, and, most of the time, elegant. The modern concepts of "trendiness" and "vogue" sound too artificial, calculating, and monotonous in comparison.

5

REFLECTIONS ON TRADITIONAL CHINESE WOMEN'S EMBROIDERY: THE SUBJECT OF BODILY EXPRESSION, GENDER IDENTITY, AND FASHION

In her book, *Women's Work: The First 20,000 Years*, Elizabeth Barber posed the following question: "Why have women all over the world sat together spinning, weaving and sewing for millennia and turned the work into women's craft par excellence, rather than the work of men?" Her answer includes the compatibility of this pursuit with gender construction, and with the demands of childcare and related means of avoiding economic catastrophe due to the nature of the productive process.[1] But women's textile production also made them subjects of artistic and bodily expression, which in exchange gave them social identities and values. A case in point is women's embroidery in China.

A Brief History of Women's Embroidery in China

Embroidery, popularly known as *xiuhua* (making ornamental designs on cloth with a needle), is one of the finest and oldest national arts of China. Applying various stitching techniques, embroidery is usually performed on finished fabrics using needles and colored silk threads according to designed patterns. Needles and threads are to a skilled embroidery artist precisely what brush, ink, and colors are to a painter.

As Nancy Berliner suggests, a long time ago embroidery in China became a basic celebratory act, which in turn encouraged and allowed women from all classes to create their own forms. Archaeologists have found beads sewn into animal-skin clothing in Xinjiang as far back as 25,000 years ago. Sericulture—the breeding of silkworms and the production of silk fabric—may also have emerged during the Yangshao culture (5000–2500 BC). Sericulture enabled the fine art of embroidery.[2]

The organization and human skills necessary for the production and trading of silk were present during the Shang dynasty, a time of great cultural advances. Elaborately embroidered textiles made of the finest of silks were luxuries for only the wealthy, who could afford to hire embroiderers, but the poor also poured a great deal of energy into embellishing clothes and mementoes. The poor developed embroidery techniques for themselves and shared others with the wealthy, for whom they often worked. An example was found in a Shang tomb at Houjiazhuang, where sculptures of human figures were dressed in robes and skirts, the hems and cuffs of which were heavily decorated with embroidery.[3]

The number of embroiderers under government control increased greatly during the Zhou dynasty (11th century–256 BC), which succeeded the Shang. Women from the countryside were employed or enslaved to do embroidery work. The patterned silks and embroideries discovered in tombs in Changsha are examples of this fine work. Later in the Han dynasty (206 BC–AD 220), eight different kinds of stitches were recorded, namely chain, couched, seed, satin, stem, appliqué, buttonhole, and quilting. No new stitches were employed until the Ming dynasty (1368–1644), when the canvas, Florentine, and petit point stitches became fashionable.[4] In 1972, the discovery of a well-preserved Han tomb demonstrated the degree of sophistication of Han artisans; the tomb revealed embroidered mittens, shoes, robes, and fifty works of embroidered silk and brocades done in a grand variety of colors and designs, such as exquisitely intertwined bird figures.[5]

Embroidery reached a peak during the Tang dynasty (618–907). Chang'an, the capital and international center at the time, employed thousands of seamstresses and embroiderers. Again, peasant wives did much of the work to bring in extra income for their families. Gradually, the clothes of the upper classes became more and more elaborate during the Song dynasty (960–1279); embroidery of this era was even more fanciful than in previous times. Stitching decorated everything from silk parasols to silk fans, wall hangings, and screens. The art of embroidering paintings developed into a respected art form in itself, particularly among the daughters of the affluent.[6]

The Mongols who invaded the Song empire to found the Yuan dynasty (1279–1368) enslaved many silk workers, embroiderers, and other craftspeople. The Mongols brought these workers to the capital to continue production of the much-admired goods until around 1368, when rule returned to the Chinese with the Ming dynasty. During the Ming period, the custom of wearing the imperial square—an embroidered badge on the front and back of officials' robes—emerged; these squares became a wonderful focus for embroidery. Official ranks were assigned animal symbols, ranging from cranes to dragons, embroidered on the badges; these symbols changed when officials were promoted (Figure 5.1, Appendix). The celebrated official costume, with its series of colors, was seen as a sacred institution and passed from generation to generation until the end of the Qing dynasty (1644–1911).[7]

In the early stages of the Qing, with the revival of the national economy, a handicraft textile industry produced household articles. Local embroidery products from Suzhou, Guangdong, Sichuan, and Hunan appeared and competed in the market. Embroidering techniques kept improving, while the dress of the upper classes became more and more luxurious. Next in order of achievement were products made in Beijing, Shanghai, Shandong, Hangzhou, Wenzhou, Fujian, and Kaifeng. Also, minorities in northwest and southwest China, such as the Miao, Mongolians, and others, used their various historical backgrounds and traditions to produce a great variety of exquisite and functional embroideries.[8]

For designs, miscellaneous embroidered patterns and signs had a variety of themes: landscapes, trees, flowers, the sun, the moon, clouds, gardens, animals, insects, characters from famous stories, geometric patterns, and auspicious symbols. Well-conceived compositions and varied stitching techniques and skills were used to achieve harmony or contrasts in color (Figure 5.2, Appendix).

The spatial and cultural contexts of the south (for example, Guangdong) provided its embroidery with a preference for warm and bold color schemes uninhibited by tradition; while the extensive grasslands and deserts of the northwest, sparsely inhabited by a nomadic population, allowed its artists to favor vivid colors to offset the dullness of the natural environment.[9] The costume of the Peking opera, embroidered with richly colored patterns, is one example. In the late Qing period, the number of colors used in embroidery was said to be eighty-eight, producing a total of 745 different shadings. "Shadings" means graduated tones of the same color, or the effect of the washing and blending of colors according to aesthetic formulas like feather gray and blue; sunflower yellow and green; jade white; pale blue and sapphire blue; silvery gray, tile gray, and pigeon gray, and so on.[10]

The designs, workmanship, and patterns of color in a good piece of embroidery carried the wisdom, labor, experience, knowledge, and feelings that had accumulated through generations. In China, women embroiderers were also traditional rulers who regulated the diversity of skills and colors and the robust and splendid styles used in embroidery (Figure 5.3, Appendix).

Embroidery and Women's Lives in China

Women of all classes in traditional China were judged not by their beauty but by their inner natures and especially by their skills in sewing, weaving, and embroidery, known collectively as female skills (*nügong* 女紅). Women from wealthy families stayed concealed in embroidery rooms until the day of their marriage. A matchmaker who went to speak with a potential groom's family often took with her a sample of the young woman's embroidery. A woman in the Ming dynasty would spend hours making and embroidering her own shoes, as she needed sixteen pairs before her wedding, four for each season, including sleeping slippers and red shoes for special occasions. Typically, a matchmaker carried one shoe to the prospective mother-in-law. If the needlework was fine, the potential bride was considered self-disciplined and skillful. A woman usually started embroidering the goods that would constitute her dowry long before her match was confirmed. She also embroidered gifts for her new in-laws and her own wedding dress, which she would keep in storage for the rest of her life.[11] In their leisure, these women embroidered paintings based on contemporary representations of flowers and birds. Women from poor families supplemented their family incomes by embroidering for the wealthy, but also did it to enrich their own surroundings.

For the potential bride, acceptance by the new family was considered crucial. Demonstration of her skills with a needle would smooth the entrance into her new environment. The usual process was that the bride would embrace her new family, by dedicating and disciplining herself into producing the finest embroideries that she could, which would be functional items displayed in the home as forms of art. The mother-in-law would evaluate the new bride's skills, which would then pass through her daughters from generation to generation. Old fortune-tellers would often predict a woman's embroidery skills by interpreting the direction of the point of the needle she threw into the water.

The embroidering of clothes also invited good fortune and chased away bad spirits and bad luck. For instance, the lotus-shaped collar worn at the wedding symbolized the bride's fertility, while the tiger motifs and designs on the clothing of little boys symbolized protection. There were also special embroideries for burial clothes. The creation of embroidery represented and fulfilled the Confucian roles of women as wives, as mothers of sons, and as teachers of daughters.

There was frequent interchange of ideas and mutual influence across classes. During the Song dynasty, paper-cuts functioned as stencils to assist women of the upper class with their embroidery. The images were cut out, pasted onto the material, and then stitched over to conceal the paper. Books were printed to demonstrate clothes patterns and embroidery ideas; art forms passed from the upper classes to the lower in this manner. Eventually, unique styles developed that distanced embroidery from its aristocratic origins. Women living far from urban centers did not get their inspiration from these patterns but from the work of their mothers and grandmothers.[12]

Female Skill and Expression in Chinese Embroidery

The involvement of women in creating a vivid and meaningful iconography leads one to question to what extent women's art, crafts, and cultural creations were a medium of expression for women. While the female sphere of embroidery seems to have expressed specifically female concerns, the creation of embroidery gave Chinese women value and identity. First, outstanding embroidery skills comprised one of the very few talents that a woman could have to make herself famous and popular in the community. Second, women's work often represented their yearning for a better life as well as their love and affection for their lovers. Traditional handmade clothes embodied a Chinese mother's love, attention, and tenderness for her children. When people were far from home, the very sight of a piece of embroidery reminded them of their loving mothers, as expressed in numerous Chinese literary works and folk songs.

A child might wear a tiger hat, collar, and shoes, and sleep on a tiger pillow on his birthday and on other festive days, such as the New Year. The animal was supposed to protect the child. The mother would continue to make larger hats as the child grew through those ages during which he was supposed to be most susceptible to disease.[13] A typical Hebei tiger hat was orange, with black stripes; its eyes were stuffed with cotton until they bulged, and its tiny cotton teeth and curling fangs looked ready to sink into any threatening spirit. In its ears, little children rested—demonstrating that, though fierce, the tiger is also protective. Mothers and grandmothers also made shoes and embellished them with enchanting embroideries of animals such as rabbits, pigs, and frogs.[14]

Wedding dress collars were formed into the shape of a lotus flower, stressing fertility. The lotus seeds symbolize the many children and descendants who will honor the family. Staying within the restrictions of the shapes and symbols, each woman created a different shape, style, and image. A woman might simply follow her mother or grandmother's methods, or she might design the empty space according to her own fancy, recombining or adding to images from her visual vocabulary.[15]

Scholars have been concerned about how the skillful Chinese female hand was connected to knowledge and the construction of subjectivity in the everyday practice of embroidery. Women were believed to be able to create a space of limited empowerment for themselves and for other women. There have been studies of the poetic writings, treatises, and manuals women produced about embroidery that indicate their self-perception and awareness of their position in knowledge production in China, dating from the late imperial through the early Republican period. All these productions were traced back to the earliest times of the development of sericulture. Originally, weaving played a significant social and economic role in the classical gendered division of labor, as reflected in the phrase "men plough and women weave" (*nangeng nüzhi* 男耕女織), until the Single Whip tax reforms (1581) of the late Ming, when cash replaced textile and grain as household tax payments to the government.[16]

While weaving often appears in women's self-representation as the trope for a virtuous, honorable means of livelihood through which a woman might support herself and her close relatives, embroidery acquired status as the refined occupation of women in economically wealthy and higher-status households. Embroidery became very much a part of women's daily experience. Art historian Marsha Weidner has observed that Ming and Qing women trained their hands and eyes through embroidery. They became attentive to the smallest details, refined their sense of color, and mastered a large repertoire of motifs and compositional formulas. Weidner states that, although the high demand for embroidery in the context of Chinese social, ritual, aesthetic, and official life made it into a commodified skill that had to be supplied or supplemented by the labor of women from the lower classes, it remained a consistent learning component of elite young women. In Weidner's words, "needlework was the premier feminine art, one measure of a woman's worth."[17] An autobiographical poem by a woman recorded, "at thirteen I learned how to embroider/at fifteen I learned how to chant poetry."

One hundred and ninety-one collections of poetry written by women have been noted to begin with the character "to embroider." Numerous poetic works by women also begin with "tired of/by embroidering" and "stopping/giving up embroidery," demonstrating resistance to orthodox demands or the turning away from embroidery to writing. These contrasts proved only that embroidery was indeed an everyday activity for women; they wrote about it to signify their emotional, intellectual, aesthetic, or spiritual experiences. Embroidery also featured among the memorable moments in a shared girlhood of emotions and dreams. The practice of it, alone in inner quarters with concentration and in the repetition of the stitching took on a meditative, religious quality. Embroidery was also described as a feminine activity that fit into a contemplative mode requiring patience and diligence. Embroidering images of the Buddha, particularly those of the bodhisattva

Guanyin, was a popular act of religious devotion for women in the seventeenth century; they embroidered these images with their hair, as noted in the biographies of women with authority on the subject.[18]

The Gendered and Aesthetic Space of Embroidery

Women's writings confirmed that embroidery required a rectification of the mind. The art should involve a kind personality and good disposition; the ideal embroiderer was defined through a series of attributes that implied class and proper upbringing. The skill was also compared to calligraphy and painting. The needle was likened to the calligraphy brush, and the varied density of stitches was compared to painted images of the Buddha, seasonal scenery, architecture, specific birds and flowers.[19]

Classical records noted that an idealized female space for embroidering was an aestheticized environment in an elite household that had incense, flowers in a vase, painted standing screens, a lacquered table, an emerald-green window screen, rose water, young maids, and so on. The optimal production times were fine days with warm breezes, long nights in autumn, chilly spring days when the shadows of bamboo fell on the window, and when swallows came in through the curtains.[20] This space had four components: *xian* 閒 (unhurried quality), the internal state of mind and the external condition of being unhurried and relaxed; *jing* 靜 (tranquility), a tranquil mood required for good quality of work; *ming* 明 (brightness), placing the embroidery loop in the source of light; and *jie* 潔 (cleanliness), an uncontaminated environment. The records aimed to underline the expertise, concentration and discipline preferred in embroidery as well as to emphasize the sacred physical and mental space for the activity. The aesthetic evaluation of embroidery was also suggested in eight categories: *neng* 能 (capable), *qiao* 巧 (skillful), *miao* 妙 (marvelous), *shen* 神 (divine), *jinggong* 精工 (expert), *fuli* 富麗 (beautiful), *qingxiu* 清秀 (simple and natural), and *gaochao* 高超 (exalted). The first four appeared to be ranked in ascending order.[21]

All these emphasized that embroidery as women's art was not a trivial or minor craft but equal in status to reputable, elite male cultural practices like painting, calligraphy, and composition, which valued structure and vitality, coherence and continuity.[22] Embroidery showed the talent, skill, knowledge, and expertise that a female author could possess, as well as the mental state she could enter into that confirmed her status as a knowing, moral, and spiritual subject. While a few men in the Ming tried to achieve the precision, concentration, and attention to detail through embroidery, this did not change the overall gendered nature of the work.[23]

Chinese Embroidery in Contemporary Markets: Technologizing and Engendering

While embroidery was closely associated with the cultivation of women in families of the gentry in the late imperial period, its class basis and status changed rapidly with modernity. From the beginning of the twentieth century, embroidery shifted from an art practice by elite women to a modern craft that provided a means of livelihood to women workers. Because of the market economy and mass produc-tion, women's claim to embroidery as their field of knowledge and expertise, gender and personal expression became lost with social and class changes.[24]

Embroidery became a township enterprise—like textiles, silk, tea, knitwear, and toys—produced by women employees, earning the most foreign exchange for the country. Recent figures show that women workers in the rural areas of Longkou City and Shandong Province carried around seventy four percent of the production tasks of township textiles, clothing, and embroidery enterprises. In 1990, the embroidery articles women made for export earned US$2.5 million for the country.[25]

In terms of both women's hobbies and labor skills, embroidery became trendy again in the modernized Communist regime. Books and manuals were published, workshops conducted, and societies founded. Some of these activities became a new form of entertainment and leisure, displacing the old social meanings and implications of *nügong*. Ritual and religious fervor was replaced by a desire for vogue in busy, postmodern living. Young women began to use their talents and energy to make money and buy European fashion brands to craft new identities, as China's economic structure began incorporating capitalistic fervor for a modernized identity. In recent years, Western fashion has utilized a lot of Oriental embroidery. Working-class women have begun to make their living by producing traditional embroidery for export. Embroidery skills have been revived as a new form of production technique and thousands of training programs attracting women workers have sprung up all over China.[26]

Here I would like to use Vivienne Tam's fashions to illustrate the situation of Chinese embroidery in contemporary consumer space. Vivienne Tam was born in mainland China and raised in Hong Kong. She moved to New York in the early 1980s and launched the label "Vivienne Tam." Her trademark East-meets-West style clearly signaled her Chinese identity in Western society, practicing a new form of Orientalism. As an example, Tam's Spring 1998 collection was inspired by the five universal elements of Chinese cosmology: metal, wood, water, fire, and earth. A common belief is that these five elements are related to one another to form an organic whole. The patterns of this collection were poetic and originated from the traditional Chinese art repertoire: waterlilies blooming on a lake; leaves vibrating in the wind; a tiger roaming through mountains; Chinese children playing games—all infused with delicate embroidery, dainty beading, and the bright colors of cloisonné jewelry. A lot of Tam's designs are worn by Hollywood celebrities such as Julia Roberts, Cindy Crawford, Madonna, Demi Moore, Jodie Foster, Helen Hunt, and Nicole Kidman, both on and off the screen. Vivienne Tam is regarded as the quintessential designer of Oriental style because she transforms embroidery into ornamental art, and because her fashions combine Asian beliefs and aesthetics.

During the handover of Hong Kong from Britain to China in 1997, Tam created designs with themes representing the old and new Hong Kong. Her well-received designs projected serene and spiritual effects that expressed her belief in a peaceful transition, featuring the Golden Buddha, bamboo prints, and embroidered goldfish. And Tam explained that the Golden Buddha brocade coat and Guanyin print signaled the Asian values of good health and happiness.[27] Tam once claimed that she did not want to see Chinese craft disappear, and that her goal was to bring all its colors and skills into fashion. Her Fall 1999 collection was inspired by the costumes of Chinese opera. This collection utilized pagoda sleeves and fabulous embroidery. She said her work was a result of the "reinterpretation of opulent Chinese ornamentation, which could be whimsical when revisited by Western eyes."[28]

In this collection, Tam did not do her embroidery in the traditional method but used mohair instead. The embroidery was applied to fresh fabric, which was later treated technologically, shimmering in the spring 2000 collection and demonstrating an innovative technique. Her Fall 2000 collection continued the combination of romanticism of the Orient with sensual silhouettes, creating a feminine, yet hard-edged look. In her designs she frequently used the handiwork of embroidery and beading as tools to signify femininity, which is another key register of her work.

Vivienne Tam was obviously quite able to develop the intricate handiwork of beading and embroidery, which became her trademark and which appeared frequently in her collections (Figure 12.4, Appendix). Her mother taught her how to crochet and embroider when she was eight. She claims of her work that "the delicate beading and hand embroidery add a warm touch to the clean modern designs," and that she regarded beading as "very pretty and feminine." Her work beautifully combined traditional skills with modern patterns and textures.[29]

Tam's favorite icons include the ocean, bamboo, and flowers of the peony, lotus, and chrysanthemum; goldfish; tiger; bat; and dragon, all in the style of Chinese watercolor painting. Dragons figured in her collections of Spring 1997, Fall 1999, Spring 2000, and Fall 2000. It should be noted that descriptions of the dragon, said to have first appeared during the mythical reign of Fuxi 伏羲 (2852–2737 BC), had been embellished for thousands of years. The dragon supposedly ascended to the skies in the spring and returned to the seas in the fall, controlling the rain on its way. This ability of the dragon explains its worship among China's early agricultural population. The rain-giver was believed to bring riches to the kind and humble. Beginning in the Shang dynasty, the dragon became the symbol of the imperial throne. The five-clawed dragon designated only the emperor; the embroidery of the mythical creature with silk and gold threads became an institution during the Qing dynasty (1644–1911). But when the dragon and phoenix are shown together, they represent the never-ending happiness of a married couple; this pair has been popular in folk art for years.

Tam's appropriation of the dragon enriched it with particular meanings. Tam said, "Dragons represent individuals who are always full of life and enthusiasm with a reputation for being loving and innovative. This perfectly describes the woman for whom I design."[30] The strong, masculine image of dragon has thus been modified to be feminine and soft. In this reading, the dragon is not only a totem or symbol of China but also an icon of women. Furthermore, the red dragon and the face of Tam's model are always pointing to the same direction, implying their having some common values. The icon in red seems to provoke an immediate revolution, just as the sky becomes red and quiet before a thunderstorm. Some read this as a signal to the West that China is waking up.

While the traditional Chinese use of ornament was for appearance and identification, social ranks were expressed through colors and embroidery. In the early Communist regime, meticulous ornaments were therefore regarded as extravagant, trivial, and irrelevant. There was an anti-adornment movement in Communist China in which dress ornaments were viewed as "unhygienic, obscuring natural beauty, and making a woman look trivial." Yet in Tam's embroidery, the beading and sequins are treasured used in the trimming of her clothes; they have become the favorite of her clients.

Tam's East-meets-West design appropriates exotic, traditional, and mysterious Oriental elements with new and modern edges, but it is also gendered. She often mixes brocade and embroidery with experimental modern elements like leather and fake fur, producing what she describes as an "eccentric approach of Orientalism" and her development of femininity. Her signature generates a new Orientalism, one with a more positive sense. On one hand, the Orient is an Other passively under the gaze of the West. On the other hand, now the Orient gazes back; it is no longer a negative stereotype in the eyes of its own Others. Tam's fashion work also brings out a new femininity in traditional women's embroidery work, which not only creates a successful market space, but also reconstructs cultural and gender expressions. Tam's work is a notable contemporary attempt to show traditional ornamental embroidery in the making.

6

KISSING IN CHINESE CULTURE

In various cultural contexts, kissing may signify respect, social ritual, friendship, romantic feeling, passionate love, sexual temptation, and momentary or eternal happiness. Kissing in Hollywood movies is always portrayed as mainly a romantic act that may or may not lead to further sexual acts. A long and steady in modern visual or literary Western representations implies the beginning of intimate relationships. It enhances the plot of a love story, declares new roles or identities, and engages passionate imaginations. Yet kissing in China was specifically regarded as a form of sexual behavior. Traditionally, the act had been restricted to the private space of the bedchamber, which explains why Western visitors to eighteenth- and nineteenth-century China left no record of the Chinese kissing each other in public. We will see shortly that, for a long time in China, there was no specific word in Chinese for kissing, and very few public discussions of it except in a few Daoist discourses related to the art of the bedchamber. In this chapter, I want to examine kissing in China as a form of eroticism by deploying traditional points of view as well describing it in its contemporary social context.

Definition of (Erotic) Kissing

Erotic kissing is said to be a common component of sexual play in many, but not all, cultures. Erotic kissing as an expression of desire and as an effective erotic stimulant in sexual play is not restricted to human beings. Behavior resembling human kissing can also be observed in primates and other animals like mice, sea lions, and elephants. As a fundamental act of human sexuality, erotic kissing develops gradually and requires sensitivity and timing, making it distinct from other social forms of human bodily contact. The definition of erotic kissing need not be restricted to the sexual partner's lips, but can be extended to the neck, ear lobes, breasts, genitals, and so on: that is, to any bodily part that has the erotic potential of fulfilling the function of sexual stimulation. However, I would like to set aside discussion of other oral sexual acts, like cunnilingus or fellatio, and concentrate on lip contact to illustrate the Chinese theories that I want to introduce. Initial lip contact is usually followed by a light rubbing of both sets of lips in alternation with tentative tongue caresses and gentle nibbling of the more accessible lower lips of the partner. Then in gradual progression, the tongue can range freely in the mouth of the partner, who may also suck on it in turn. It is inappropriate to reduce voluptuous kissing only to the opening act of sexual foreplay, as it may also continue throughout the entire coital process.[1] But in several writings about sexuality, kissing can be found only under the category of sexual "foreplay"; so far it has not received the kind of attention it deserves.

Because of the erect posture of *Homo sapiens*, kissing between human beings can be conducted more freely and with more stylistic variety; the meaning of kissing has been enhanced by various cultural interventions. Kissing is said to be an index of advanced evolution and sexual civilization, as it has more spiritual implications compared with more direct coital contact. We will find out shortly how Chinese traditional theories of kissing support this assertion.

History of Kissing in China

Findings in archaeology disclose more than 2,000 years of the history of kissing in China. The earliest pictures of erotic kissing between men and woman were discovered on Han dynasty stone tombs in Sichuan and Shandong. We should note that the modern Chinese word for kissing, *wen* 吻 , is quite recent; there was no special word for the act in ancient days, but there were some other words used to describe oral activities, like *wu* 嗚 (crying and sobbing), *chuo* 啜 (to suck, to smack the lips), or *han* 唅 (to hold in the mouth). In a few Tang dynasty (618–905) literary texts, realistic phrases were used to describe kissing. During the Song (960–1279) and the Yuan (1280–1368) dynasties, the importation of Lama Buddhism, with its kissing Buddha images, led to a flourishing representation of erotic kissing in the literature of the Ming dynasty (1368–1644). The famous erotic novel of the Ming, *Jinpingmei* 金瓶梅 is a good example: it describes erotic kissing in immense detail and in various styles, reflecting the advanced development of the art of kissing in that era. This development extended to the Qing dynasty (1644–1911) in which kissing was expressed in different forms, even in erotic folksongs. The term *wen*, used these days as a term for kissing, first appeared in a Qing erotic novel in 1791, implying that kissing at that point had gradually been accepted as a distinctive erotic act.

Daoist Theories of Erotic Kissing

Contemporary research in physiology reveals that the pleasure in kissing results from elevated blood pressure and accelerated circulation during the act, which in turn enhances the rate of glucose decomposition in saliva. But in traditional Daoist theories, the entire process of kissing is broken down into totally different levels and terms. According to the ancient Daoist sex handbook, *Dong Xuanzi* 董玄子 (Book of the mystery-penetrating master), written in before the Tang dynasty around the fifth century, kissing was seen as more important than just a transitional phase toward sexual intercourse, though it was usually initiated at an early stage. To quote from the handbook:

> When first coming together for the purpose of intercourse . . . the man, sitting in "winnowing basket" pose, embraces the woman to his bosom. He clasps her slender waist and caresses her jade body. Expressing their joy and speaking of deep attachment, of one heart and one mind, they now embrace and then clasp, their two bodies

> beating against each other and their mouths pressed together. The man sucks the woman's lower lip and the woman sucks the man's upper lip. Then simultaneously sucking, they feed on each other's juices. They may slowly bite each other's tongues, or gently nibble each other's lips; they may cradle each other's heads, or urgently pinch the ears. Caressing above and patting below, kissing to the east and nibbling to the west, a thousand charms are revealed and a hundred cares forgotten. Then let the woman take the man's "jade stalk" in her left hand, while the man caresses her "jade gate" with his right. At this moment, the man senses her *yin-chi* and his "jade stalk" is aroused like a solitary peak reaching up to the Milky Way. The woman senses the man's *yang-chi* and liquid flows from her "cinnabar hole" like the trickling down of a secluded spring spilling from a deep valley. This is the result of *yin* and *yang* stimulating each other and not the product of human effort. When conditions reach this stage, then intercourse is possible. If the man is not aroused or the woman is without copious secretions, this is a manifestation of internal illness.[2]

Tang physician Sun Simiao's *Qian Jin Yao Fang* 千金要方 (Priceless prescriptions) said:

> The classics on immortality say that to live long and remain youthful one must first play with a woman and drink her "jade fluid." "Jade fluid" is the secretion within the mouth.[3]

What is the function of this "jade fluid" that refers to the woman's "saliva"? I found more discussions of "jade fluid" that other Daoist texts of sexuality suggested men should "drink" during kissing. To quote one paragraph from *Yu Fang Mi Zhuan*玉房秘傳 (Secrets of the jade chamber) composed around the fourth century:

> The Dao of *yin* and *yang* is to treasure the semen. If one can cherish it, one's life may be preserved. Whenever you ejaculate you must absorb the woman's *chi* to supplement your own . . . Position your mouth opposite the enemy's mouth and exhale through the mouth. Now inhale, subtly drawing in the two primary vitalities (the *yin* and the *yang*), swallow them and direct the *chi* with the mind down to the abdomen, thereby giving strength to the penis . . . One must use a

> woman to restore oneself to health. The method is to have the woman lie straight on her back with her thighs nine inches apart. The man follows her, first drinking of her "jade fluid." After a long time begin to play with her "vast spring" and then slowly insert the "jade stalk" . . . [4]

In an earlier text called *Xiu-chen yu-lu* 修真語錄 (Record of cultivating the true essence), presented to an emperor in the Han dynasty around 108 BC, the following instructions and meaning of erotic kissing were already suggested for sexual foreplay and dallying:

> When one desires to have intercourse, first concentrate the spirit and settle the temper. Embrace the woman and gently play with her. Suck her lips and tongue and twirl her breasts with your fingers . . . Continue to slowly carry out your methods, and the woman will surely experience bliss and be first to go down in defeat.[5]

And for the great natural "medicine" that facilitates the sexual benefits of men, the text states:

> [medicine from the uppermost is the "jade liquid" which] issues from the two openings beneath the woman's tongue. Its color is emerald green, and it is the *ching* of the saliva. The man should suck it up with his tongue . . . It should be sucked and swallowed to be deposited in the *tan-tien* . . . It generates *chi* and blood . . . Expel a breath from the mouth and embrace the woman with both arms. Suck the woman's tongue, gather her saliva and swallow it five or six times, sending it to the lower *tan-tien*.

According to the text, kissing is not only a part of the sexual foreplay but is also the last phase that most benefits the health of the male. It states:

> One first absorbs from the lower peak [the vulva]. When the lower absorption has reached great intensity, the woman's *chi* becomes expansive and stimulates the middle peak [the breasts]. I slowly embrace her, suck the juices from the left and right [breasts] and swallow them. After obtaining their wonderful essence, one may stop. This then is absorption from the "middle peak" during which the

> absorption has reached great intensity, the woman's *chi* expands again and penetrates all the way to the "upper peak." I allow my tongue to explore freely beneath the opponent's tongue. Probing the two openings there, I suck the secretions, swallowing again and again . . . When the upper absorption [of the kissing] is complete, the woman will be at the height of ecstasy and the "true *chi*" of her private parts will be released . . . Take in the opponent's *chi* and absorb her secretions, circulating them throughout your body. At this point, the three absorptions are complete.[6]

But no matter if kissing functions at the beginning or the completion: there could be a number of interpretations grounded on basic Daoist theories of sexuality. These interpretations could begin from the Daoist emphasis on the significance of sexual life for health. A classic of religious Daoism, *Bao-pu-zi* 抱樸子 (The work of Ge Hung 葛洪), written around AD 320, presents a representative attitude toward sex. It said:

> If a man in the vigor of youth attains knowledge of how to revert his years [by the art of the bedchamber] absorbs the enchymona of the *yin* to repair his brain, and gathers the Jade Juice from under the Long Valley . . . he will not fail to live for three hundred years . . .[7]

The belief, based in religion, that appropriate sexual behavior could contribute to health and even longevity led to the development of a variety of special sexual techniques recorded in old Daoist texts. The background of this belief is cosmological and is generally referred to as *yin-yang* theory. The key elements here are the familiar *yin, yang,* and *qi (chi).* This cosmology is already present in early writings of Chinese culture, such as the *I-Ching*. Chinese sexual understanding was profoundly elaborated by later Daoist writings that reflected a deep-rooted belief in the magical, therapeutic, and health-giving properties of sex. Sexual coupling, seen both symbolically and actually as the harmonious balancing of the *yin* and the *yang,* was believed to preserve life through the preservation of *qi*. These traditions held that *yang* manifested as heaven and (hu)man while *yin* manifested as woman and earth.

These two elements were believed to be the polar forces of the cosmos, and the sex organs were believed to possess elemental forces. However, as we have read, the vulva not only represents the *yin* and the penis the *yang*, both of which refer to the lower absorption. The mouths and saliva of both male and female are also organs that have elemental forces, representing the upper absorption that happens during kissing and thereby completes the process. By following a number of sequential sexual progressions and reactions, a mutual supplementing of each sex would lead to a state of harmony in which one's vital essence (*qi*) would be nourished and one's life would be prolonged. By the same logic, failure to adhere to the sequence would result in illness. Sexual engagement was to be conducted in a harmonious and tranquil mood. Daoist texts generally caution against sudden and violent sexual behavior because improper intercourse in terms of speed and posture would lead to physical afflictions. This may explain why sadomasochism is absent in Chinese erotica and is replaced instead by harmonious, cooperative, and playful sex.

However, the above citations easily give the impression that these texts are basically male-oriented and concerned only with male benefits. But the ancient Daoist texts on sex also stated that men and women should cooperate, with the *yin* and the *yang* nourishing each other, and with male relaxation and female excitement combining for equality between the sexes. The texts emphasized that during intercourse the man "chants" and the woman "harmonizes." Most texts stressed the man's nourishing intake of vaginal flow from the *yin* element, stating that the process further increases his vitality if he preserves his semen, which is also his life force. For instance, the main principle is that longevity can be achieved by reversing the flow of semen in form of energy upward to the brain. This belief made frequent or premature ejaculation a taboo. Thus, the man on the verge of emission was instructed to change partners immediately or to control the woman during sexual intercourse so that he could be nourished by rich female elements. Conversely, the man was advised not to be prematurely excited by the woman's responses. This explains why the woman was always described as the "enemy" or the "opponent." Likewise, monogamy in sex was not encouraged, for if a man was to constantly control the same woman, her emission force would weaken and its benefits to the man would be reduced. The prescriptions for multiple partners were usually accompanied by reference to the fact that semen must be retained to ensure a constant supply of the *yin* energy. Thus, there is the following Daoist saying:

> *Yang* is modeled after fire, *yin* after water. Just as water can quench fire, so *yin* can diminish *yang*. If the contact lasts too long, the *yin* essence (absorbed by the man) will grow stronger than his own yang essence, whereby the water will be harmed. Thus what the man loses through the sexual act will not be compensated by what he gains. If one can copulate with twelve women without once emitting semen, one will remain young and handsome forever. If a man can copulate with ninety-three women and still control himself, he will attain immortality.[8]

These techniques are of vital importance. This applies as well to the art of erotic kissing, a significant form of the sexual act, as it also involves exchange of the *yin qi* and the *yang qi* and the beneficial influx of the *yin* element into the male's internal organ.

The Confucian Perspective

There is a conventional impression that sex is taboo in traditional Confucianism, formed as an institution since the Han, though sex was more liberated in some dynasties due to external influencesuch as in the Tang. Though Confucianism and Daoism are usually viewed as two conflicting traditions in China, they share much in common as part of the background of the cosmological Dao, but with different philosophical emphases. The interplay of the two maintained the so-called super-stable equilibrium of Chinese culture. The domination of Confucian education and its ritual practices were effective in advocating a harmonious society and a patriarchal family life. One may say that Daoist thinking balanced Confucian constraints with its romantic carefree lifestyle and its enthusiasm for the "way of nature."

We should note that Confucianism never considered sex as harmful or unhealthy; but, since sex was integral to human nature, it was imperative to regulate it for the stability of relationships and family, as both are necessary for the orderly functioning of society. It was understood that, within a normal family structure, sexual hedonism was permitted only in its proper place and relationship. Moreover, sex involved ritual and discipline, but under the Confucian patriarchal social structure, the path to harmony presupposed male dominance and female submission.

The Confucian ideology of male dominance was strictly promoted, according to which the female must know her place and behave correctly, or else society and even the universe would fall out of balance. We could say that the Daoist emphasis on the man's benefits was due to influence of Confucianism, which was usually the dominant official culture. However, female sexual pleasure in certain "proper ways" was permitted within the Confucian context. Such pleasure at least functioned to keep women content and under control.

But it is fair also to consider the spiritual aspect of Confucianism instead of concentrating only on its secular practices that adhered to patriarchal and political constraints. The Confucian philosophy of love employed the word *qing*, which, compared to "love" in the Western sense, presupposes a subject-to-subject relationship rather than a subject-to-object one. *Qing* is related to the meaning of *ren*, the first principle of benevolence in Confucianism, which aims at treating others as oneself. Thus, the famous five relations speak about the *qing* between father and son, lord and minister, brother and brother, husband and wife, and friend and friend. Confucians understand love to be the conscious activity of a subject and a mutual empathetic experience in which each party treats the other equally as a subject, which is the foundation of human values.

How about sexual love in this "spiritual" philosophy? According to the *I-Ching*), the female and male also represent the two polarized qualities of the *yin* and the *yang* respectively; in their union they complement each other to become a complete whole like a microcosm. In the Confucian model of the correspondence of heaven and man, sexual love has metaphysical implications, but it is also a conscious, human, moral, and spiritual activity. In the Confucian concept of proper relations, sexual love between male and female, usually between husband and wife, should be based on mutual commitment and respect. It is a moral union. Unfortunately, the notion of loyalty in this union—as applied in secular life—resulted in the subjection of women's chastity to the benefits of Confucian patriarchy. We could say that both the Daoist and Confucian spiritual traditions do not imply the dichotomy of subject and object in sexual activity but the union—and mutual benefit—of subject and subject. It was only under the discourse of patriarchy that the female subject became the object of desire and a tool of sex.

The Aesthetic Dimension of Kissing in China: A Study of Late Qing Erotic Painting

Records of erotic activities, including kissing, are easily found in some late Qing erotic paintings that were mass-produced in popular and vulgar styles and widely circulated in brothel areas. Now, nineteenth-century China was rife with an interesting tension and divergence between the Manchu ruler who adopted Confucian policies and the lifestyle of nouveau-riche merchants. The background of most of these paintings featured the newly prosperous towns of the lower Yangzi river valley, where there was demand for a more hedonistic lifestyle wrenched from the extreme Manchu policies of the central government in Beijing. Erotic behavior in these paintings reflected the complex cross-currents of society, including bureaucratic values and "immoral" and "heterodox" ideas that the government tried to ban. The traditional, leisurely approach to sex was replaced by a "frenetic" mode of sexual excitement and sensation, even of decadence.

Under the pressure of social and economic changes, there was an explosion of sexual hedonism that may be interpreted as repressed Daoist discourse. This interpretation is confirmed by paintings in which women participating in the act of love appear submissive and cooperative. Most of the women portrayed were either concubines or prostitutes whose roles were to please the master, and who enjoyed more sexual intimacy with the master than did the wives. These women were therefore the favorite subjects of Chinese erotic painting. Another factor supporting this interpretation is that prostitution was important in the development of popular erotica, with the portrayed love scenes either inspired by or recorded in the brothel bedchambers, where the paintings themselves functioned as entertainment. Late Qing erotica inherited many ideas and beliefs from Confucian and Daoist sexual traditions. These include ideal female bodies and women's ability to adjust their movements to those of men. Though female characters were often represented in active sexual postures, kissing was not a favorite subject of depiction. More common were men examining women's vulvas or playing with their "golden lotus," that is, bound feet considered the sexiest part of a woman's body and the main tool of sexual hedonism. It was not until the late nineteenth century, when Chinese erotic painting came under the influence of Western painting and when the import market increased, that kissing became a popular subject. Women were kissed in these paintings, their breasts were fondled, and their bodies were usually in full blossom.

Because of the abstract calligraphic tradition of Chinese painting, it is difficult to interpret the emotional expressions of the characters in figure paintings. The female experience may be read only via basically ambiguous, subtle, and implicit forms. Therefore, it was cultural context and not individual character that was the main frame of reference. We should remember that, in the Daoist theory of sex, women are also supposed to enjoy sexual pleasure. The important step of "harmonizing the will" to sexual pleasure requires that the feelings and intent of both man and woman combine as one. This may explain why the harmonious acts of women were often portrayed. The requirements for becoming a successful female sex partner, as recorded in manuals for training prostitutes were focusing on artificial beauty, manner, and posture; displaying sexual skill in keeping men company; disguising one's true emotions with apparent sincerity when necessary; and the ability to be flexible and lively in sexual activities when dealing with customers.

It is difficult to determine genuine responses of the women portrayed in the paintings according to apparent cooperative and harmonious attitudes of sex. Maybe we should consider this: that when the Qing authorities imposed puritanical rules, the well-controlled social and political environment failed to eliminate the deeply ingrained Daoist culture. Late Qing erotica may be seen as a monument to the resilience of a Chinese spirit expressed eloquently through female figures that articulated the interplay of harmonious attitudes in both Confucian and Daoist senses. Finally, we should emphasize that it is extremely difficult to connect the study of behavioral patterns in art forms with an analysis of values and beliefs; moreover, this connection cannot be established with certainty.

The Contemporary Situation

Now, we know well that instead of being a purely biological function, human sexuality, including erotic kissing, is a construction of various psychological, sociological, cultural, historical, and even economic factors. In China today, progress in modernizing sexual relationships and education has frequently been hampered by a generally repressive political atmosphere. For most of the history of the People's Republic of China, any social activity that implies sexual expression—including even women's mode of dressing—has been severely restricted. Plays, films, and songs that the government considers "obscene" are banned. Until the comparative liberalization of the 1980s, there was no public nightlife in towns and cities. One exception to the ban of social gathering on the sexes was the occasional meeting at dance halls, since the mainland Chinese especially enjoy Western social dancing, as they have since the 1930s. With limited improvement of freedom of expression through the years, the Democracy Wall in Beijing is being used to advocate the sexual liberation that young people want.[9] Moreover, with the open economic policies and influx of Western capitalistic ideology in the 1990s, the younger generation of Chinese has learned different modes of expression quickly, including those of love and desire. For various economic reasons, prostitution has become an uncontrollable, growing industry, having been well suppressed only as recently as the 2010s.

These days we can easily see couples kissing each other in public in the PRC without arousing strong reactions from people. As modernization overtakes China, sexual freedoms like kissing in public may lead to the false hope that people can now enjoy vital human rights in general.[10] Nevertheless, the act of kissing is still not a strong subject of interest in contemporary films, television, or visual images among Chinese communities in the PRC, Hong Kong, Taiwan, and Singapore. Romantic scenes depict brief kissing, inserted for story-telling purposes. Erotic films are the only exception, tying kissing to sexual foreplay. The contemporary portrayal of kissing no longer serves as a demonstration of the old Daoist discourses, which focused on health or longevity. It belongs to a space that aims to be free from, or subversive against, the Confucian social and political mainstream.

7

EXTREME EXPRESSION AND HISTORY TRAUMA IN WOMEN'S BODY ART IN CHINA: THE CASE OF HE CHENGYAO

This study is inspired by Amelia Jones's arguments for body art that has developed in the late capitalist, postmodern, and postcolonial Western world. Her conclusions are that body art practices are performative, enacting subjects in "passionate and convulsive" relationship, aiming at dislocating the effects of social and private experience. She argues that these practices, desirous and erotic in nature, participate in the subversion of formalism in art.[1] This study, while not aiming to describe how modernism and formalism are subverted through body art, coincides with most of Jones's intention to highlight the position of the body as the locus of a "disintegrated" or dispersed "self," and as an elusive marker of the subject's place in the social, while locating it under art in the context of a new China.[2]

The human body as an art medium has a history as old as that of dance. In this sense, body art has the normative framings of expressive art. Yet its later development leads to a specific category within performance art, including that which transgresses social and political boundaries involving body parts. As Andrea Pagnes explains, performance art is culture-bound, always related to the specificity of a particular context, situation, and circumstance. Body art as a special form of performance art, according to Pagnes, is a discipline "that moves along the interface that exists between an action that just refers to itself, and a live art work intended not just as a mere 'corpus of actions', but mainly as possible instrument of expression and communication, aimed to create or decipher a particular experience."[3] In this sense, body art is something specific to contemporary Chinese art, which flourished during the 1980s but slowed down after the 2000s when visual arts in China entered the globalized art market. The situation leaves body art to those who utilize the art form for personal reasons, as well as to make political statements and who lag behind the capitalization of the art market.

The reading of a case study in Chinese body art echoes Jones's argument:

> Body art . . . laces the body/self within the realm of the aesthetic as a political domain . . . In its opening up of the interpretive relation and its active solicitation of spectatorial desire—[it] provides the possibility for radical engagements that can transform the way we think about meaning and subjectivity (both the artist's and our own). . . . (body art) demonstrates that meaning is an exchange and points to the impossibility of any practice being 'inherently' positive or negative in cultural value.[4]

This study will also review Jones's proposition of how body art opens out subjectivity as performative, contingent, and always particularized rather than universal, within the meanings and cultural values ascribed to the work of art.[5]

The case study of the Chinese woman artist He Chengyao will not only come to political conclusions (when it is engaged with through a phenomenological and feminist model as Jones suggests) but will also attempt to arrive at social, historical, and psychological ones as well.[6] The gendered body is a common subject for disseminating and promoting thought that is central to the understanding and the subversion of gender identity issues and related social conventions and constructions. Exhibitions and performances portray how artists explore gender through representations of the body, sometimes by using their own bodies in the creative and performing process. The female body, idealized in traditional depictions, has been reclaimed by feminist artists through a variety of reformist representations. For many artists, using their bodies in performance has become a way to both claim control over their own bodies and to question issues of gender. This chapter further engages Jones's other arguments by demonstrating how He's work departs from those representations of female body in the dynamic of fetishism or consumerism, which the rapid development of cosmopolitanism and capitalization in China has nurtured in the present day.[7] This address, together with the Confucian patriarchal tradition and its suppression of female physicality, has turned gendered body art into a specific category of contemporary Chinese visual and performance arts. Body art, in this sense, has rich meanings beyond just being a recognized genre.

Contemporary Chinese Body Art: The Work and Its Background

Lisa Rofel used the term "cosmopolitanism with Chinese characteristics" to describe the contemporary state of the PRC, which may be seen as a replacement for the official term "socialism with Chinese characteristics," as adopted in the country's political propaganda.[8] While Rofel's term is controversial, the author uses it in a broader sense relating sexual, material, and affective desires to the country's economic development.[9] Rofel describes the tension facing the rapidly changing country as between "an universal progressive identity through its formation of a consumer identity, and a domestication of cosmopolitanism by way of renegotiating China's place in the world."[10]

Rofel also argues that the way contemporary China domesticates cosmopolitanism is through a series of structured "forgettings" that reinvent the past. Here is what she refers to as the backwardness and the political turmoil that China has gone through in the last century.[11] After Deng Xiaoping's economic reform in 1979, China was opened to international investments and trade and involved itself vigorously in the global economy. Cosmopolitanism often accompanies images of a newly global capitalism; body representation is within the politics of representation in the globalization process in China, which Rofel sees as providing the staging for contemporary enactments of cosmopolitanism.[12] Now that China has become one of the greatest consumers in the world, and that consumption is about embodiment, consuming selves produce bodies and social selves through food, sex, and fashion, all revolving around the making of bodies.[13] Slowly migrating to world citizenship, China has extended its influence beyond its geographical borders to the international arena. This study agrees with Rofel's suggestion that the elaborative effort in building up a unique form of sexiness and other bodily practices that try to capture the desire to be a cosmopolitan state is also a national discourse about normality and about the kinds of citizens representing China to the world.

The contemporary, dichotomous discourses of private and public also operate in China, whereby, with regard to the regulation of social bodies, political domination and traditional ethics are yielding to growing individual choices. "People's bodies" are situated in tensions and contestations among age, gender, ethnicity, regions, and cultures, all striving for identity and uniqueness. There are new Chinese faces and bodies in the media representing and legitimizing classes, sexualities, and ethnicities of a wide variety. These processes of publication are inevitably steeped in political and economic factors, which represent bodies in ways that enhance the related desires of vision. The desirous excitements created through body performance and visual pleasures negotiate with the traditional discourses of the body, as discussed below. This process works more vigorously in places with a repressive past like China, which is catching up through its search for new identities and images.

New media art has displaced body art in China these days; the marketing of paintings among art dealers has been very competitive both nationally and internationally. Body art has functioned as decorative art in large exhibition events, though people still recall those pioneers in the 1980s and 1990s with their innovative and stunning performances that made a strong social impact. The liberated strengths they achieved came along with the economic reform of the country in the 1980s, which created a big psychological craze for explicit linkages between the normative framings of expressive art and the boundaries being transgressed by performative art utilizing body parts, nudity, or other expressions in contemporary Chinese art. Chinese artists realized the power of the body, as well as its rich and multiple layers of meaning. This realization parallels those about conceptual and other new forms of art that have not yet been properly recognized in China. One can understand the gratification aroused by the artistic and bodily expression in such a background, while most of the works favor personal, psychoanalytical, and accidental styles opposed to the mainstream political and social discourses.

The mainstream artistic and political discourses were gradually revised and replaced by new ideologies of a China that has blossomed in the last two decades. Contemporary art, including popular genres like "political pop" and "social cynicism" are concerned with social reality and addressing public issues in more direct ways; they refrain from oppositional fervors. Body art, in particular, has been producing social commentary through the integration of individual artists' personal sensibilities and social existence. The common features presented are identified as violent, masochistic, mutilational, exhibitionistic, scandalous, and even immoral. The art form, therefore, is not embraced by official parties and regional curators, who are wary of possible uncontrollable and unexpected scenes. More and more Chinese artists have turned away from body art to visual art for its booming market.

It is said that body art, in general, using specific representations of the object body, has embraced notions around sickness and health, ugliness and beauty, abnormality and normality, and other oppositional pairs.[14] They are also stimuli of visual desire when the body is regarded as both demand and supply of images.[15] How may female bodies, in the form of artistic expression, enact their political statements addressing issues like gender, social suppression, and human rights in the content of New China, where male gaze in its broadest sense has been so penetrating?

Moira Gatens argues that traditional philosophical conceptions of corporeality are counterproductive to the attempt to construct an autonomous conception of women's bodies.[16] Iris Young—under the influence of Merleau-Ponty's account of the "normal" relationship between human bodies and their environment in action—states that female bodily existence is commonly distinguished by three features: "ambiguous transcendence," "inhibited intentionality," and "discontinuous unity." The discussion is for women, there is a sense that the body is a "subject" as well as an "object." It is the object of the gaze of others, frequently experienced as limited and limiting. Young notes that it is important to recognize the specific and historically changing forms of restrictions that have been placed on the women's movement, including such things as restrictive clothing and constricting conventions about female deportment and demeanor. She points out that these modalities do not remain constant but are culturally variable, subject to changing circumstances and lifestyles.[17] Young's suggestions make a lot of sense when one reviews the issue of female body expression in the Chinese historical context, only that the notions of "ambiguous transcendence," "inhibited intentionality," and "discontinuous unity" would refer to different and more specific meanings in these conventions.

In female body art, works usually involve the artist's enactment of her body in all of its sexual, class, and other particularities; the "overtly solicit spectatorial desire" (suggested by Amelia Jones) will unhinge the very deep structures and assumptions embedded in particular societies and their engendering processes.[18] It will therefore be necessary to conduct an understanding of He's body performance in its cultural context.

The Body Art of He Chengyao

Deng Xiaoping's opening reforms brought about a whole series of changes in the public sphere. The art world, for instance, allowed artists not only to exhibit but also to try out new attempts of expression that went beyond the canvas. Yet the contemporary art scene at the beginning of reforms met with restrictions. Performance art emerged, known as *xingwei yishu* 行為藝術, whereby the "behavioral" aspect or "conduct"' (*pinxing* 品行) of a meaningful "action" (*xingwei*) is articulated in art (*yishu*).[19]

Chinese contemporary art responded in general to the political and social climate of the time, yet any novelties introduced in artistic practice were treated as a pernicious influence brought into the country from the West. Restrictions were imposed by political and official art institutions, but they soon became important incentives that enhanced the creativeness and boldness of new Chinese artistic productions, though they met the restrictions on behaviors in public spaces, like nudity. This places the expressive extreme of the work of He Chengyao in context, who presented about twenty pieces of body art from 2001 to 2006 in Asia, Europe, and North America.

He Chengyao was born in the 1960s in Chongqing, Sichuan, to an unmarried couple. Her father was a photographer. He left her mother, who suffered from mental illness initiated by the condemnation she had received from society, due to her illegitimate pregnancy and birth of

Chengyao. Soon after Chengyao was born, her parents were dismissed from their public jobs and moved to Rongchang, a very small village in Sichuan Province. After her mother failed to withstand the criticism and psychic pressure from her community, she had a nervous breakdown. During the Cultural Revolution, Chengyao recalled, her mother used occasionally to take off her clothes and scream and run around the village. She was then forced by her community to take medicines and to receive all kinds of treatment, including acupuncture and folk practices, which inflicted physical wounds all over her body. One may see that the wounds Chengyao later inflicted onto her own body were intended to be equivalent to those that her mother carried. Madness and family traumas have gradually become the main references of her artistic creativity.

He Chengyao graduated in 1989 from the Sichuan Art Academy, where she trained as an oil painter. In 2000, she moved to Beijing, where she was enrolled in the contemporary art research program at the Central Academy of Fine Arts. Her oil painting was described as surrealistic and expressionistic, focusing on relational themes between person and environment. She admitted suppressing her childhood memories and her deep feelings for her mother, which were just too strong for the medium of oil painting. The illness of her mother, and the poverty and suffering of her family left a deep scar in Chengyao's soul. It is believed that the scar started to heal after her first improvised body performance at the Great Wall.

This first work was a nude piece presented at the Great Wall in 2001; it kicked off a series relating bodies and family history. This first public performance was a real breakthrough and a turning point when Chengyao attended the opening event of the installation "Trash People" by the German artist H. A. Schult. The work displayed artificial human figures made of industrial waste, arranged in two rows, at the Jinshanling part of the Great Wall. Suddenly, Chengyao stepped out of the audience, stripped off her red shirt, and walked in between the two rows of figures all the way to Beacon Tower. This entirely unexpected and improvised performance did not only shock Schult and the audience, but also drew the attention of the media and the press. People at the site then walked with her; the line of action was given the title of *Open the Great Wall* afterward. This scene at the Great Wall was immediately reported, followed by severe attacks and criticisms from the public and Chinese art circles. People regarded it only as a ploy for attention. Chengyao concluded that she did not plan the work; it was an unintended first piece of body art. She attributed it to a "mysterious" call from within, and only became aware of what had happened as an epiphany when the walk ended. Yet when one reads another work of hers, *Homage to Joseph Beuys*, produced the same year, what the previous work was supposed to manifest has yet to be deciphered.

Contemporary Chinese visual artists have been paying homage to Beuys in some sense, especially for his notion of art as therapy, in which creativity originates from trauma in war.[20] Chengyao reworked Beuys's idea by holding a photo of her mother. Her face was painted with red fluid and her upper body was naked in her performance *Homage to Beuys*. She raised her head and her right hand, indicating that the strength of her work came from her deep feeling for her mother, which called for therapy. Yet Chengyao used the Aristotelian word *catharsis* instead during interviews, stating that, despite the attacks and pressures she had received for her work, she succeeded in overcoming her fear of her mother's madness and had come instead to understand, accept, manifest, and reconstruct it.

A series of works were presented by Chengyao after *Homage to Beuys*, including *My Mother and Me* in 2001.[21] Chengyao photographed her own self and her mother naked, inspired by a time when she saw her mother playing naked with a rotten apple on the rooftop. She felt for her and thought that her mother resembled an innocent child living in a lost world. She then stood behind her mother, also naked, and took seven photographs for the series.[22] One notes the facial expression of Chengyao's mother, who looks at her daughter behind her with perplexity and curiosity. In six of the seven photographic pieces, one finds Chengyao's mother as the only subject, her naivety and innocence captured in the center, looking at her daughter beyond herself and the frame, unable to tear her gaze from Chengyao.

The work *Witness*, produced later in 2002, is a continuation of the theme, this time with the naked body of Chengyao's son inserted in the series. Grandmother, mother, and son all posed for the photograph. Chengyao regards her son's body as being just as minoritized and marginalized as her mother's.[23] Yet in addition to this reading comes also the fear that Chengyao has held, that she may have passed madness from her mother to her son, just as her mother might have inherited it from Chengyao's grandfather. It is obvious that Chengyao fears the madness within herself; the manifested nakedness is a statement, a therapy, and a form of catharsis. The occasion of the photographic shoot marked the first time that Chengyao's son met his grandmother; the pose struck suggests a continuation of some sort, related to trauma and family history, and the struggles of a mother and a daughter.

Despite the political context of China in the 1960s, the social treatment of the mentally ill remained violent, full of folk superstitions and beliefs. Chengyao's mother received all kinds of treatment, echoing Foucault's reading. According to Chengyao, her mother was once held down onto a wooden board by the People's Liberation Army and forced to receive acupuncture. The woman screamed and struggled in vain as ninety-nine needles were inserted all over her body. Chengyao produced the work *99 needles* in 2002 (Figure 7.1, Appendix), memorializing the event. She stated clearly that she dedicated the work to her suffering mother, to atone for her own helplessness. After receiving ninety-nine needles by an acupuncturist, her body was red and swollen. She made a series of photographs of her naked body pierced from the waist up by the needles. Some of the needles were not put in correctly, so that the artist started to bleed from her right wrist and fainted. It was obvious to Chengyao that enduring the same pain that her mother had gone through acted as a form of physical and mental compensation. She confessed that she had been indifferent to her mother's suffering and had tried hard to forget the fact that her mother had suffered for carrying her in a premarital pregnancy.

After *Open the Great Wall*, Chengyao took up body art to the extent that she reconstructed peasant village history and projected it onto contemporary city life through her work, which became durational, repetitional, and ritualistic. Critics read the repetition in her work as necessary for its effects in initiating empathy, firstly in reproducing the pain in the artist, and secondly among the audience.[24] Yet Chengyao realized that her mother was indifferent to what she had done, as she shut herself within her own world.

These works of body art would be therapeutic only to the artist herself. However, when the extreme expression in these works is read into the historical context in China, they would seem to offer much for people to relate to. One of the controversial performance pieces produced by Chengyao in 2004 demonstrated this. The piece, titled

Public Broadcast Exercise (Figure 7.2, Appendix), sees the artist's body wrapped all over in white tape while doing a series of exercises that was usually broadcast on the radio in public places all over China during the Mao era. The tape was sticky so when the artist was moving, her limbs got stuck. It produced awful sounds when she was trying to unbind it. The sounds were so annoying that they made the audience feel extremely uncomfortable, as it sounded like her body was being ripped apart. The performance recalled the time when the Socialist regime tried hard to suppress any form of individualism and promoted collectivism. The work also echoed Chengyao's realization that her mother's disrupted body and soul had acted in a way to survive various forms of pressure exerted from the outer world.

Chengyao attempted body art in more different styles starting in 2003, but maintained the extremity of expression. She was then concerned with materialistic exchanges in human relationships, of serious concern since the economic reform in China. She asked for physical exchange with and collaboration from her audience through her tongue and mouth. Her work also reflected on the hegemony of Western culture and issues related to globalism and post-colonialism. She had her long hair cut when she presented *The Possibility of Hair* in Manchester in 2006, announcing a new phase of creativity by denouncing the long entanglement in her personal history. A long text was gone as well, together with her therapeutic efforts through art.[25]

Extreme Expression, Nudity, and Body Trauma

Even before *Open the Great Wall*, He's works were read as challenges to patriarchal culture. Her oil paintings from the beginning were described as a post-modern woman's lament by her academy in Sichuan; critic Gao Minglu regarded the nakedness in her work as "extreme appeals on women's suppression and torture."[26] The story of Chengyao's mother demonstrates notions like "male gaze," "female insanity," and the "history" of male-centered discourses. Her body work *Illusion*, in 2002, was an example of her reflection of gender, in which males in the audience were given a mirror and asked to reflect sunlight onto the surrounding wall. Chengyao dressed in white and followed the reflected light everywhere, demonstrating females' daily practices of passivity and subordination.[27]

Yet Chengyao rejected the label of feminist artist, perhaps in reaction to the clichéd Western art labels that had frequently been stamped onto contemporary Chinese art from the 1980s on. The label "feminist art" has not been positively received in China, even with some of the more subversive works. The comments are that most of the feminist art in China at He's time had not succeeded in posing strong criticisms of the root or ground of its patriarchal culture; there were no common gender issues, only personal accusation and statements. As Gao had suggested that contemporary women's art in China emphasized personality rather than minority in the sense of a gendered class, there were no attempts to deconstruct or reconstruct the power within, nor were there discourses on core gendered norms and values as those in the West, only some revisions of male languages.[28] But Chengyao's work did come close, addressing social, political, and cultural suppression through personal trauma and a family history of madness. Her works also fit perfectly with the parameters of peculiarity that Amelia Jones suggests, in both personal and contextual dimensions, and with some of the common agendas discussed in feminist aesthetics.[29]

The elements of madness and the therapeutic attempts in Chengyao's work are two "peculiar parameters," with madness as a cultural construction resulting in social marginalization and oppression in the context of the modern history of China. The family trauma of the artist could be read as a page in the nation's history, both in its internal turmoil and ideological reform. The calm and speechless artistic treatments of Chengyao proved to be as powerful as the body art of Hermann Nitsch or the famous Marina Abramovic. They are also in a sense more effective than the shocking work of some of Chengyao's contemporaries, like the baby-eating performance of Ju Li and the self-mutilation of Yang Zichao. They demonstrate that the re-enacting of personal memories through real bodies could tell all.

It should be noted that body art in Chinese tradition has long been normalized in symbolized, operatic, and ritualistic ways. Nudity did not become a tradition in Confucian history, especially after the Song and Ming schools of Confucian discourse, which had successfully promoted a strict suppression of bodily desires. As analyzed in previous chapters, the depiction of female bodies in traditional Chinese paintings and sculptures has always been linear, simple, and devoid of sensuous elements, while more detail could be found in poetry and literature. Visual nakedness and nudity were rare. Body aesthetics was greatly molded under Confucian and Daoist discourses; the former dominated public presentation. Particular social constraints on female bodies and related codes were strictly practiced in the traditions, with their internalized moral codes and values. This continued until the nineteenth century, when Chinese painting came under strong Western influence and in which shady and vulturous female bodies were portrayed in the Western style.

Chengyao's representation of nudity is, therefore, a form of extreme expression and very effective in making its strong statements on madness and marginalization in her country, echoing Foucault's ideas of the synchronic emergence of madness and artistic creativity.[30] According to the artist's confession, she started to do body art as therapy for her wounded soul and as a personal, inner urge. She further believed that her art could be therapeutic to many others who were neglected and marginalized in the shared social and political contexts. The madness involved was not merely personal nor a family matter but a social issue. Chengyao soon started to make documentary films of her surroundings. She taped the families of mental patients from her hometown, Rongchang. Critic saw this as a transformation from personal declaration to social criticism, involving stronger expressions of "body politics."[31] Susan Brownell and Jeffrey Wasserstrom note, in the afterword of their edited volume *Chinese Feminities, Chinese Masculinities*, that the Cultural Revolution in China in the 1960s was a period of excess and madness in its aftermath, for Chinese trying to make sense of their own experiences, including of the centrality of gender in revolutionary action and violence. To the extent that these categories of people were more constrained by gendered social norms in everyday life, they were more likely to engage in excesses when they finally broke free from those constraints. This observation matches the life of Chengyao's mother, who descended into madness, and Chengyao's own extreme body art.[32]

Amelia Jones defines body art as one of the most dramatic and radical types of cultural production to destroy the modernist subject; one wonders about the implications of Jones's statement for He Chengyao's body art. It is certain that Chengyao incorporates socialist, family, and gender peculiarities in subversive and accusational gestures. The boldness, roughness, and violence with which she treats the female body are demonstrations of body politics; the juxtaposition of the bodies of her mother and her son posed significant readings of a political history. The liberation of Chinese bodies and their public showing in the artist's work refer to notions of freedom and captivity. The pain induced is in service of social therapy and the catharsis she suggests is collective.

According to John Berger, nakedness reveals itself and nudity on display is a form of dress.[33] Chengyao's body work is nudity in the form of performance, which she performs to recollect and to heal. It also meets the expectation and the convention of a particular culture and situation. In Kenneth Clark's distinction between the naked and the nude, nudity is not fragile but a balanced, prosperous, and confident—it is a body re-formed. This thesis negates some critics' reading of the bodies of Chengyao as huddled and defenseless. Instead, it is the central subject of her art, providing the means and occasion to figure forth something meaningful.[34]

François Jullien suggests that nakedness implies a diminished state, stripped and laid bare, carrying with it a concomitant notion of shame or pity. Yet nudity, on the contrary, is a state of plenitude; it is total presence, offering itself for contemplation.[35] Echoing this suggestion, one sees no sense of shamefulness, shyness, or guilt in Chengyao's performance, but willfulness on her face and innocence on that of her mother's. This also confirms Jones's statement on body art, that the position of the body becomes the locus of a dispersed "self," and an elusive marker of the subject's place in the social world.[36]

Body Art as Recuperation

Contemporary Chinese visual artists, including He Chengyao, have good reason to salute Joseph Beuys. It is said that Beuys's charisma and eclecticism have polarized his audience into those who uncritically accept Beuys's own explanations as interpretive solutions to his work, and those who are "relentlessly critical" of Beuys's rhetoric and reduce the potential of his work to the specific material properties of the works themselves.[37] But perhaps some of the common legacies of Beuys that have been well appropriated among Chinese artists are art's restorative, healing powers, despite the fact that contemporary Chinese works of visual art may require close attention to the cultural specificity of their iconographical and visual references, as the artists themselves have proclaimed. Some suggest a strain of thought extending back to the 1980s, which distanced itself from a straight-forward alignment of post-revolutionary Chinese culture with the notion of postmodernism, and is different from Jones's discussion on post-modern bodies. It was read as a re-negotiation between present and historical Chinese cultures beyond the rupture of the Cultural Revolution, arguably the Chinese counterpart to Nazism in Germany, to which post-war German artists such as Joseph Beuys and Anselm Kiefer have addressed themselves.[38]

It is obvious that He's idea of art as cure or recuperation might have been inspired and motivated by Joseph Beuys. Her work *Homage to Beuys* was based on a copy of a performance Beuys made in 1964 at the auditorium of the Technical College in Aachen in Germany. It was performed on the date of the twentieth anniversary of an assassination attempt on Adolf Hitler. Chengyao should have noted that Beuys's performance irritated the audience and was interrupted by physical attacks. The artist, in return, provocatively saluted the audience by raising his arm in the Nazi style while holding a cross in the other hand. Instead of holding a cross, He Chengyao in her homage held a picture of her semi-nude mother in one hand and with the other gave the Nazi salute. In one of the artist's interviews, she admitted that the piece was her way of expressing gratitude to Beuys, who had shown her the way in which art could recuperate and heal.

Chengyao started to make documentary films as a method of self-recollection and rediscovery. As one critic commented, the shift from photography to video documentary demonstrated a transformation from personal declaration to social concern.[39] The silent way of directing and conducting the production of images regarding a prohibited space is a strong protest in itself. The particularization, as pointed out by Jones, involved the dimensions of gender, "madness," social marginalization, and political repression in contemporary Chinese history.

It is interesting to read Chengyao's work in exhibitions with the theme "Global Feminism."[40] He Chengyao was a featured artist in Global Feminism at the Brooklyn Museum, curated in 2007 by Maura Reilly and Linda Nochlin. While the event was criticized for the unresolved contradictions in its underlying concept, the exhibits of Chengyao would seem to have fulfilled its objectives in the sense that the event demonstrated different obstacles and circumstances faced by women in different cultures.[41]

During the "awakening period" in the late 1980s, following the fall of the Gang of Four in 1976, female characters in new fiction or the so-called scar literature were liberated figures who emerged as individual spirits, undergoing sexual awakening and in search of real meaning in life, love, and gendered being. Yet the economic reform promoted by Deng Xiaoping in the 1990s produced currents within the market economy that re-enhanced and re-legitimated the male gaze and desires of women's bodies. The trend was the globalization of slim bodies and homogeneous standards of female beauty, whereby developing countries competed with the West by duplicating the process of modernization, confirming the observation that they are the big consumers of technological devices, fashions, and cosmetics. Female bodies then became contested sites and symbols of modernization, economic growth, and national pride in the new China. Standardized female faces and bodies were stamped on pictures at beauty parlors and magazine covers all over the country. Their sexual awakening was clearly tied to the dynamics of the state and the world beyond, when people began to discuss cosmopolitanism with Chinese characteristics. One may see from these particular social changes how Chengyao's body art was subversive, in the sense of healing, recuperating, and protesting.

"Global feminism" refers to a movement of women's rights on a global scale; it is claimed to dismantle the currently predominant structures of global patriarchy, and from this sense comes the notions of "transnational feminism," "world feminism," and "international feminism." Yet the impact of First World women, as consumers within the global economy, upon the living and working conditions of Third World women, and "the levels of culturally validated oppressions, exclusions, violation and surveillance that women experience . . . are very high."[42] Under global feminism, there is a common utopian project of emancipation, yet post-modern discourses confirm conceptualizations of difference. There are calls for respecting different histories and situations, and the related different tactics and strategies, including those in art.

He Chengyao made the following artist statement for the event:[43]

> Feminism is a remote topic in my country where I live. China is always a male-dominated world, although the Chinese Communist Party had tried to abolish the old male-dominated system so that

> everyone had a right to obtain an occupation. We had already shortened the discrimination between male and female and established the "equal rights" constitution between female/male. In fact, the equality is not based on rights from individual liberation and fair opportunity. There is still existing sexual unfairness, discrimination in social status as well as between female and male. Most people still conform to the traditional sexual division of labour. Individual value and rights of female are still ignored. . . I (also) wish that I can speak about the feminism topic with my own voice through taking part in such kinds of exhibition and making more and more artworks. Women . . . are able of holding of the world.

It is obvious that He's body art is more powerful in its own articulation, in demonstrating particularities, than the common utopian project of emancipation.

8

NOTES ON A CHINESE GARDEN: COMPARATIVE RESPONSES TO ARNOLD BERLEANT'S ENVIRONMENTAL AESTHETICS

In this chapter, I present a comparative study of Arnold Berleant's recent essay, "Nature and Habitation in a Chinese Garden"[1] from his book *Aesthetics Beyond the Arts: New and Recent Essays*. In addition to reviewing Berleant's thoughts on the subject and object relation, bodily reaction, and aesthetic experience in relation to the Chinese garden environment, I compare his reading of the nature of Chinese gardens with the real case of Geyuan Garden and the architectural aesthetics of the contemporary Confucian scholar Tang Junyi. In his influential work, *The Spiritual Values of Chinese Culture*, Tang proposes a metaphysical manifestation of traditional Chinese architecture and garden design and the interactive relation between man and Nature, or Dao.[2] The comparison of the two works demonstrates the strength of Berleant's reading of the subject, and its proximity to Tang's bodily notions of "hiding" (藏), "cultivating" (修), "resting" (息), and "wandering" (遊) in a Chinese garden. The correspondence between the two works also allows me to examine the relevant comparative aesthetics and critical responses.

In his earlier work, *Rethinking Aesthetics*,[3] Berleant elaborates on the notion of "aesthetic engagement." Recognizing that art does not simply consist of objects but of situations in which experiences occur,[4] Berleant points out that the numerous oppositions that are used to describe aesthetic relations, such as surface and material, form and content, illusion and reality, spectator and work of art (that is, subject and object), beauty and use, and interestedness and disinterestedness, have a philosophical rather than an aesthetic basis. Berleant proposes that these oppositions have led aesthetic inquiry in fragmentary and oppositional directions.[5] Although the language of art has since changed, one would have to agree that we are in need of a broader theoretical language that can embrace both the contemporary and traditional arts.[6]

I would like to start with painting to convey a basic understanding of Chinese aesthetics before discussing landscape aesthetics. Both aesthetics emphasize integrated and unified experiences, and that art is identifiable but not distinct from other activities. Berleant's notion of "continuity and engagement" sees art as integrated into the full range of individual and cultural experiences and aesthetic perception as incorporating the numerous social, historical, and cultural factors, and different meanings, associations, and memories that penetrate perceptual awareness. These aesthetic concepts correspond fully with early discussions on Chinese aesthetics. Chinese ancient painter Gu Kaizhi, introduced in Chapter 3, suggests that art should involve "continuity and engagement," and the importance of depicting the relation between the subject and the environment in portrait painting.[7] He also states that artists need to care about the personality and social class of their subjects (especially historical or legendary figures), and the relations between the subject and other characters in a painting. Of equal importance are the reaction of the subject, the social constraints or rituals that affect the subject's bodily behavior, the places where the subject and other characters are situated, and the related setting or environment. To realize the above principles, Gu suggests that artists should make efforts to observe, study, analyze, and understand their subjects, because the essence of the subject and the related artistic transformation can only be grasped through hard study. The example of this approach, *The Admonitions of the Instructress to the Court Ladies* 《女史箴圖》 was discussed in Chapter 3.[8] This painting reminds us of the dwelling that Berleant mentions, the dwelling in the aesthetic situation and the broader social and personal uses of art. Accordingly, the painting also portrays the basic connection between what art does and the larger world of meaning, perception, consciousness, and knowledge—in short, the totality of human being.

When talking about art as an original unity, a unity as the condition of primal being that precedes all divisions and separations, Berleant uses the term *embodiment*, which denotes a condition of being before the divisive acts of thought that alienate consciousness from the body, thought from feeling, and people from their world.[9] In this sense, he evokes the aesthetic principles of Daoism this book has discussed in previous chapters, the unity of the subject and the environment in the "calmness of mind" described by the original Daoist, Zhuangzi.[10] In contrast with the Western epistemological sense of cognition, in which things are perceived as objects, the subject and object relation in this unity is a "host and guest" relation, according to the traditional Chinese aesthetics of the neo-Confucian scholar Tang Junyi.[11] I here find it necessary to recap briefly some of the previous discussion, as it is crucial to the understanding of Berleant's reading of aesthetic experience in a Chinese garden. There are several features to this unity or encounter. It emphasizes the communication with nature in gaining a form of human totality; and refers to a unifying way of thinking in contrast with Western mainstream aesthetics, which implies dogmatic and subjective elements. The aesthetic experience that takes place is a fundamental process that presents a "pre-existing inner structure" that exists before the objectification process in which the relationship between the object of art (the text), the author, and the audience is formed. The process claims to be the continuation of life as a cycle of rebirth in the sense of the circulation of life (*qi*) in Daoism. It also demands that we should adapt ourselves to nature, which includes our bodies and our immediate environment, leading to the harmonious correlation between a change in nature and a spiritual change in the self.

This ancient wisdom echoes Berleant's view in *Rethinking Aesthetics* that art functions as a present and active factor in the participatory engagement that is the sign of the aesthetic.[12] It is also in this sense that Berleant reminds us of Daoism. He is correct in stating that the notion of intuition is a characteristic feature of much of the art of the Orient, that by examining the varying facets of intuition we may come to realize more fully how the artistic process engages the reality of experience, and that intuition shows that it is impossible for art to be subdued by reduction and division.[13] Accordingly, the idea of intuition is an important commonality between Berleant's reading of Chinese aesthetics and the unity of aesthetic experience described in neo-Confucian thought, as proposed by Mou Zongsan and Tang Junyi, reviewed in Chapter 2. In fact, as I shall discuss, Berleant's notion of intuition closely corresponds to the aesthetic experience of a Chinese garden. In Berleant's words, intuition involves absorption in the dynamic nature of form as it moves across space and time, in vertical and horizontal dimensions of experience. It is a total vision instead of a fleeting impression. Art (in this case a garden) is not a finished object or a completed process in intuition, but rather a coming into being, as the artist shapes a path, which the viewer follows in the wonder of personal discovery. And aesthetic intuition reflects a merging of one's consciousness with the art object or the intimate bond by which we engage with the object in experience.[14]

In this earlier text, Berleant regards the aesthetics of intuition as a general illumination in art and states that Eastern philosophy seems to have expressed this trait most openly. He suggests that there is a special kind of intercourse between art and the world that is best captured by the intuitive impulse.[15] He also proposes to examine the varying facets of intuition to realize how the artistic process engages the reality of experience by grasping the sharpness, clarity, and directness or immediacy of that experience. I wish to describe this reading of intuition as a genuine form of experience of walking through a Chinese garden, which is echoed in Berleant's later essay.[16] Berleant describes this intuition as one that leads the eye, the ear, and the hand across the surface of perceptual experience with more delight in the caress than in the direction or the content. All the sensory intuition is the cutting edge of consciousness. It is the focal point of all the phases of intuition we have reviewed here—sensory, formal, creative, appreciative, and ontological, or, in Berleant's summary, the totality of human being in a primal state or an embodiment in the sense of being a unified organism, an experiential unity.[17] The aesthetic experience is a non-transcendent perceptual unity that joins object and perceiver together. These descriptions parallel Tang Junyi's discussion of the unity of aesthetic experience.

In a recent essay, "The Art in Knowing a Landscape," in *Aesthetics Beyond the Arts: New and Recent Essays*, Berleant states that contemporary scholars have opened aesthetics to the environment of everyday life and to comparative aesthetics, thereby deepening and expanding the field of environmental aesthetics.[18] Here, Berleant specifically refers to landscapes, and the text forms a quartet of readings that integrate art, the environment, landscapes, and knowing in the sense of appreciation.[19] He argues that landscape appreciation offers an important challenge to the prevailing view of the subjectivity of experience in Western philosophy, because it does not come in parts but emerges in a situational context in which the activity of appreciation is embedded and to which it contributes. The revealing point is that human presence creates the landscape, otherwise the "landscape" is simply a geographical area. The appreciation involves the dynamic presence of the body with its full range of sensory awareness.[20]

For comparative purposes, I summarize Berleant's reading of the body in landscape.[21] He first defines distance receptors and suggests that the distance receptors discern light, color, shape, pattern, movement, and distance, within the corresponding abstraction of space. We also have the awareness of climbing and descending, turning and twisting, and encountering obstruction and free passage. The notion of synaesthesia plays an important role in Berleant's sense of bodily experience, as it fuses the analysis of sense modalities with the directness of immediate experience in landscape appreciation, which engages the entire, interactive human sensorium. (This reminds us of the notion of intuition, and Berleant describes landscape appreciation as a process through which we become part of our environment through the interpenetration of body and place.) The differentiation of the senses only occurs after the integrated, unitary wholeness of aesthetic experience is encountered during reflection and analysis.

These definitions of bodily experience resemble Tang's notion of unity, which transcends the difference between the physical and metaphysical paradigms. In Berleant's words, "(landscape) appreciation is this entering into the experience as direct knowing, knowing that is engaged and replete. Its aesthetic is what makes a place come alive as a presence to those who live, work or visit it."[22]

Nature and Habitation in a Chinese Garden

Berleant has a special interest in Chinese gardens, which he correctly describes as varying in scale from the extensive grounds of emperors, wealthy merchants, and officials to small urban gardens and the private countryside retreats of scholars and retired officials of more modest means. A significant number of these centuries-old gardens have been restored as public treasures, some of which are designated as World Heritage Sites.[23] Here, I use the Geyuan Garden (個園) in Yangzhou, in China's central Jiangsu Province, as an example to illustrate Berleant's meticulous reading. I visited the garden in March 2014 (Figure 8.1,

Appendix), which is the best month to visit Yangzhou as suggested by the traditional literati, with Berleant's recent work in mind.

The official information states that Geyuan Garden was known as "the garden of the long-lived Ganoderma" during the Ming dynasty.[24] In 1818 (the twenty-second year of the reign of the Jiaqing Emperor), the salt distribution commissioner, Huang Zhiyun, bought the property and rebuilt the garden as a private retreat. The name Ge means individual personality, which echoes Berleant's view of the moral implications in the design of Chinese gardens.[25] In China, the form of bamboo is considered to be straight and persistent, illustrating an honest, fair, modest, upright, and loyal personality. Huang's name, Zhi Yun (至筠), also means bamboo, which explains why he named the garden Ge; the word Yuan means garden.

Geyuan covers an area of 2.5 hectares (6.2 acres), and is primarily composed of bamboo and rocks (Figure 8.2, Appendix). Rocks of different hues and shapes are used to represent scenes from the four seasons (Figure 8.3, Appendix); hence, the rock garden is named the "Artificial Mountain of Four Seasons."[26] This fits Berleant's description of a classical Chinese scholar's garden perfectly. The aptness of Berleant's description can best be shown by comparing Geyuan with Berleant's own depictions of a Chinese garden.[27] He writes,

> The overall plan of a scholar's garden is usually irregular, as are the shapes of its discrete sections. It is unusual to discover geometrical forms, from their boundaries to their details, apart from the rectilinear outlines of some pavilions and halls, and sometimes a straight perimeter wall.
>
> Structures for study, contemplation, and conversation occupy a major part, perhaps as much as half, of the garden area. They are carefully integrated into the landscape, embraced by trees and shrubs, and usually connected by covered walkways. They are interspersed by equally important semi-enclosed natural areas that contain a profusion of rocks and vegetation (Figure 8.4, Appendix).
>
> Water is almost always present, often as a central large pond but also in smaller pools connected by narrow waterways traversed by small foot bridges. The ponds and waterways are usually framed by shrubs and trees, often displaying a profusion of lotuses on their surface

while beneath is the constant movement of colorful large and small goldfish (Figure 8.5, Appendix).

They are natural sculptures of arresting presence and absorbing detail: the Chinese consider them 'a concentration of the creative forces of the Dao.

Berleant continues:

Scenic "rooms" are separated by walls and connected by doorway openings and passageways through halls and across pavilion, invite the visitor to wander along a circuitous route through a succession of scenic spots from one partly enclosed area to another.

These gardens are generally relatively small in extent, so when possible they are expanded by 'borrowing' the landscape outside its perimeter, adding the view of trees, distant mountains, a temple, or a pagoda to the garden's ambiance.

These features of the garden structures convey a sense of continuity. As one wanders contemplatively through the garden, the visitor becomes part of the landscape and nature. Nature is habitation and habitation is nature.

Wandering through a Chinese garden can evoke an association with a scroll painting and perhaps even its embodiment.

One moves slowly and meditatively through scenes that are continuously changing with an awareness enhanced by the meanings associated with the trees and plants.

Classical Chinese garden, most especially, is shaped by and for human participation. It requires a peripatetic human presence to be completed and fulfilled.

Although Chinese gardens encourage a reflective, contemplative mood, this is not a state of passivity or inactivity. It is a roving contemplation, an immediacy of thoughtful presence in the activities of walking, noticing, listening, contemplating, and sensing bodily the garden's constantly varying environmental experience.

> It is due less to the layout and the formal arrangement than to what vibrates through and around the various elements of composition, enhancing their power to bring out the rhythm of nature.

Tang's "Wandering in Art": Chinese Aesthetics and its Manifestations in Art

I want to highlight Berleant's reading by referring to Tang Junyi's beautiful phrase "wandering in art," which is one of the four themes of his conception of landscape appreciation, namely, "hiddenness," "cultivation," "rest," and "wander." Tang's insightful analysis contributes to the understanding and appreciation of Chinese landscape aesthetics that Berleant has promoted. Moreover, Tang's ideas on the Chinese garden in *The Spiritual Values of Chinese Culture* can be regarded as a companion to Berleant's landscape aesthetics.

Tang suggests that the notion of "wandering" (*you* 遊) in Chinese landscapes embodies both the physical and the mental and spiritual, as manifest in the appreciation of different Chinese architectural forms, such as towers, palaces, gardens, and home interiors. Tang writes:

> A tower is called a tower when it is high enough for people to climb to and have a bird's view over the surrounding. Its height is why it is being praised for and it allows one to travel up vertically. Chinese palaces are elegant not for its height, but more on its width and extensiveness . . . because one can wander—travel—in it.[28]

Tang states that, unlike the churches and castles of the West, Chinese architecture allows and enables the visitor to travel in the space, even if it has a deep courtyard, and layers of curtains and draperies.[29] He subsequently discusses corridors in Chinese architecture, stating that walking around the house and strolling along the corridors allows one to rest while "wandering." The concept of travel has another layer of metaphysical meaning, as it echoes the Daoist concept of the intertwining relationship of the concreteness in the empirical world and the vacuous (*xu*) in the metaphysical world (虛實相涵). Tang further suggests that, in addition to "wandering" (遊), the notions of "hiding" (藏), "cultivating" (修), and "resting" (息) emphasize the unity of the visitor's inner feeling with the outer space when wandering in landscape.[30] He states,

> The meeting point of the concreteness and the vacuous is where one's mind and soul travel freely. The beauty resulted from this is the realization of a free-mind and openness . . . that is why I compare the aesthetics of Chinese architecture to that of wandering.[31]

When wandering in a Chinese garden, one can appreciate the landscape by hiding alone ("hiddenness"), reflecting on one's moral life ("cultivation"), sitting around and resting the body ("rest"), and walking through the aesthetically natural or artificial space of the garden ("wander"). Tang also shares with Berleant that the experience transcends the rigid binary opposition between subject and object in Western aesthetics, and that the visitor gains an overall understanding, self-nourishment, and enrichment when the mind departs from the garden and travels into the realm of the Dao and back again.[32] To conclude, Tang conceives aesthetic experience as the capability of going beyond our usual perception. In the realm of the Dao, this going beyond enriches the viewer and results in his or her aesthetic appreciation of the fluid nature of the work's artistic qualities. This is best illustrated by Chinese landscape painting in ink.

In his article on Chinese gardens, Berleant claims that Daoism is key to understanding the Chinese scholar's garden, and that its philosophy functions as a pervasive perceptual presence and cognitive undertone.[33] Berleant considers the Chinese garden as a landscape that represents the Daoist idea of *wuwei*, or no action. Tang regards the Daoist idea of wandering as the key to the aesthetics of the gardens, as it integrates the physical freedom of the body and metaphysical transcendence of the mind. Moreover, Geyuan Garden demonstrates Berleant's observation that all of the elements and parts of the garden are designed to blend gently together to show the harmonious forces of nature. In his words, to experience landscape aesthetics is "to follow the Dao of nature, getting oneself in tune with the underlying rhythms of the seasons, the plants, the very universe, so that there was no discrepancy between inner being and outer reality."[34] With this in mind, I can see only the correspondence between Berleant's landscape aesthetics and Chinese aesthetics, which supplement and enrich each other in different languages.

The above comparative discussion also echoes James Cahill's findings on Chinese gardens. In one of his lectures on the subject, in which he relates Chinese garden with painting and its representation, Cahill said those who built gardens as sequestered places thought of themselves as inhabiting work of art, with all the attendant sense of escaping from real world and all its cares and clutter.[35] Close affinities between gardens and the painting of them affirmed this feeling. The typical wandering process is described by Cahill as one moves into the garden, pauses to participate or observe, then moves out. The wanderer or the aesthetic subject situated in a garden has the experience of a demarcated passage in one's life. Cahill even quotes this paragraph from Charles Jencks's essay, "Meanings of the Chinese Garden": "although there is a complicated order that can finally be perceived, the Chinese did not lay out their gardens to be conceptualized from above, in a cerebral helicopter, as the French and Italians did. The Chinese garden was to be perceived as a linear sequence, 'the scroll painting you enter in fancy.'"[36]

Section III

BODY AND GENDER MATTERS

9

FEMALE BODILY AESTHETICS, POLITICS, AND FEMININE IDEALS OF BEAUTY IN CHINESE TRADITIONS

Chapter 1 of this book provides discussions of post-modern thinkers, including Moira Gatens and Judith Butler, on how male and female are not just biological categories but historical and cultural constructions.[1] There should not be any sharp distinction between being "female" (in the biological sense) and being "feminine" (in the social sense), as "femininity" represents a dissolution of the self, which is fragmented into a fleeting array of desires and impulses driven by certain symbolic and cultural impulses that come from beyond the self.[2]

I understand that "femininity" does not refer to a mind-body dichotomy in Chinese philosophy, as there is no such dichotomy in Chinese philosophy. I would therefore like to focus on two overlapping issues while discussing the development of female aesthetics and the notion of a feminine ideal in China: (1) how this development can be understood within the particular historical and cultural context in China and how it can be related to various factors such as economic and political situations; (2) with man as the speaking subject in the Chinese patriarchal system, how male imaginations (especially those represented by the literati) construct the ideal and the aesthetic quality in woman as the projection of their wishes or regrets and of the various forms of their fantasies.

Susan Brownell and Jeffrey Wasserstrom claim that the notions of femininity or masculinity include anatomical details, behaviors, discussions, and ideas. Unique judgments about femininity and masculinity are made by specific people in particular contexts. In a word, the notion of "Chinese woman" is never a single basic category; femininity and masculinity were reconfigured as well as re-created in different phases.[3] This book attends to issues of power and meaning between the two sexes, between individuals and society, and between conventions and developments. It agrees with Brownell and Wasserstrom that masculinity and femininity are mutually constructed phenomena that should not be treated in isolation from one another.[4] It also agrees that, in China, beginning from ancient times and persisting to the present day, social gender overshadowed sexuality in the definition of the categories male and female.[5]

Aligned with the basic ideas above, this chapter introduces the philosophical discussion of female beauty in the Chinese tradition. It continues with a contextual case study of the development and construction of the feminine ideal in the courtesan culture of late imperial China. This critical study illustrates how the notion of female beauty in China was redefined and represented by male literati under certain political and economic contexts. Lastly, this chapter outlines the contemporary notion of female beauty in Communist China, a notion that has departed from tradition to follow that of the capitalist West.

The Notion of Feminine Beauty in Classical Confucian and Daoist Texts

Vision and Other Senses of Beauty

The term *nü se* 女色 (literally, woman color) is used to describe the beauty of women in traditional Chinese texts. It basically refers to the visual sense, which is believed to originate in the heart. In the old dictionary *Shuowen jiezi* 說文解字, *se* (color) is formed when the heart manifests its feeling in *qi* (the metaphysical element), and when *qi* expresses itself between eyebrows and turns into the color of physical appearance. This meaning is echoed in other Confucian texts like *The Analects* and *Xunzi* 荀子. Besides the common meaning of color in the present day, *se* in classical Chinese also refers to femaleness, the skin color and erotic qualities of a woman, which include her bodily beauty, the shape of her limbs, the gentleness of her behavior, the charm of her voice, the way she dresses and makes up, and so on. All these qualify a *meiren*, a beautiful woman (see Figure 9.1, Appendix). In addition to the role of the visual sense in the definition of a *meiren*, there is also the sense of touch, as the erotic factors just mentioned are conceived through physical contact with the beholder, which produces sensual pleasure. The sense of smell is another factor, as the scent of women is always mentioned in the description of a *meiren*; likewise the sense of hearing is mentioned in relation to the sound of her voice.

The following are some basic criteria summarizing the attributes of beautiful women listed in ancient literary and philosophy texts, in both Confucian and Daoist works, including *Shijing* 詩經 (*The Book of Poetry*), *Liezi* 列子 , *Zhuzi* 朱子 , *Huainanzi* 淮南子 : young; small; slim but fleshly; soft bones; drooping shoulders; smooth, white skin under colorful and tight silk underwear; clean, slender fingers; long neck; broad and white forehead; long ears; dark and thick hair with stylish hairpin; thick and bluish black eyebrows; clear and sentimental eyes; charming smile; tall and straight nose; red lips exposing small, seashell-white teeth; relaxed and elegant bodily gestures; and, finally, gentle behavior. Basically, it is the vitality of the body that counts, the sensuous qualities and curvatures of which must be conceived by the integration of all our senses.

According to most of the classical writings, a woman's beauty has also to be judged through (hetero) sexual sensations; that is, the attributes of a *meiren* are in the passionate eye of a male lover or admirer. The beauty of goddesses and *meiren* in classical myths and stories is basically grounded on male desire, fantasies, and devotion. Though the notion of beauty later departs from physiological and sexual considerations and is rather shaped by cultural and normative constraints, it is meaningful first of all to take a closer look at the sexual implication, as this dimension has never vanished.

The Sexual Implication of Female Beauty in Daoist Texts

Not only do the female physiognomy and feminine attributes reveal more than a skin-deep aesthetic judgment, but they also indicate the Chinese faith in the goodness of what nature makes beautiful.[6] As the previous chapter on kissing in Chinese culture notes, some of the Daoist theories related to female beauty made values or judgments according to female gestures that might facilitate sexual enjoyment and provide physical benefits presented to male partners.

The main recommendations given by early Daoist texts, like *Sunü jing* 素女經 (The classic of Sunü) of the Han dynasty (206 BC–AD 220), *Yufang mizhuan* 玉房秘傳 (Secrets of the jade chamber) of the Northern and Southern dynasties (4th century–AD 581), *Qianjin yaofang* 千金要方 (Recipes of priceless gold), written between 630 and 650, and so on, typical feminine ideals are also the suggested requirements of the ideal female sex partner. In summary, the texts recommend that she should be young and not yet a mother, amply covered with flesh, and have swelling breasts that fill the whole hand when held.[7] She should have silken hair and small eyes with the whites and pupils clearly defined; her face and body should be moist and glossy; her voice should be harmonious and low; the bones of her four limbs and hundred joints should be buried in ample flesh; and her private parts and underarms should be bare—but if there is hair, it should be fine and glossy. In contrast to the above definition of an ideal woman is a woman with tangled and yellowish hair, a fearful countenance, mallet-like neck, prominent Adam's apple, irregular teeth, husky voice, large mouth, high nose bridge, dull pupils, chin whiskers, prominent large joints, scant flesh, coarse skin, or copious, rough pubic hair. The texts warned that to associate with a female of these qualities would only bring harm to a man.[8] An example is the Daoist belief that women with rough pubic hair usually had a tough, short life; they would not bring any luck to their male partners.[9]

The above criteria are related to some fundamental theories of sex in Daoism, basically that it is for sexual pleasure, physical benefits, and longevity of the male. The background of the belief and practice concerned is cosmological and is generally referred to as the *yin-yang* five elements (*Yinyang wuxing* 陰陽五行) with the key elements *yin*, *yang*, and *qi* as outlined in the *I-Ching*. As is well known, the Daoist understanding of sexuality was profoundly affected by other ancient texts, like *Huangdi Neijing* 黃帝內經 (The Yellow Emperor classic of internal medicine), written around 475–221 BC, and later Daoist writings by Dong Xuanzi 董玄子 in the seventh century. These texts reflect a deep-rooted belief in the magical, therapeutic, and health-giving properties of sex. Sexual coupling is seen both symbolically and practically as the harmonious balancing of the *yin* and the *yang*, preserving life through the preservation of the *qi*. These traditions hold that *yang* manifests as heaven and man while *yin* manifests as woman and earth. These two elements are believed to be the polar forces of the cosmos but related to each other. Their respective sex organs possess the elemental forces. As the penis is the *yang* and the vulva is the *yin*, when a man and a woman conduct sexual intercourse, the moment of orgasm is a form of metaphysical harmony that transcends the couple's corporeal existence through the fusion of the two polarities. Consequently, sex leads to a sacred experience.

According to Dong Xuanzi, if one follows the natural laws of sex to the state of harmony, one's *qi* is nourished and one's life prolonged. Furthermore, by following a number of sequential sexual progressions and reactions during sexual intercourse, one might attain longevity. Failure to adhere to the sequence could cause illness. Thus, it is important to learn the proper procedures and to choose a partner who is cooperative and desirable. Dong's sex guide, *Art of the Bedchamber*, is a favorite source of such knowledge, and gained a wide following after the Tang period when it was compiled into a catalogue of some thirty basic postures. Even though the ancient Daoist texts on sex all stated that men and women should participate together in sex, it is obvious that the texts are basically male-oriented and concerned mainly with benefits to males. As I suggest in the previous chapter on kissing, under the influence of the dominant Confucian patriarchal system, this bias was reinforced by the idea that, during intercourse, the man "chants" and the woman "harmonizes."

Returning our attention to the criteria for the feminine ideal, we should note that these judgments are not only made according to bodily characteristics, but are also related to the sexual reaction of the woman, which finally leads to sexual consequences for the male body. One example is that an ideal woman partner must not have a manly voice. One of the main interpretations of this is that a woman with a manly voice manifests an excess of *qi*, which would make it difficult for her to harmonize with a man in sex. Thus, it is believed that certain bodily attributes of a woman would downgrade her beauty, as they would be inimical not only to sexual enjoyment but also to the health of the male partner. Women over forty were more likely to have many more of these negative characteristics: hearts and bellies out of order; cold, stiff, and hard bodies; smelly armpits; and spontaneous vaginal secretions. Other negative tendencies include inclination to jealousy, bad disposition, and eating binges.[10] In summary, we could cite the following excerpt from the Daoist text *Xiuchen yulü* 修真語錄 (Record of cultivating the true essence), written in the Han dynasty around 108 BC:

> When mounting women one must first have a clear understanding of the "five avoidances." Women who have manly voices and coarse skin, yellow hair and violent dispositions, and are sneaky and jealous constitute the first avoidance. Those with evil appearances and unhealthy countenances, bald heads and underarm odor, hunched backs and jutting chests, and who hop like sparrows or slither like snakes constitute the second avoidance. Those who are sallow, thin, frail, and weak, cold of body and deficient of *chi*, and whose channels of circulation are out of harmony constitute the third avoidance. Women who are mad, deaf, or dumb, who are lame or blind in one eye, who have scabies, scars, or are insane, who are too fat or too thin, or whose pubic hair is coarse and dense constitute the fourth avoidance. Women who are over forty, have borne many children and whose yin is weak, whose skin is loose and breasts are slack, these are harmful and confer no benefit. This is the fifth avoidance.[11]

But is physical appearance more important in determining a woman's beauty? In the ancient Daoist myth Sunü Jing, this priority is made clear when the legendary goddess Sunü said the following to the emperor:

> A woman's virtue is her inner beauty; her appearance is her outer beauty. First observe her skin and then observe her inner qualities. If a woman's hair is burnt black, her bones large, or her flesh coarse; if she is disproportionately fat or thin, exceptionally tall or short of an unsuitable age, then she will be barren, manly of speech, or violent and abrupt in her actions. Her private parts will be dry and her womb cold. She will leak red or white discharge and have a savage odor. This is extremely harmful to one's *yang-chi*.[12]

It is clear that, in the old Daoist teachings, a woman's physical appearance is the primary requirement for sexual purposes, while her virtues are secondary. This resonates with other elements of Daoist philosophy, which emphasizes affinity to Nature and regards (Confucian) moral codes as forms of constraint.

The Moral Meaning of Female Beauty in the Confucian Texts

However, it should be noted that aesthetic objects in Chinese culture are not restricted to objects of sensation or physical desire. Their meaning and value have acquired spiritual, social, and material properties. The root of "beauty" in Chinese denotes material benefits and connotes wealth, abundance, longevity, vitality, good reputation, and power. The word also refers to one's behavior and to outstanding abilities of many kinds. The old Confucian teachings in *The Analects* and *Mencius* relate beauty to moral practices. The sages are beautiful people, parables and analogies of which are found in *Mencius*, as in the following:

> Mencius said: "The trees of the Niu mountain were once beautiful. But can the mountain be regarded any longer as beautiful since, being in the borders of a big state, the trees have been hewed down with axes and hatchets? . . . Is there not a heart of humanity and righteousness originally existing in man? The way in which he loses his originally good mind is like the way in which the trees are hewed down with axes and hatchets. As trees are cut down day after day, can a mountain retain its beauty?"[13]

Beauty refers to the good qualities and positive dispositions of personality that define a human being. Female beauty refers to those attributes that define a good woman. When beauty is used to describe a moral saint, a righteous minister, or a kind emperor, it has transcendental moral and social meanings (that is, ensuring happiness and peace in a country); when it is used to describe a woman, it is subject to social norms. The old Chinese teachings for women in the Han dynasty say that "a man is great because of his strength, a woman is beautiful because of her weakness" (from *nüjie* 女誡). The term *weakness* means humility in human relation. Other words used to describe female beauty are *rou* 柔 (gentleness), *ruan* 軟 (softness), and *zhi* 稚 (innocence), all of which imply the feeling of superiority involved when one is involved with women of these qualities. These women are defined as virtuous women with inner beauty. It is interesting to see how these ideas are developed to extremes, so that virtuous women are praised as saints who possess incredible moral courage manifesting the humanity for which Confucians strive. It should be noted that the moral code for women in the old Confucian culture stresses basically the virtues of chastity, piety to their parents-in-law, and marital fidelity. These considerations make a woman outstanding in her inner beauty. The more consistent women were in keeping these virtues, the more they would be remembered in history. *The Records of Lie Nü* 烈女 (women of admonition) from the Han dynasty reveal how Chinese women in the old Confucian context were willing to die for patriarchal values. Numerous suicide attempts were made by widows as protests against forced remarriages, as well as by young women whose fiances had passed away after they were engaged. The ideas of love, chastity, and marriage were internalized by women of various dynasties and attained the status of religious cult, which ensured the success of Confucian teachings among Chinese women.

We can conclude that, in the Chinese tradition, both the external sexual and inner moral dimensions determine the beauty of a woman as in other cultures, but the presentation and definition of female beauty in the Chinese context (especially under Confucian influence) generated its own specific forms and meanings. Though Confucianism and Daoism are usually depicted as two conflicting traditions in China, they shared a common philosophical background in the Dao; the interplay between the two maintained the so-called super-stable equilibrium of Chinese culture, as I explicate in the previous chapter on kissing in China. The notion of female beauty comes from both traditions. The Daoist notion emphasizes natural physicality, while the Confucian one stresses behavior control or "inner beauty." This is best illustrated in the courtesan culture of late imperial China in the eighteenth and nineteenth centuries. The signification of *meiren* in the era is the result of a long history of adaptation and modification in response to political, cultural, and economic restraints. We will now turn to the development of the feminine ideal in late imperial China, as represented in courtesan culture, for a case study further exploring the notion of feminine beauty in China.

The Feminine Ideal in Late Imperial Courtesan Culture

The images of courtesans are various, ambiguous, and even contradictory in late imperial times; scholars attribute this to class differences and the change of sovereignty from the late Ming to the Qing.[14] Courtesans in the era ranged from street and brothel prostitutes who entertained men at home to high-class courtesans who could be commissioned for a trial relationship. Therefore, before investigating how a courtesan's role affected the judgment of her beauty as a specific form of female beauty, it is necessary to outline the background of a woman's social existence at that time.

The General Life Pattern of a Woman in Late Imperial China

The age of six or seven was an important turning point for both sexes in the late Qing. For boys, it was time to begin formal schooling, the transfer from maternal to paternal authority, and the conferral of a formal name. For girls, it was time for foot-binding to begin. The tight, painful binding of the toes and wrapping of the feet was intended to keep them the small size deemed desirable by men. This will be discussed later in this article. Foot-binding, which began in the Song dynasty (960–1279), was a sign of social status, as it meant that the woman concerned was not available for work in the fields or that required physical mobility. The onset of a woman's puberty at this age was also signified by special codes of hairstyle. In general, for women this was also the age for formal instruction in cooking and sewing, and for decreased mobility outside the home.[15] Marriage was at age seventeen or eighteen for women, by parental arrangement. About ten percent of marriages were polygamous. Marriage patterns varied according to class, depending on conditions in society, but in general, the Chinese preferred to select brides from families that were slightly lower in social status than their own. Female literacy was more likely in cities, where private tutors were available for the daughters of the elite. Education was to prepare women to marry into better families. A lucky woman would marry into a rich family. Her family would provide a portion of the family estate as dowry, which would help to give the daughter honor in her husband's household and also encourage favorable treatment from the mother-in-law.[16] An unlucky woman would enter a wealthy household as a maidservant or a child concubine. Worst off were those sold into prostitution for cash, but if these girls survived and succeeded in the training, their beauty and talent would be valued and marriage or concubinage was possible.

Wives, concubines, and courtesans had to meet different expectations. First wives and concubines had different duties. The former were householders, while the latter were the love-objects of the husbands, helping to procreate to enlarge the family. The basic responsibilities of wives were to perpetuate the family and to manage the household. They were not asked to be good lovers. Concubines were supposed to please and serve the master by different means; they enjoyed more intimacy with the master. Courtesans—as distinct from lower-class prostitutes, who basically fulfilled the sexual needs of clients—were literate and skilled in a variety of entertainment arts, and their services were not confined to the sale of sex.

Courtesans of high-class brothels were the only group of women besides the daughters of good families who received literacy training. Though they could produce wonderful literary works, their livelihoods did not depend on it. In that era, access to women was unequal, as males outnumbered females. Intermarriage was common between the literati and merchant classes, but the elite still frequented high-class brothels. Erotic novels, prints, and scrolls, produced in great volume in the era, reflected an openly sensual urban culture.[17] The beauty, performance, and literary talents of popular courtesans qualified them for work in such high-class establishments. In fact, some courtesans had even become honorary literati; they occupied the only place in the culture where women could openly socialize with men who were not their husbands. The most prominent among them, usually at the upper levels of the profession, enjoyed a level of renown unattainable by any other type of woman. Among the literati, these courtesans were ideal lovers, objects of adoration and admiration, and sources of inspiration.

Though courtesanship stood entirely outside the kinship system of Chinese society and so did not pose a real threat to that structure, it was built securely into the structure of a Chinese society that was at once very hierarchical and surprisingly fluid. However, in a Confucian culture, courtesans could not escape the taint of notoriety.[18] Even the most famous of courtesans aspired to leave the brothel, to be purchased and "redeemed" into "respectability," and to be taken as a concubine by a wealthy or talented client.[19] Chinese women in their old age were entirely dependent on males and their close relatives.

The Depiction of Female Beauty in Late Imperial Courtesan Culture: The Cases of Painting and Writing

Nudity was taboo in Confucian culture, which explains why it was not a common subject in Chinese art. The depiction of female bodies in traditional paintings and sculptures was linear, simple, and devoid of sensuous elements, but more detail could be found in poetry and literature, especially in erotic literature. A good example is found in the 200 linear wood- block prints related to the story and characters of the famous seventeenth-century erotic novel *Jinpingmei* 金瓶梅 . However, crude portraits of nude women were also found in paintings in albums, on porcelain bottles, and on glasses circulated in low-class brothels for the entertainment of customers in the late Qing. Literature provides a more detailed and sophisticated discussion of female body aesthetics especially that related to courtesan culture.

Interesting readings may be made from the perspective of class differences. Low-class brothel culture tended to depict *changji* 娼妓 — a special term referring to prostitutes rather than *jinü* 妓女 (courtesans), which was comparatively a less pejorative and ambiguous term— in paintings or writings in ways that illustrated the Daoist criteria. In "pillow books" or "albums" circulated in the brothels, female bodies were quite often engaged in sexual activities, demonstrating various sexual positions for arousing desire. These activities were usually conducted in the harmonious and tranquil mood advocated by Daoists, who believed that sex was a joyful journey aimed at a sacred experience, as mentioned in Chapter 6. Thus, women participating in the act of love in the paintings appear submissive and cooperative. Late Qing erotica also reflected the criteria mentioned in classical Daoist texts for the most desirable female bodies. Some of the criteria recommended that bodies should be young, unmarried, and under thirty; they should not be full bosomed but amply fleshed, with silken hair and small eyes. Visible ribs and hair below the vagina were undesirable; pubic hair should be sparse and smooth; women should have slender limbs, soft flesh, and pure white pale skin of an elegant texture. These had become items on a checklist for the female body as portrayed in the late Qing erotica.

In quite a number of erotic paintings of this era, as described in the previous chapter on kissing, male characters examined the female vulva, *yin*, so named because it was seen as the repository of the elemental force of *yin*. Other parts of the female body, including the breasts, received less attention and appreciation, which explains why women's breasts were usually bound and flat in paintings. Facial beauty was also not of great concern, as it was not considered the center for sexual pleasure. Again, foot-binding, the so-called cult of the golden lotus, is a custom depicted in late Qing erotica that most clearly illustrates attitudes toward sexual pleasure. We can criticize this sexual adoration of miniature female feet as a "Confucian patriarchal aesthetic perversion." Until the late imperial era, bound feet had been the main feature of a *meiren*. The practice enhanced the sexual appeal of women and the intensity of sexual pleasure, but it also controlled the mobility and behavior of Confucian women and tied them to their homes. Late Qing documents contained a detailed grading system in nine categories, used by the literati to evaluate a woman's bound feet. The best grade was given to small, fleshy, soft, and "boneless" female feet. Van Gulick once pointed out that it was easier for a man to lose control when he got hold of a woman's bound feet than of her body.[20]

Dorothy Ko's study of "lotus feet" states that the practice of foot-binding spread from the thirteenth to the fifteenth century in China. Its function was to enhance a daughter's marriage prospects; beyond stimulating male desire, bound feet fulfilled the familial expectation of modesty and morality.[21] Ko's reading echoes the discussion in Chapter 5 on Chinese women's embroidery. She relates the domestication of foot-binding to women's textile work, which was a form of female education taking place in the inner chambers of a Chinese household. Ko describes how a Chinese daughter's first binding session took place in the inner chamber in a women-only ceremonial process, marking the first step of her becoming a bride.[22] Ko proposes that it was by this process that a woman gained power and value to her family by way of her body, be it through her bound feet or her physical labor. Her detailed depiction of the foot-binding process and its use of materials reveals that the function of the act is more than erotic.[23]

Yet male imagination of women's foot-binding in Qing erotica continued to elaborate on the role of the golden lotus in sexual activities. Miniature feet were considered to be the sexiest part of a woman's body, as they were originally designed by dominating Confucians to act as constraints on a woman's behavior. Foot-binding soon developed into the main object of visual pleasure and tool of sexual hedonism. Beautiful women were attractive mainly because of the ways they walked and carried their bodies on bound feet. However, this tradition started to change in the latter days of the Qing. The literati and courtesan clients of that era commented that a thin waist, not bound feet, was the most fashionable trait.[24] Later, as mentioned in the chapter on kissing, Western erotic images were supplemented with the traditional linear expression of beauty, portraying full-bosomed female bodies. Moreover, according to the detailed manuals compiled in the nineteenth century by some female brothel managers for training *changji*, the requirements for becoming popular were as follows: *se* (beauty), which focused on artificial beauty, manner, and posture; *yi* (artistic skill), which included the skill of keeping the master company; *qing* (emotion and affection), which demanded disguising one's true emotions with apparent sincerity; and *biantai* or variation of attitudes (變態), which required the ability to be flexible and lively in dealings with customers. Chapter 13 discusses one of these manuals, *Hunrupian* 渾如篇 , in detail. The criteria reflected very different standards for evaluating courtesans in low- and high-class groups. For high-class courtesans, serious and genuine displays of emotion and poetic talent were required, in addition to a flirtatious wit.[25] We can trace the images of this group back to records earlier than the late Qing era for evidence that a tradition had already been formed.

Good portraits of courtesans depicted their external appearance with most of the characteristics that comprised the old criteria of *meiren* already mentioned, but these were not the most important features. Because of the special function they served and the particular culture they were in, there were extra requirements for a courtesan to be judged as great or beautiful. Elaborate dresses and hairstyles with flowery hairpins were some necessary items, in addition to bodily features and bound feet. Detailed descriptions of dress had always been part of the literati's repertoire. Since an upper-class courtesan's service was not confined to the sale of sex, the literature related to high-class brothels that flourished in late imperial China contained few direct descriptions of the sexual performance of courtesans or the experience of the clients. The literature contained instead a detailed record of the ways the courtesans dressed and the decoration of their residence. Emphasis was placed on their posture, the atmosphere of their meetings, and their artistic talent. As mentioned, most popular courtesans had received good literary training and had the talent to write and paint. They collaborated with their elite customers in creating literary works, and they read their work in public.

Harriet Zurndorfer provides a vivid depiction of the atmosphere mentioned here. She writes that a courtesan of high class had the ability to write poetry; literary exchanges were fundamental in the communication between her and her clients. Her survey shows that talented courtesans functioned as counsellors and were responsible for creating an "aesthetically pleasing atmosphere," including in gardens—" in these beautiful, rustic, and artistic sites people congregated to enjoy leisure pursuits in the open air. Here courtesans met their patrons to enjoy intense cultural exchanges on poetry and singing. In some cases, courtesans actually owned gardens and used them as a form of financial investment."[26]

One could say that the positive inner dimensions of a beautiful courtesan were her artistic talent and her sentimentality and emotional loyalty to her literati lovers. Thus, in the representations of high-class courtesans, Confucian criteria were applied to this group rather than the Daoist sexual ones. Some courtesans could and did become powerful symbols of morality and virtue, as they were memorialized and praised by their literati fans. In sum, a great courtesan was evaluated according to her personality, talent, sensitivity, strength of character, and capacity for passionate and declared devotion to the man she loved. Art historians and literary critics have investigated the writing and reception of women in late imperial China. Wu Hung points out in his brilliant study that systematic accounts of *meiren* did not come into existence until the late Ming and early Qing dynasties.[27] There were dominant models in literary and artistic production, like those circulated in Qing court painting and popular New Year prints, which seemed to conform to the standard, impersonal female imagery of late imperial China. But there were also deliberate variations that served creativity and other functions. Beauty in courtesan culture was a good example of how female images assumed different meanings in different contexts.

Wu correctly points out that, in the popular writings and famous paintings of the seventeenth and eighteenth centuries, Chinese female beauty was represented within a feminine environment. This feminine space was replete with details of decorative items and architectural layouts. Individual items offered static features while architectural layouts provided the space with a dynamic spatial or temporal structure and points of view. These environmental elements usually took the following forms: particular kinds of buildings, paths, railings, trees, flowers, plants, rocks, decorative objects, painting, and calligraphy; personal attributes like clothes and ornaments, makeup, standardized facial and bodily features; and, finally, tableaux of female activities, with maids in attendance. This kind of depiction appeared long before the Qing dynasty and had formed a tradition.

Portraits of women produced by famous court painters like Zhou Fang 周昉 in the Tang dynasty already carried the structure of this kind of feminine space, though not as elaborated. A typical depiction was groups of beautiful women playing with butterflies or engaging in various leisurely activities inside a garden. We can easily find abundant handscrolls portraying women in this kind of manner, only the tendency to itemize the iconographical features of a beauty and her place achieved more extreme forms in the early Qing—with reference to the lifestyle and culture of high-class courtesans.[28]

How may one interpret the function of this feminine environment and its relation to female beauty? Art critics suggest the concept of feminine space as a totalizing entity. In Wu's analysis, a beauty was essentially the sum of all the visible forms one expected to find in her space; all the pre-arranged components of this space were actually features identified with herself. One identified a woman as a *meiren* not by recognizing her face but by surveying her courtyard, room, clothes, her servants, and her expression and gesture. In other words, what one found in her and her space were numerous signifiers. At a deeper level of reading, a beauty was by definition idealized; this explained why the outlook of Chinese beauties was epitomized in classical texts as a woman with star-bright eyes, willow-leaf eyebrows, cloud-like hair, and snow-white bosom.[29]

The "Manual of Beautiful Women," written by Xu Zhen 徐震 around the mid-seventeenth century, was a popular text to which art critics refer when discussing female beauty. Xu compiled the iconography of an archetypal beautiful and talented woman based mainly on the lifestyles of courtesans and concubines of his time. Wu has produced a faithful translation of the ten-part iconography consisting of physical appearance, style, skills, activities, dwelling, seasons and moments, adornment, auxiliary objects, food, and special interests:

- *Physical appearance:* cicada forehead; apricot lips; rhinoceros-horn teeth; creamy breasts; eyebrows like faraway mountains; glances like waves of autumn water; lotus-petal face; cloud-like hairdo; feet like bamboo shoots carved in jade; fingers like white shoots of grass; willow waist; delicate steps as though walking on lotus blossoms; neither fat nor thin; appropriate height.
- *Style:* casting her shadow on a half-drawn curtain; leaving her footsteps on green moss; leaning against a railing while waiting for moonrise; holding a *pipa*-guitar at an angle; glancing back before departure; throwing out an artful, captivating smile; having just finished singing and becoming fatigued from dancing.
- *Skills:* playing the lute; changing poetry; playing *weiqi*-chess; playing kickball; copying ancient calligraphy before a pond; embroidering; weaving brocade; playing the vertical flute; playing dominoes; comprehending musical pitches and rhymes; swinging; playing the "double six" game.
- *Activities:* taking care of orchids; preparing tea; burning incense; looking at the reflection of the moon in a gold basin; watching flowers on a spring morning; composing poems about willow catkins; catching butterflies; fashioning clothes; harmonizing the five tastes [fine cooking]; painting her fingernails with red paint; teaching a mynah to recite poems; comparing posies collected on Duanwu day.
- *Dwelling:* a gold room; a jade-storied gallery; a pearled door curtain; a screen inlaid with mother-of-pearl; an ivory bed; a lotus-blossom pink bed-net; a curtain of kingfisher feathers for the inner chamber.
- *Seasons and moments:* flowers blossoming in the Golden Valley Garden; bright moon over a painted pleasure-boat; snow reflected on a pearled curtain; silver candles above a tortoise-shell banquet table; fragrant plants in the setting sun; raindrops pelting banana leaves.
- *Adornment:* a pearl shirt; an eight-piece embroidered skirt; a raw silk sleeveless dress; a pair of "phoenix-head" shoes; rhinoceros-horn hairpins; hairpins made of "cold-preventive" rhinoceros

horns; jade pendants; a "love-birds" belt; pearl and gem earrings; head ornaments made of kingfisher feathers; gold "phoenix" head ornaments; embroidered tap pants.

- *Auxiliary objects:* an ivory comb; a "water-chestnut flower" mirror; a jade mirror stand; a rabbit-fur writing brush; patterned letter-paper; an inkstone from Duanxi; a "green silk" *qin*-lute; a jade vertical flute; a pure silk fan; rare flowers; a volume of the *Odes* with Master Mao's commentaries [*Maoshi*]; a rhyming book; collections of love poetry, including the *New Songs from the Jade Terrace* [*Yutai xinyong*] and the *Fragrant Dressing Case* [*Xianglian ji*]; witty maidservants; a gold incense burner; ancient vases; jade boxes; rare perfume.
- *Food:* seasonal fruits; fresh lichee; dried fish; "kid" wine; various kinds of delicious wine; delicacies from hills and seas; famous tea from Songluo, Jingshan, and Yangxian; various kinds of pickles in clever shapes.
- *Special interests:* leaning drunkenly on her lover's shoulder; taking a noon bath in fragrant water; laughing seductively beside the pillow; secretly exchanging glances; picking up a pellet to shoot a yellow bird; showing slight jealousy. (*Tanji congshu* 檀几叢書, 141–142)[30]

This kind of *meiren* manual was supposed to have originated in places where a courtesan culture flourished, like the southern cities of Suzhou and Hangzhou. There were reasons to believe that the idealized feminine space described in the writings and paintings concerned were an exaggeration and idealization of some of the high-class brothel scenes in these places.

There were a number of significant "coded" images suggested in the reception. First, readers were reminded of the fictionality and idealization of these portraits of beautiful women. The linear method in the case of paintings was used to represent the "types" of ideal female face and body instead of individual and particular ones. The use of the "weeping willow" metaphor (*liu*) had become standard for portraying the "willow-branch" waist (*liuyao*) and "willow-leaf " eyebrows (*liumei*) that were regarded as beautiful. Even the background and stories of the female characters portrayed were stereotyped. It was observed that the *meiren* was always anonymous, enclosed in an isolated world, being an object of the gaze of her male painter or author. Wu summarizes:

> The woman in a courtesan-concubine painting is nameless and often appears in an opulent interior or a garden setting. She may be engaged in leisurely activities, but more frequently she is alone, either looking at her own reflection in a mirror or gazing at a pair of cats, birds, or butterflies. In both cases, the subtext is that she, as an "amorous beauty," is thinking about an absent lover and suffering from "spring longing." Differing from a portrayal of a palace lady, however, a courtesan-concubine" picture often delivers a bolder erotic message. Although the painted woman rarely exhibits her sexuality openly, her sexual allure and accessibility are represented through certain gestures (such as touching her cheek and toying with her belt) and sexual symbols (such as particular kinds of flowers, fruits, and objects) that a Ming or Qing spectator would have had no difficulty understanding.[31]

As a beautiful courtesan or concubine must possess intellectual and artistic talents, there were always calligraphy supplies, books, and poetry ready for use in the ideal feminine space. This note, and the bolder erotic message mentioned, reflected again the special role of courtesans as the ideal lovers of men and as the idealized fantasies of female beauty in the eyes of men. Courtesans satisfied both the physical desires and spiritual demands of their clients that wives were not supposed to fulfill.

An additional reading of the *meiren* painting and writing in late imperial China was given to those Qing court productions patronized by Manchu governors like Yongzheng 雍正 in the eighteenth century. A form of exotic "Chineseness" was supposedly projected onto and identified with the feminine space of these works. The vulnerability, passivity, excessive refinement, and melancholic expression illustrated in the space of the beautiful characters were read as the images of a lost and subordinated country waiting for the power of the new foreign ruler. The late imperial feminine ideal that basically followed traditional standards with certain elaborations was said to have been reinvented to fulfill the desire and fantasy of the ruling patrons.[32] But besides these particular political implications, what were the general meanings of this popular genre of female beauty in the era indicated? How did the image construction relate to the economic, class structure, and cultural factors involved?

Deconstructing the Feminine Ideal of Courtesan Culture in Late Imperial China

I was reminded of Beverly Bossler's reading, which details the origins of the late Imperial cult of fidelity and concludes that women's fidelity or loyalty stemmed from a complex amalgam of political, social, and moral agendas.[33] I use here Qing courtesans as an example.

We have already analyzed the transformation of the portraits of the courtesan from the late Ming to the Qing, as well as the polarization in the courtesan world between low-class prostitutes and talented and prominent courtesans. When China was taken over by the Manchurians, the changed political context also altered the significance of the literati's identification with the life of courtesans. The lifestyle of famous courtesans had been said during the Ming to symbolize freedom, self-creation, heroic action, and the embodiment of elite cultural ideals. After the Manchurian conquest, courtesans came to represent the loss of these ideals.[34] The busy brothel area around Jiangnan and Nanjing was completely destroyed by the Qing court in the seventeenth century. Brothels later resumed their business, but when compared with the late Ming era, prominent literati seldom published poems or essays celebrating their liaisons with well-known courtesans or took them into their homes as concubines. Instead, these beautiful women were seen as objects of pity. There was a parallel drawn between the suffering of the literati under the Manchurian dynasty and the exploitation and loneliness of a courtesan, which meant she had become a representation of the literati's "lost world."[35] The following example given by Paul Ropp in his discussion of ambiguous images of courtesan culture in late imperial China is excerpted from a representative courtesan song written by a popular poet in the early nineteenth century, entitled *Sighing Through the Night's Five Watches*:

With sly flirtatious glances
        I had to encourage the guests to stay.
When the night drum sounds the second watch,
        The moon casts a cold shadow on the window.

How pitiful, entertaining guests is so difficult;
How annoying
To have to talk with every guest who comes and goes.
Tobacco and tea I serve with my own hands;
Maintaining friendly smiles all the while.
What is truly frightening:
To encounter drunken guests at the banquet table;
"Ill-fated beauty" does not begin to capture the shame.
How many days until I can escape this mire? (My God!)
Yet for the sake of money I have to endure it all . . .

Sadly singing, I enter the curtained bed
Accompanying my guests;
No matter whether young or old, he becomes my partner;
No passion for me in this lover's tryst;
Clouds and rain are all his doing;
He wants to crush my flower's heart to pieces;
We toss and turn, my agony is endless . . .

I can only
Muster all my strength to seem warm and compliant;
Pressing my cheeks against his;
Whispering sweet and flattering words;
Exhausting every bit of my cunning;
To swindle him out of his money. (My God!)
Even with the most disgusting of men,
I dare show no sign of resistance . . .[36]

The poem revealed a poor economic situation and hard business attitude on the one hand, and a change of attitude regarding the life of courtesans on the other. It was well known that the Qing government reinforced orthodox neo-Confucianism while ruling China, as previous foreign rulers had in the country's long history. This reinforcement aroused prejudices and negative attitudes toward courtesans. Throughout the Qing dynasty, this group of women had more difficulty joining the circle of refined letters; they were transformed in representation from elite subjects to erotic objects, or objects of hardship and misfortune—as shown in the above poem. Among the Confucian, paternalistic, and condescending views of these poor courtesans, there was the literati's own sense of inadequacy and failure as regards the courtesans. The self-love and self-pity of these intellectuals had been projected onto the romanticized, pitiful, but beautiful images of courtesans. In the nineteenth century, the low-class erotic portraits of prostitutes we discussed previously had instead become popular in the brothel districts, which flourished again later in the era but lost their previous prestigious position and fervor.

The bodily images of the Chinese courtesan reflect what Christine Battersby has clearly stated, that biology is a mode of discourse that cannot be separated from other symbolic codes and practices in the social networks of power. Beauty refers not to "facts" but is socially and historically constructed.[37] As Susan Suleiman said, the question of women's bodies and women's sexuality has implications both for politics and literature; the production of verbal constructs about them in some ways reflects and creates these relations.[38] It also illustrates very well what Naomi Wolf has observed about the beauty myth, that beauty reflects emotional distance, politics, finance, and sexual repression.[39] The image of the ideal courtesan in the late Qing was projected by the psychological disappointment of the literati in that era. The pretty but pitiful female images were also formed in relation to political and ideological suppression by the Manchurian government with the aid of powerful Confucian orthodoxy. The life of courtesans working in both high- and low-class brothels was hard because of the anti-prostitution campaign organized by the new rulers. Courtesans sold their bodies to earn a living, most of the time against their own will. Under both the male literati and the Manchurian rulers, courtesans demonstrated that beauty was not about women but about men's institutions and institutional power. Moreover, the "feminine space" represented in the writings and paintings also prove Wolf's statement that the qualities that a given period calls beautiful in women are merely symbols of the female behavior that that period considers desirable; beauty is always actually about prescribing behavior and not appearance. However, the feminine ideal in the courtesan culture of the late Ming and Qing also contradicts some of Wolf's analyses, whose basic frame of reference is the contemporary West. Wolf said that when women in culture show character, they are not desirable; also, that a beautiful heroine is a contradiction in terms, since heroism is about individuality, interesting and ever-changing, while "beauty" is generic, boring, and inert.[40] This is just the opposite of the case we have been discussing. Beautiful courtesan figures in late imperial China were constructed as heroines with unique talent, vital personality, and free will. Wolf said beauty is amoral, that the moral lessons of male culture exclude "beauties."

On the contrary, the devoted passion and loyalty of a courtesan to her male lover (who sometimes represented the country or its ruler) was invested with moral merit in the Confucian sense. Finally, Wolf said that Western culture stereotypes women by flattening the feminine into beauty-without-intelligence or intelligence-without-beauty; women are allowed a mind or a body but not both.[41] Again, artistic and intellectual talent were not only treasured but regarded as necessary and positive at the upper levels of late Ming and Qing courtesan cultures. These contradictions only affirm that the notion of beauty is actually a particular cultural, social, and historical construction.

The Contemporary Notion of Female Beauty in Communist China

Nevertheless, what Naomi Wolf deconstructed in the beauty myth might be applied to the general notion of female beauty in Communist China during the nineties. The development of the feminine ideal in China after the Qing had been as confusing as the modern history of the country. It is difficult to trace and discuss the notion during the first half of the twentieth century when the country was undergoing ceaseless civil war and the disastrous Sino-Japanese War. Discussion of beauty was then restricted to a few elite groups of women from distinct political and social classes. After the Communists took over in 1949, the notion of female beauty became tied up with the love of labor, the party, and the nation. In the first thirty years of Communist China, women nationwide had their hair either tied up or cut; the plain party uniforms had suppressed every individual characteristic or taste. Women were at the time devoting their energy to economic and political practices and reforms. The plain look was for action; it had been brought to its apogee during the Cultural Revolution in the sixties, when nearly all the women in the country wore only blue and gray with neither makeup nor accessories. The only "fashion" was the shapeless, socialist look; the one acceptable exception were brides, who wore red and had their hair made up during their weddings. At that time, external beauty was not important, but the inner beauty of women who sacrificed themselves for the nation, the people and the party according to the Communist ideas. Women with flamboyant looks would get themselves into trouble, as they would be accused of succumbing to bourgeois ideologies.

Only when China opened its door in the late seventies did its women brighten up their looks again. The influx of foreign economic investment brought along with it famous brands of European fashion and cosmetics. The flourishing commercial market brought various trends and colors to big cities like Beijing, Shanghai, and the southern Guangdong areas near Hong Kong. Women's consumer products filled up the country markets during the eighties. It seems to be a common phenomenon that women's fashion is always the fastest sector to develop when a developing country takes off. Furthermore, when the country's power structure became more fluid and economic classes appeared again, fashion and beauty were necessary symbols and signs of personal and class identification. Mainland women urgently wanted and shared a new look. This phenomenon echoes what was happening to women's fashion in the 1960s, with the same motives and drives, which I explicate in Chapter 12 of this book. Advertisements for women's products were everywhere; foreign magazines were imported and translated to promote new female images from Western culture. Under the urge to modernize, to correct the backward past, and to forget the "wrong" history of the Cultural Revolution in the sixties, contemporary discussions of female beauty in China closely followed those of the West.

Fashion Models Wearing European Brands as the New Models of Female Beauty

The traditional standards of external beauty were less well emphasized during the Socialist period, and the "inner" dimensions of beauty, like moral effort and intellectual qualities, were mentioned only in the party's propaganda or some "politically correct" publications. These publications continue some traditional discussions, for instance, that external beauty originates from an inner beauty that aims at benevolence, commitment to one's community, self-improvement, and unique personality; the aesthetic principle involved is the natural principle that avoids exaggeration and distortion of reality. However, after China opened up, the traditional discussion became just empty talk and was taken for granted. Instead, urban women in China put up photos and posters of top fashion models at home and wished they could be like them. The following are some physical standards of beauty promoted and well-studied in Shanghai women's magazines that followed a Western model:[42]

Physical appearance

- Height: ideally 1.74 to 1.8 meters, a little shorter than Western models.
- Proportion: the lower part of the body from the belly button should be longer than the upper part. The lower thigh should be a little longer than the upper thigh with the shape of the leg slim and slender. The difference between the size of the breast and the waist should be 22 to 24 cm while that between the breast and the hip should be equal or 2 to 4 cm. The shoulder should be broad enough to form a "V" shape at the back and the ideal shape of the head is oval, which joins the neck to form a "?" shape. For facial features, the distance between the two eyes should be one eye in length; the length of the ear and the nose should be close; upper and lower lips should be equal in thickness and red in color.
- Others: Hair should be smooth, healthy, and dark. Limbs should be slender. Eyebrow should be longer than the eye and tidily trimmed. Skin bright and soft.

Temperament

- This is the only aspect that considers inner beauty. It is said that the temperament of a woman is the sum of her psychology and behavioral traits. One's cultivation would have good influences on one's gesture, posture, and verbal expression. The difference from the past discussion is that it has nothing to do with Confucian morality but with layman psychology.

Performing ability

- It is said that bodily movement should be rhythmic and form a special style of one's own. It should be noted that the traditional "feminine space" has been replaced completely by a stylish Western look; nothing traditional remains except the physical composition, which is still a Chinese make up.

Both this chapter and Chapter 12 adopt Susan Kaiser's reading of fashion, which is said to symbolically provide individuals with a mechanism for detaching from the past, to allow people to cope with the present in an orderly way by helping to define what is appropriate, and to prepare for the immediate future by providing a sense of anticipation or a clue to emerging issues and tastes.[43] Fashion also provides consolation to individuals, as it promotes self-esteem and the language of identity. It explodes out of enthusiasm, as the fashion codes of identity always represent leisure, fun, youth, health, open-mindedness, playfulness, energy, independence, courage, and subjectivity, no matter how controversial. A fashionable woman reflects the image that she is fully aware of her femininity, that she is free and sovereign, and that she makes her own decisions. All these explain why women fashion models have become new feminine icons in contemporary China.

The construction is also made possible by external business investments and related promotions. Within consumer culture, advertisements, popular press, television, and films all provide a proliferation of stylized images of the body. It is easy to detect the contradictions and confusion involved: the image built by the cosmetics, garment, and diet industries—the so-called beauty myth essential for economic markets—mixes with and contradicts the real working abilities, growing intelligence, and fluid individualistic characteristics of contemporary Chinese women. Whereas the ability and appearance of a beautiful woman might have been in great harmony in the past, as illustrated by the courtesan tradition, the two dimensions are in great tension today for commercial interests.[44] The developing self-confidence of Chinese women today does not make them aware of the fact that one can become a slave of fashion commodities, which simply repeat bodily constraints in a new form.

The brief historical survey given above of some developments of notions of female beauty in China seems to confirm the recent feminist statement that sexual bodily difference, gender behavioral, and affective differences are manifestations of a transformative relationality constituted by various modes of power relations. The so-called "feminine ideal" or female beauty is not immediately and biologically given, but, as Christine Battersby has said, a historically and socially emergent norm that "does not describe, but prescribe categorical 'fit' based on the perception of bodies."[45]

10

BEAUTY AND THE STATE: LITERATI FANTASY, IRON GIRLS, AND THE OLYMPICS HOOPLA

The global economy has an impact on female beauty today, regardless of the multicultural and historical factors in its formation and construction processes, resulting in homogenizing tendencies in women's fashion and appearance. But when the issue of contemporary female beauty is brought up in China, its contestation within the turbulent modern history of China deserves serious consideration, together with the policies, promotion, and regulations imposed by its state apparatus.

As discussed in the last section of Chapter 9, certain factors have been constant in discourses of female beauty. Ideal bodies, in all their specifics, are represented by physical standards that very few women can attain. They are accompanied by demeaning characterizations of women who fail to achieve these standards and who are then destined to be discontent. It is now necessary for feminist theorists to examine the social and cultural roles of the body in terms of gender, power, the established patriarchy, and its oppression of women.[1]

The oppression of women has been complex and multifaceted in China. In recent history, beauty standards were tied up with the political necessities of the state, injecting another patriarchal element into the agenda. If sexist beliefs about and hostility toward women are associated with the endorsement of Western beauty ideals and practices, these dimensions in China have been, at least recently, more fluid, practical, and closely related to perceived national benefits. A review of them will contribute to a deeper understanding of China's reception of Western standards and their related development.[2]

Socially pervasive ideals of femininity are in dialectical relation with women's lived experiences. It is important to review the interaction between images of beauty and the actual living conditions of Chinese women in the country's recent discourses. This has implications for the self-enhancement and fulfillment, and the emotional and mental states of female subjects. These ideals are promulgated through the media and propaganda; it is interesting to see in these media strong political and national agendas in their portrayal of ideal women's bodies. Contemporary portraits of female beauty are constant in terms of their depiction of ideal bodily parts, irrespective of race and class, and those in present-day China—focused on young, female bodies—have integrated the imagination of them with the imaginary future of the state. The emphasis of social cognitive theories on the effects of prevalence and incentives initiated by the media and social propaganda echoes the case of the national promotion of ideal female bodies in China at the turn of the twentieth century. One can see the chronological influences and the dialectical development of these impacts on feminine ideals in the country today.

The discourses on female beauty in twentieth-century China have been divided into three phases by historians.[3] These are the "enlightening period," from 1919 to 1949; the "degradation period," from 1949 to 1978; and the "awakening period," from 1978 to 2000; all had built-in political burdens and social implications. One can see how these discourses of Chinese male intellectuals shaped and constructed the body and mind of the "new women" (*xin nüxing* 新女性), and how they themselves developed through related cultural, political, and economical discourses. This chapter follows Susan Brownell in advocating that feminist thinking about Chinese gender issues should move out of the realms of text and film and into the realm of mass demonstrations and everyday life.[4] Scholarly research on contemporary China has been very productive when gender practices are placed at the center of the formation of national identities in China. This is also the approach adopted in this book.[5]

National Discourses of Feminine Beauty in Recent China: The Movement of *Jianmei*

During the "enlightening period," immediately following the May Fourth Movement in 1919, women's liberation became a part of the new cultural movement. The introduction of Western sciences and of democracy promoted the concept and values of gender equality in order to build up the new image of women, which was anti-traditional in its thrust and emphasized freedom. This contributed to the new images of feminine beauty. In contrast with traditional fashion, new women wore less jewelry and their clothes were more tightly cut, emphasizing feminine body curves. Juxtaposed with this was a new taste for cross-dressing in male suits and schoolgirl uniforms, usually with matching white socks and shirts, black skirts and shoes, presenting a carefree and reforming style that matched well the revolutionary slogans of the May Fourth Movement. The traditional female dress was changed to shorter or "moderated" *qipao* 旗袍 , the one-piece long dress originating from the Manchu costume that had become so popular among Chinese women at the time. This new look, together with short hair and unbound feet, were the main signifiers of women's liberation at the time, in contrast to the elaborated, long, and sexy *qipao*, which was popular in celebrity circles in Shanghai (Figure 10.1, Appendix).

A study by Gao Haiwen on the *Jianmei* Movement demonstrates in detail how female bodies had long served as signifiers for competing nationalist and feminist knowledge on womanhood in modern China.[6] Gao refers to the period in China following the 1931 Mukden Incident, which launched a series of aggressive Japanese military maneuvers in the north and east coasts and lasted until Japan was defeated in 1945. During that time, Chinese nationalists encouraged Chinese men and women to become physically strong in order to build up the overall strength of the nation. The government enforced the development of strong physiques and participation in *tiyu* 體育(sport, physical education, physical culture) as part of women's civic obligation. When the current national leader Chiang Kai-shek 蔣介石 and his wife, Song Meiling 宋美齡, launched the New Life Movement during the 1930s to instill ideas of self-discipline and moral regulation, the female body was taken as a site for the embodiment of the unchanging essence and moral purity of the Chinese nation.[7]

Women trained in gymnastics and dance; they promoted hygiene through open-air exercise, diet, clothing reform, and natural therapies. Gao points out that women's advocates in the movement built a cult of "health" and "beauty" called *jianmei* 健美, which was backed by a populist feminist agenda affecting the popular culture. This promotion of women's bodies in plain, makeup-free style with bare legs and feet (in contrast to female nudity, which was viewed as "harmful to public morals") echoed the May Fourth Movement's liberation fervors in China through the 1920s. The movement gained a female space that enabled complex interactions with the nationalist agenda, as *jianmei* and *tiyu* became prevalent in fashion and the mass media, especially in highly successful pictorial magazines that circulated in major cities across China. Gao mentions in particular the literary and visual influences of the magazine *Linglong* 玲瓏, which repeatedly called on women to make sacrifices for the nation, to educate themselves in politics, to develop courage, power, and their bodies in order to prioritize nationalist concerns; women's liberation was sought through national liberation.[8]

Gao's interesting visual analysis of *jianmei* reveals that the movement presented examples of Western women's bodies in the early 1930s. Chinese magazines featured photographs of white women in miniskirts, bathing suits, or gym shorts; they were ice-skating, jumping over vaulting horses, standing on their heads, and dancing, in order to show that "Western women have gained *jianmei* physiques through athletic exercise."[9] Photos show that camera angles frequently accentuated bare, strong legs; magazines used paintings and photographs of nude Western women with "healthy curves" and robust physiques. To balance and shift attention from the traditional, conservative angles, these physiques were elevated to a spiritual level in the pure, reverential contemplation of nature. Images of glamorous Hollywood stars reinforced *jianmei* as fashionable and Western.[10]

In this way, national ideals of health and beauty during the Sino-Japanese War were set; women's strong physiques were promoted as the "science of the normal" with manipulated, managed, and disciplined workout routines in conformity with specific measurements. The national discourse also incorporated Western standards in terms of health and beauty. It was suggested that the approximate standards for women of the Chinese nation be five feet tall, weighing 130 pounds, with "wide chest," "large and erect breasts," "high nipples," "ample behind," "slender waist," "even-proportioned figure," and "strong legs." Most attention was drawn to women's breasts and legs, which had never before been considered an important aspect of Chinese feminine beauty. Dancing as a significant *tiyu* activity linked *jianmei* with fashion; illustrations in magazines appeared of Chinese dancers wearing short dresses, sleeveless shirts and gym shorts showing *jianmei* legs and arms.[11]

This Chinese national phenomenon of young female bodies in the 1930s paralleled the national body movement in Germany during the same era. Both phenomena promoted bodies as the nation's pride and high hopes through unembellished faces, fit physiques, healthy skin color, and lively gestures. The display of the female body became part of a new public discourse related to modernity in everyday life, which ushered in an ideological war. A 1929 *tiyu* law addressed the need to fight against traditional, conservative attitudes toward female bodies that would hamper a successful *tiyu* program for women. This also included modern girls' preference for extravagant clothes and permed hair.[12] In June 1936, Chiang Kai-shek instructed officers on the streets to enforce the law by accompanying violators to their homes to change their clothes, and by jailing and fining those who resisted.[13]

I agree with Gao that Chinese modernity was built in a discursive way via the *jianmei* movement, on Western ideas and motifs. Through an emphasis on clean, strong female physiques and simple, practical clothing, the interpretation can be read as indigenous, culturally authentic, and moral—engendering new national strength and pride. The movement is a strong demonstration of female bodies as a national site of contestation.

Female Bodies and State Control: The Notion of *Funü* and "Iron Girls"

The New China founded in 1949 brought strong Communist fervor, in which women were called *funü* 婦女, interpreted as female proletariats, workers, and laborers. Their new image was of physicality and strength; in contrast to the cult of health and beauty of *jianmei*, their new feminine beauty substituted toughness and iron-like strength. The New Chinese women were also sexually neutral, in the sense that they were not sexy or romantic but devoted all their sexual and emotional energy to loving their nation. These inclinations were represented by short hair and loose revolutionary outfits of workers' green, gray, and blue. Political discourse dominated; individual *eros* was replaced by nation-building and reforms. It was titled the "degradation period" in terms of female beauty, because former female ideals of beauty had been degraded into genderless norms of a working-class ethic.

Historical records routinely connected women to the state, like the *femme fatale* version of "a woman's beauty can subvert a city and a country," which has become a common saying. For instance, there were only the words *fu* and *nü* to designate inferior women's labor and the perception of women as the second sex. The combined term *funü*" appears at the turn of the twentieth century and after the May Fourth Movement, when the discourse promoted individualism and gender equality. It should be noted that Communist China also publicly adopted the term *funü* for women—in an attitude of respect. The term glorifies women and is similar to the terms *proletariat* and *laborers*, in designating commonly suppressed classes, while at the same time approving women's self-actualization and liberation. It also conveys ideas of chastity, sexual loyalty, and purity: with moral and political implications in the context of the state, referring to a national entity or a federation. While new terms for women commonly used in later eras connoted sexy and innocent subjects, implying superficial values, like *nülang* 女郎 (sexy girls) and *nüseng* 女生 (girl students), customary terms for female beauty imply inner qualities and have undergone an evolutionary process alongside that of the state.

In New China in the 1950s, female beauty was combined with political purity. The inner qualities of a woman dominated the notion of femininity. The propaganda around "iron girls" is an outstanding example. Studies show that, at the end of the 1950s, under the Chinese Communist Party's radical policy of rapid industrialization, women became the first reserve labor force and peasants the second. Urban women entered heavy industry—construction and mining (Figure 10.2, Appendix).[14] The phrase "iron girls" originated with the Dazhai Iron Girl brigade in 1963, who could bear hardship with their iron-like shoulders. These female laborers also participated in the revolutionary agenda and embodied liberated ideals of gender equality.[15] Their work performance was more efficient than that by mixed gender groups. But since only female youths with a solid political consciousness and good health could be admitted, the aesthetic appreciation of the masculine woman—expressed in the Iron Girl—eventually received harsh criticism. Yet the movement had become a dynamic political force and the working-class Iron Girl had become an inspirational role model created by the state.

In the 1960s, class consciousness and class struggle dominated. The female figures in political propaganda dramas, like the characters in *White Haired Girl* and *Red Women Soldiers*, are straightforward in their political orientations and revolutionary attitudes.[16] Again, the traditional virtues of tenderness and modesty gave way to heroism and toughness, enhancing the revolutionary agenda (Figure 10.3, Appendix). Women's loyalties, in the patriarchal sense, were extended to the new country for which they were presumed to sacrifice and fight. The mixture shifted to a combination of toughness and tolerance after the Cultural Revolution of the 1970s, befitting survivors of that political disaster. These female characters populated "scar" literature and paintings, which depicted the sufferings and tragic stories of the victims of the Cultural Revolution. The term "scar" refers to the unforgettable wounds left on the mind and body of these victims, who were accused, beaten, and cursed for their landlord and bourgeois backgrounds and identities. It was not until the 1980s that female sexual bodies were depicted with a new liberating fervor; bodily sexual beauty—together with lively personality—became the qualities of the main female characters in novels and films. Young female bodies finally replaced sophisticated and loyal women fighters and intellectuals; in response to the growing beauty industry brought by foreign investment, female bodies were elaborated and physical appearances prioritized.

The Female Body in China and Contemporary Discourses

The "awakening period" began in the late 1970s, following the fall of the Gang of Four in 1976. Female characters in "scar literature" were liberated figures who emerged as individual spirits, undergoing sexual awakening and in search of real meaning in life, love, and gendered being. Yet the economic reform promoted by Deng Xiaoping in the 1990s impacted the market economy in ways that re-enhanced and re-legitimated the male gaze on and desire for women's bodies. The trend was toward the globalization of slim bodies and homogeneous standards of female beauty; developing countries competed with the West by duplicating the process of modernization and becoming large consumers of technological devices, fashion, and cosmetics. Female bodies became contested sites and symbols of modernization, economic growth, and national pride. Standardized female faces and bodies were plastered all over beauty parlors and magazine covers throughout the country. The sexual awakening of women was clearly tied to the dynamics of the state and the world beyond.

"Cosmopolitanism with Chinese characteristics" was a phrase promoted by party followers of Deng's economic reform of 1979, signifying that China was open to international investments and trade and involved itself vigorously in the global economy. Today, China has extended its influence beyond its geographical borders to the international arena. The Olympics held in Beijing in 2008 was a major opportunity for the country to gain glory on a cosmopolitan scale. In Lisa Rofel's reading, *cosmopolitanism* serves as one of the key nodes through which contemporary Chinese sexual, material, and affective desires bind citizen-subjects to state and transnational neoliberal policies. The cosmopolitan discourses on feminine beauty in China mesh with Rofel's suggested tension between two desires: on the one hand, that of a self-conscious transcendence of locality, accomplished through the formation of a consumer identity; and on the other, that of a domestication of cosmopolitan cultures by way of renegotiating China's place in the world.[17]

Through structured losses of memory that reinvent the past—that is, in the case of China, the "scars" of the Cultural Revolution, the World Wars, and the civil war—young women are pulled into this negotiation. Women's fashion definitely has the power both to forget and remind; with the young woman as the ultimate consumer, it is all about how to embody a new self.[18] Rofel casts women as desiring subjects in this context, including desire for sex and consumption of various sorts. The elaborative efforts in building up a unique form of sexiness, and other bodily practices that try to capture the desire to be a cosmopolitan state, is also a national discourse about normality and about the kinds of citizens representing China to the world that naturally involves feminine representations.[19] This ideal is in tension with the self-conscious transcendence of locality, which is posited as a universal transcendence through the formation of a consumer identity.[20]

The contemporary dichotomous discourse of the private and the public also operates in China, whereby political domination and traditional ethics are giving way to growing individual choice. "People's bodies" are situated in tensions and contestations among age, gender, ethnicities, regions, and cultures, all striving for identities and uniqueness. There are new Chinese faces and bodies in the media representing and legitimating classes, sexualities, and ethnicities of a wide variety. These processes of representation are inevitably steeped in political and economic factors, which represent bodies in ways that enhance related visual desires. The excitement of desire created through bodily performance and visual pleasures is in negotiation with traditional epistemologies and ethics of the body. This process works more vigorously in places with a repressive past like China, which is catching up through its search for new identities and images.

In one understanding of consumer society, the value of objects is more than their function; additionally, the fashion represented in them is about more than beauty. These two main components, function and fashion, have social meanings as signs and symbols; they may act as social or even national identities, providing comforts and imaginary gratifications. This reading offers a good description of pictures in China in which bodies have already become "the finest consumer object(s)," functioning as both capital and fetish. Fashionable female bodies are marketed as more than objects of desire; they are also functional entities in various senses. Jean Baudrillard, for example, points out that, in a culture of sensibility, woman's sensible, expressive body is disciplinary rather than pleasurable.[21] Media representations and advertisements of ideal female bodies demonstrate secular, mundane pleasures—beauty and happiness on the surface—but at the same time, they reconstruct the social and cultural, psychological and sensational paradigms of the state at the cost of female physical and mental constraints. It is thus both surprising and predictable to see the rapid changes of female body aesthetics that occurred after China's economic reforms kicked off in the late 1970s.

Social researchers on female self-imaging, mainly concerned with the perception of obesity and its relation to social comparison and social support, demonstrate similar findings among countries whose national economies have become integrated into the international economy through trade, foreign direct investment, capital flows, and migration. In 2001, half the advertising for health products in China were for weight-reduction products, which have also kicked off the slim body culture leading to disciplinary bodies that Baudrillard mentions. Research shows that slimming commercials in Beijing, Shanghai, and Guangzhou target young and middle-aged women with the promising of sexy, slim figures, fostering a morbidly slim culture.[22] Though obesity is shared equally by males and females, and elder women are more obese than younger women, weight-reducing products nevertheless target younger females. The names of these products are Chinese adjectives designating slimness; they are advertised through female celebrities who are symbols of beauty and success. Moreover, slimness is regarded as enhancing rather than reducing sexiness; it is regarded as the equivalent of health, normality, and emotional balance. While slim female bodies are seen to attract love, public praise, and admiration, it is suggested that the ideal body is attainable through product consumption rather than disciplinary measures taken upon oneself, as Baudrillard states.[23]

Women's magazines share at least half of the magazine market in China. International fashion magazines like *Vogue*, *Elle*, and *Marie Claire*—in their Chinese versions—are no doubt shaping the female beauty standards of the country. They are directing Chinese women to dress and carry themselves in internationally fashionable ways. At the same time, they enhance readers' sexual, emotional, and materialistic desires. Even mainland scholars realize that women's bodies have become a specialized area, professionally and economically, no longer being autonomous subjects. Both conservative and contemporary women appear simultaneously in various media, including the internet; these representations fulfill various imaginary desires and purposes.

Desirable female bodies and characters have also become popular in the best received literary works and films from the 1990s. Chinese critiques point out their double function: to satisfy marketable, imaginary pleasures and to shoulder moral judgments and comments. In the process of evolution from revolutionary woman in the 1950s to individual woman in the 1970s to sexy or "bad" woman in the 1990s, the notion of female purity has become ambiguous. When the notion is placed in a political context, it has swung from an extreme leftist domain to the global capital economy, in which female body ideals appear on the public stage. The body has always been the site of identity tactics; socialist female bodies have been replaced by desirable, fashionable bodies, without regard for class, religious, political, or social background, and with little ideological judgment. Female bodies and feminine ideals remain important signifiers of the modernized country; their related discourses are also the languages of national strengths and resources.

Changes in the Representation of Female Bodies in Consumerist China

In meeting consumer desires, female bodies in the global economy have become superficial and flattened. Their visual exposure in media and advertising takes spectacular forms, depriving them of aesthetic depth and genuineness, so richly depicted in classical Chinese literature and the arts. The women's portraits created by traditional Chinese literati were resources of imagination and interpretation, operating within the spiritual domains of ethics and aesthetics. They were more than representations; they held meaning and expressed aesthetic qualities waiting to be appreciated and contemplated. The famous ancient literary work, *The Book of Songs*, introduced in Chapter 4, features a large range of adjectives relating to beauty and praise of femininity. As mentioned, they were projected onto female historical characters and figures of the songs, in which morality played a secondary role to daring emotional and erotic expression. The songs recorded vitality, intuitiveness, spontaneity, joy, passion, and variety in females.

There was also a time when women were described as "holding half of the sky," with regard to their labor input under the economic campaigns of the Mao regime; after that came the discourse of female beauty that revolved around the political promotion of virtuous wives and good mothers. Rofel suggests that the post-Mao economic reform legitimated its specific imaginary of the modern body politic as it revolved around the natures of women, while the naturalization of womanhood promoted in post-Mao politics has shown that women in China lead an uneasy and provisional existence as subjects of the nation.[24] When the state's economic reforms failed, it asked women to perform domestic roles as wives, daughters-in-law, and mothers, so as to leave work positions to men. This suggests that the national construction of female ideals was for the social and political benefits of the state. But the objectification of female beauty in the current commodification process has departed from past practice; it may have led to the dissolution of personality traits that past Chinese arts used to glorify. There are no subjects here; one has no knowledge of the particular females being represented when depictions of them are all shown in the monotonous language of globalized cosmetic products and fashion.

It is well known that the PRC government has incorporated a capitalist economy into what the government usually calls "socialism with Chinese characteristics." Rofel's reading is that, although the content of "socialism with Chinese characteristics" is quite distinct from Maoist socialism, its manner of attempting to fasten together economic policies, moral evaluations of social life, and the emergence of new kinds of persons, in fact, closely resembles the earlier socialist articulations of power, knowledge, and subjectivity.[25] Yet my study of the *Book of Songs* shows that the current representations of the female body have strayed from subjectivity and authenticity of earlier forms. At the very least, genuine vividness and individualistic identities have all been lost or rendered pretentious in the discourse on female beauty. They have been sacrificed in the quest for a combination of national (economic) pride and cosmopolitanism.

The 2008 Beijing Olympics produced new forms of female beauty. Some of them are young female bodies from university campuses. These female students dreamed of being Olympic volunteers and frequented English training centers, gyms, and whole-body beauty parlors (Figure 10.4, Appendix). The touching story of a young female boxer tells all: in order to meet the bodily and posture requirements of the volunteer training center, she is twisting her muscular body to tender texture, aiming to become a soft-looking, ideal reception model. Her lady-in-the-making process included walking in steady, light steps, holding her body trunk in an upright position, and practicing strict smiling exercises that required training in front of a mirror three hours per day. She was required to hold her head and eyes at a particular horizontal level and to control the number of teeth exposed. Tough stories of this kind, reported in the media, are the embodiment of a new self, which is not only historically and culturally specific, but also tailor-made as items of national pride.

While "Olympic girl" image-making is another process of normalization in the history of China, one may query the ideas and reasons it has become the standard of female beauty representing China today. It is obvious that certain traditional representations have been appropriated and incorporated (such as the Qing-dynasty *qipao* and postures from courtesan culture), yet they have also been seriously reduced to and designed for the international and global imaginations of "Chinese beauty (Figures 10.5 and 10.6, Appendix)." The Olympic girl may also be read as an updated "domestication of cosmopolitanism," with the implications just stated.[26] Through tailor-made female bodily construction, this new development is negotiating for a place in the world, and is loaded with desire for a global recognition of wealth, resources, and the pride of the state.

Susan Brownell is correct in saying that, when thinking about nationalist rhetoric or regional identities or consumerism, much can be learned from analyzing and contextualizing the sexual politics involved.[27] Yet when, following her suggestions, authors favored social, cultural, economic, or strategic explanations in trying to account for the continuing subordination of women under Communism, the opposite approach may tell even more.[28] This chapter supports Brownell and Wasserstrom's response to Harriet Evans's article, "Past, Perfect or Imperfect: Changing Images of the Ideal Wife," in that there is a dramatic revival in the prominence of sexuality as a defining characteristic of Chinese gender categories, which is obviously related to the increasing presence of global culture and capitalism in the PRC.[29] Evans describes the reemergence of sexuality, particularly female sexuality, as a contested issue in 1990s China and attributes this to the state's interest in regulating sexual practice in times of market-oriented reform.[30] Yet I read from the bodies of new Chinese female beauties signs of imperialism in excess that have been carried forward from the Qing, and which have survived in Communist China in its power and control. There is also the consumption of global cosmetics and fashion commodities by Chinese women, with the new imagination of a wealthy China that the state cannot wait to show off, in declaring its competitiveness in the new world setting. The portrayal of female sexuality is particularly obvious and visible in global events such as the Olympics in Beijing in 2008. As observed in other chapters of this book, gender practices have been placed at the center of the formation of national identities.

11

PSYCHOANALYSIS AND WOMEN'S PHYSIOLOGY AND PSYCHOPATHOLOGY IN FEUDAL CHINA: A CASE STUDY BY PAN GUANGDAN

In Chapter 1 of this book, I quoted Moira Gatens's disagreement with many Western philosophers who regard the soul or mind as sexually neutral, and attribute the apparent differences among minds to the influence of the passions of the body.[1] These philosophers assume that the most superior minds suffer least from the intrusions of the body.[2] Gatens further points out that this dualist notion of the body involves an implicit alignment between women and irrationality. This chapter is a follow-up discussion to Gatens's line of argument, disagreeing with the mind-body dichotomy. In both Confucian and Daoist sexual traditions, a female's whole being, including her mind, is shaped by those traditions' constraints on female physicality, as articulated in previous chapters. Ways to regulate and represent a woman's body are incorporated into various Confucian teachings on women from the Han dynasty on; these teachings discuss the resulting impacts on women's mind and sense of morality via bodily control. This chapter aims to review the close link between, and the interconnected whole of, the mind and the body from the gender dimension and from a different and deeper perspective, the psychoanalytical perspective, through a case study.

This chapter introduces, analyzes, and reviews China's first application of psychoanalysis, in a case study of a female member of the literati in fifteenth-century China. The case reveals how psychic and physical sickness, as well as cultural and gender factors, intertwine to affect a woman's life in the Confucian tradition. The study, drafted in 1922, was conducted by Pan Guangdan on the late Qing writer Feng Xiaoqing. This chapter describes Pan's diagnosis of the woman's mental illness and his appropriation of the concepts of psychoanalysis, which were new to China at the time, though a recent volume on psychiatry in Chinese history, edited by Howard Chiang, has revealed earlier evidence of the subject in Chinese history.[3] This chapter discusses Sigmund Freud's psychoanalytical model and theory of narcissism, as understood by Pan, and reviews the application of that understanding to the historical context of 1920s China, an era in which Western modernization was seen as a model for national progress. The discussion then turns to an examination of Pan's observations on the living situation of women in feudal China and the implications for sex education in his own era. It concludes with a reassessment of Pan's views in light of recent feminist critiques, particularly criticism of Freud's narcissistic theory and psychoanalysis as a whole, and views on related gender issues.

Feng Xiaoqing: A Case of "Shadow Love"

Pan Guangdan completed his research on Feng Xiaoqing's case in 1922, while he was affiliated with the Tsinghua School of Higher Education in Beijing. He submitted the draft to *Women Magazine* in Shanghai two years later. It was subsequently published, and became the only psychoanalytic article on the so-called shadow love mental illness to have been published in China.[4] In 1927, the Crescent Bookshop in Shanghai invited Pan to revise the article. In his subsequent revision, Pan elaborated upon his reading of the case, supplemented it with Xiaoqing's own writings and related them to his reading of psychoanalytic theories that had been introduced to China only very recently. This revised version was finally published in book form and entitled *Analysis of Xiaoqing*. It was republished in 1929 and retitled *Feng Xiaoqing: A Case Study of "Shadow Love."*[5]

Pan's book is regarded as the first psychoanalytic study of mental illness in China (Figure 11.1, Appendix).[6] The author was concerned with the physical and mental health of the Chinese, and had had the opportunity to study the works of the English psychologist Havelock Ellis as well as those of Sigmund Freud. He was obviously deeply impressed by psychoanalysis, which was then being hotly debated in Europe. As Chinese sociologist Fei Xiaotong stated, Pan was interested in exploring whether sexual repression had affected the psychological development of the Chinese people in his day and whether abnormal psychology and behavior in China had the same root causes as those suggested by psychoanalysis in Europe.[7] Pan had a strong interest in Xiaoqing's mental state and her personal life; his empathetic approach to her demonstrates a different attitude from that of his contemporaries in China, who exhibited many prejudices toward women. He personally disagreed with these prejudices and with the prevailing view of women as objects of oppression or pleasure, which he believed led to abnormal psychology in Chinese women. Pan's view was that, in China, women's physical and mental diseases were both related to their abnormal physiological and psychological sexual development. His study of Xiaoqing's case demonstrated the relation between such abnormal development and the social context of traditional China, which was characterized by gender oppression and prejudice.

Feng Xiaoqing's Personality and Story

Xiaoqing's character was recorded in anecdotal biographies and legendary opera stories from the Jiangsu and Zhejiang areas of China during the Ming and Qing dynasties. Pan studied numerous Qing-era sources and recorded materials, including Feng Menglong's 馮夢龍 famous *Qingshileilüe* 情史類略 (Genres of the history of love), which constitutes a biography of Feng written by Zhou Junjian, along with commentaries written by Zhi Ruzeng. He also read the revised version of Zhi's commentaries, written by Zhang Shanlai and published as *Yuchuxinzhi*, Xiaoqing's story in Zhang Dai's *Dreams of the West Lake*, and literary commentaries on her work by Li Wen, Shi Runzhang, and Lu Lijing. Pan also examined Xiaoqing's story in Ye Junxu's study of theater and opera in the Ming dynasty and in Chen Shuji's *Memories of the West Lake*; he cross-referenced these materials with Xiaoqing's own writings to reconstruct her biography.[8]

This young woman stands out as an intelligent and creative writer who produced outstanding poetry, seven-syllable quatrains, and love songs in the late 1600s. Pan summarized her life:[9]

Feng Xiaoqing was born during the Ming dynasty, in the twenty-third year of the Wanli 萬曆 reign (1595) in Yangzhou. She died of tuberculosis in the forty-first year of the Wanli reign at the age of eighteen. She studied with her mother, who was a private tutor. She was keen on and talented in music and poetry, and demonstrated outstanding musical performance and writing skills as a little girl. She joined the Fung family in Hangzhou as a concubine at the age of thirteen. Her husband's first wife was very jealous of Xiaoqing and moved her to a mountain temple after a quarrel. She was then isolated from her husband and lived in solitude. Xiaoqing established a close friendship with Lady Yang during her stay at the temple. They read, painted, and wrote together. Yet, Xiaoqing soon began behaving abnormally, spending a lot of time looking at her own reflection in the lake. She talked to the reflection in a sad mood, and ceased only when her maid turned up.

Lady Yang was very sympathetic to Xiaoqing and suggested that she help her out of the temple and the crisis. Xiaoqing refused and told Lady Yang of a strange dream she had had. She saw herself breaking up flowers by the river; the flower petals then fell into the water and floated away. She believed that these flowers represented herself, and that her life would soon be gone. She said her marriage was arranged and not intended for her gratification, but that if she went away she would worry about other people's comments. Lady Yang finally left with her husband, leaving Xiaoqing in complete solitude. She became weak and sick, but refused to take the medicine that Feng's first wife delivered and stopped eating. The only thing she cared about was the way she dressed and her own appearance, and she continued to write to Lady Yang. One day, Xiaoqing asked her husband to arrange a portrait of her. She did not like the first one, as it failed to depict her spirit. The second portrait also failed to grasp her rich gestures, so she stood up and moved around to give the depiction more life. The third portrait finally pleased her; she put it by her bedside, wrote her name on it, and burned incense in front of it during rituals. She talked to herself while doing this, murmuring: "Xiaoqing, Xiaoqing, is the relation you have with the person in the portrait your destiny?" She died in blood and tears beside the portrait.

Pan Guangdan's Analysis of Xiaoqing's Mental Illness

In the introduction to his 1933 Chinese translation of Havelock Ellis's *Psychology of Sex*, Pan stated explicitly that he had adopted Ellis's theories and combined them with Freud's psychoanalysis, theories of psychosexual development, and Chinese references in his study of Feng Xiaoqing. He said he was twenty years old in 1920 when he first read and became fascinated by Ellis's work. One year later, he read Sigmund Freud's *A General Introduction to Psychoanalysis* (1915–17); the theories therein reminded him of Feng's story, which seemed to him to be an outstanding illustration of Freud's theory of "narcissism." This discovery led to Pan's first case study of sexual psychology, which resulted in *The Investigation of Feng Xiaoqing.*[10]

Pan wrote: "This attempt has nothing to do with Ellis, for Ellis's article on 'shadow love' was published only at a later stage. One could see it in series no. 7 of Ellis's Studies in the Psychology of Sex. As a matter of fact, I have also checked Ellis's related theories with the case of Xiaoqing and found no discrepancies between them."[11] Ellis's *Studies in the Psychology of Sex* (series no. 7) was not published until 1928, whereas Pan's study on Feng was drafted in 1922. He did subsequently revisit the abnormal psychosexual aspect of her case, supplemented with new references, but the new version, *Analysis of Xiaoqing*, was published a year before Ellis's work.[12] The main frame of reference for his case study was thus Freud's related theories in *A General Introduction to Psychoanalysis*. When Pan translated Ellis's *Psychology of Sex* in the 1940s, he inserted his findings from his study of Xiaoqing in footnotes. Bearing this timeline in mind, this chapter focuses on Pan's appropriation of Freud's theories.

Pan was particularly taken with the concepts of "auto-love" and "shadow love."[13] Freud said a child's "latent stage" begins at the age of six or eight and lasts until adolescence. For boys, sexual instinct at this stage projects the mother as the object of love, which is forbidden by society. This latent stage varies in length and degree, according to the degree of sexual repression and suppression of norms in the child's social environment. Pan stated that, "when it comes to the latent stage, the suppressed sexual instinct begins to be active. It moves along gradually and those that are held up are going to emerge and grow. They need an object for projection."[14] However, given the very repressive Confucian social norms, the object of projection tended to be the subject's own self, resulting in "auto-love." This auto-love would later extend to an outside object, usually someone similar to oneself or even someone of the same sex, thus constituting the origin of one's sexuality.

Sexual development may also proceed in abnormal ways, which Pan explained using Freud's notions of "fixation" or "regression." He said the cause of fixation was the subject's mental weakness. When the subject was also spoiled by his or her parents and had an immature or traumatic sexual experience, his or her sexual instincts might stop developing, remaining fixated at the stage of a child or even an infant. When sexual development was completed but was then confronted by a traumatic sexual experience, the individual might regress to an earlier stage of sexual development and instead develop maternal love, auto-love or "auto-love turned homosexuality."

Pan posited that the consequences of fixation and regression were the same. He used the example of a sexually mature woman faced with a traumatic sexual experience: "The woman might be sexually mature, but shocked by the sex act on her first night of marriage if she is not well informed and prepared. This shock will cool down her physical heat and emotions, and regression will follow."[15] It should be noted that this theory is the foundation of Pan's analysis of Xiaoqing's case.

Fixation or regression can lead individuals back to the stage of auto-love. Pan used the term "shadow love" to describe Xiaoqing's case, regarding the term as similar in meaning, as the subject of the shadow is the same as the self in auto-love. Pan explained the meaning of shadow love using the Greek myth of Narcissus, elements of which he saw reflected in Xiaoqing's story: "Narcissus went to the water every day and looked at his own reflection. He did not want to leave his reflection, but continued to gaze at it until he became exhausted and died. He was pitied and turned into a water lily after his death so that he would be able to accompany his reflection by the water."[16] Pan further studied the meaning of the Greek word *narcissus*, tracing its root meaning to paralysis, which is comparable to the mental state of shadow love—shadow love is a representative form of auto-love.

Pan's further explication of the story of Narcissus positioned him as a beautiful young man who fell in love with himself and was therefore unable to receive Echo's invitation, which was an invitation to heterosexual love. In other words, Pan understood auto-love as homosexual love. Is the case of Narcissus the same as that of Xiaoqing? Pan does not seem to have thought so, as he read the case of Narcissus as a case of fixation and that of Xiaoqing as a case of regression. Xiaoqing was a mature woman who was sexually shocked in the early days of her marriage, and thus entered into a state of psychological regression.

A Reading of Xiaoqing's Shadow Love

When Pan first began his reading on Xiaoqing, he discovered that there were many cases of women with the same narcissistic inclinations and behavior as Xiaoqing. In what sense then can she be considered abnormal? To delve deeper into the matter, Pan cross-referenced Xiaoqing's story as told in her various biographies with her own writings. He examined the style of her writing, the metaphors she used, the parables she adopted, their related temporality and space, and finally the details of their content, and came to the following conclusions.[17]

Pan referred to Zhi Ruzeng's biography for a record of Xiaoqing's behavior. Zhi reported that Xiaoqing "talked to her own shadow often, at dawn and at sunset, when the flowers were blooming, the air was dry and the water was clear. She came to the waterside promptly, and questioned herself and then answered. She ceased when the maid turned up but became sad and mellow." He further reported that Xiaoqing became sad whenever she could not speak to her shadow, which was obviously a sign of obsession. Pan found further proof of this obsession in Xiaoqing's poems, one of which reads: "I pity my own shadow, which is slim, as reflected on the spring water. She should pity me as much as I pity her!"

Xiaoqing's biographers report that, after she became ill and could no longer go to the water to see her reflection, she would gaze at herself in the mirror at home. In "A Farewell Letter to Lady Yang," she wrote: "I dressed up and found no shadow in the mirror. When I cried in the morning, the one in the mirror was also crying; when I cried in the evening, the one in the mirror was crying too." Pan concluded that Xiaoqing was seriously mentally ill at this point, because she cried for the person in the mirror without knowing that that person was herself. She had lost her capacity for cognitive judgment and self-awareness.

Harkening back to Narcissus, Xiaoqing used the metaphor of a water lily in one of her poems: "The water in the pond is moving slowly . . . I see my reflection in the mirror as the flower's reflection in the water—who has more autumn thoughts?" Narcissus turned into a water lily after his tragic death. Xiaoqing used the phrase "autumn thoughts" to refer to her misery, which she saw reflected in the face in her mirror. It is also noteworthy that Xiaoqing dressed and made herself up even when she was very sick, which is not normal behavior. Zhi, her biographer, reported: "When she was becoming more seriously ill, she stopped drinking and eating, taking only a little pear juice every day. But she still made and dressed herself up and never let herself down in laziness."[18] Pan's explanation was that she had come to love the person in the mirror and wanted her to look beautiful too. At the same time, she also wanted that person to think that she was beautiful. Pan here suggests the tricky merging and non-differentiation of the two beauties: "Didn't she want her love to be beautiful? And didn't she also want herself to be beautiful so as to please her love in the mirror and receive her praise in return? Under the sickness of shadow love, the two combined as one!"

Xiaoqing asked for her portrait to be revised three times before she died. As Zhi reported:

> Xiaoqing said to her maid one day: "Send a message to my husband and ask him to find me a painter." The painter came, and she requested a portrait of herself. When it was done, she looked at herself in the mirror and said, "this portrait grasps my appearance but not my spirit." When the painter presented her with another portrait, her comment was: "The spirit is there, but it fails to depict my activity." She asked the painter to sit down and watch her moving around the room in various activities, such as making tea with her maid, arranging books, folding her sleeves or preparing ink . . . She then asked the painter to do her portrait again. She checked the final work and was pleased to say that it was fine.

According to Pan's understanding of the notion of auto-love in psychoanalysis, the subject of the portrait was Xiaoqing's ideal lover. It is recorded that Xiaoqing asked Lady Yang to keep her portrait safe. In this way, her lover would become immortal. Pan regarded her obsession as a solid case of shadow love, which explains the demands she made on the painter. Zhi's depiction of Xiaoqing's death scene gives an idea of the degree of her mental illness. The end came after her portrait was finished, and she was satisfied with it. He reported: "She put the portrait at the front of her bed, prepared tea and pear juice for it, and asked: 'Xiaoqing, Xiaoqing, will we have relations together?' She then touched the portrait and cried, her tears and the blood coming from her mouth mixed, and she died in a paroxysm!"[19]

Was Xiaoqing Aware of Her Own Narcissistic Attitude?

In what sense is shadow love a form of abnormal psychology? What are the sexual implications of the case of Xiaoqing? Pan's conclusion is based on Xiaoqing's own writings and the letters she sent to Lady Yang.[20] When Lady Yang suggested that Xiaoqing should remarry, she responded: "I dreamed of myself breaking a flower with my hands. It was broken into pieces and fell into the water. If this is karma that should complete itself, I should wait before I make another wish. I am not gratified by my marriage, but I don't want to hear other people talking about it." Pan noted two elements of Xiaoqing's response: she could not be gratified by a heterosexual relationship, and she felt the weight of social pressure. She saw her sad marriage simply as her fate.

In her reply to Lady Yang's invitation to depart the temple, Xiaoqing stated that she was too weak to leave, implying that she might not be able to adapt to a new environment. Pan saw the sexual implications of her reply, however, taking it to mean that she knew she could not adjust to another heterosexual relationship. This reading suggests that Xiaoqing was aware of her burgeoning homosexual inclination. In one of Xiaoqing's letters to Lady Yang, she said that even if she became a nun and dressed like one, when seduction came and aroused her, she might not be able to cope, as there were difficulties within. Pan read the tricky psyche between the lines, and confirmed Xiaoqing's self-awareness of her changing sexual inclination. She was aware that she had sexual desire of an uncommon type, but did not identify it as a form of auto-love. Pan's further conclusion was that Xiaoqing's auto-love was a mental state between heterosexual love and celibacy. She wanted to love, but she did not want to love anyone other than her own self.

Pan made note of a revealing paragraph in Xiaoqing's poem "Fairies": "I withdrew at once when the black wind came and the fire wheel burned; I was then in the state of a cool mind. I did not belong to the group for romance, [so] why should I be a member of it? I reflected, I explained [and] discussed with myself. Where was my heart? Where was my soul? I dressed in a skirt with two robes!"

Pan read auto-love between the lines of Xiaoqing's conversation with herself, and took it to mean that she was aware of her own mental state. Such awareness would explain why Xiaoqing called out her own name when she worshipped her portrait and enquired whether the relationship might continue. However, her self-awareness did not protect Xiaoqing from mental illness for three reasons: she could not get away from social norms and her own social obligations; she had been isolated for too long and was in almost complete solitude; and she was obsessed and in a melancholic state, which finally affected her physical state.

What Led to Xiaoqing's Mental Imbalance?

Was Xiaoqing's mental illness inborn or a result of her living situation? Was it an outcome of fixation or regression in the psychoanalytic context? Pan attributed it to both hereditary and environmental factors, noting that psychoanalysis pays special attention to childhood history and development. Psychoanalytic fixation and regression, in particular, refer to the early stages of psychosexual development, which explains why Pan began his analysis of Xiaoqing when she was ten years old.[21]

According to Zhi's biography, Xiaoqing had met an old nun when she was ten. She was already articulate, and regularly demonstrated her talents by reciting literary works. At sixteen, she was able to intelligently discuss Buddhist texts with Lady Yang. However, Pan failed to further explore the relation between Xiaoqing's intelligence and her later mental imbalance, although it can be inferred from Freud that intelligence and artistic creativity are the results of the sublimation or conversion of the libido. The logic is that the stronger the instinct, the richer the resources for conversion and sublimation. We may say that, for Pan, Xiaoqing's intelligence was a sign of her shadow love syndrome.

Was Xiaoqing's narcissistic turn fixation, regression or both? Pan constructed his arguments on the basis of a letter to Lady Yang in which Xiaoqing mentioned early marital sexual relations: "He acted on me overnight without gentleness or consideration." The Qing-era biography of Xiaoqing written by Feng Menglong describes her husband Feng as short-tempered, rude, and clumsy in manner. Pan inferred that "Feng was a generous guy, but he was rude . . . Xiaoqing was young, weak and fragile, [and she experienced] her marital sexual life as trauma in both physical and psychological terms. One could read from her letter to Yang that she was suffering terribly."

Pan thus diagnosed regression in Xiaoqing's case; the cause was the traumatic sexual experiences she underwent in the early days of her marital life when she was not well prepared. This regression ended in auto-love, and later developed into narcissistic shadow love when she was isolated, sad, and lonely, but too worried about social pressure to walk out.[22]

However, Pan also suggested fixation when he reviewed Xiaoqing's adolescent days. Biographies note that Xiaoqing was always proud of her own outstanding qualities and loved to show them off, which is indicative of a strong auto-love inclination, as Pan elaborated. During puberty, her auto-love inclination exhibited a strong tendency toward psychological fixation, he said. Following the trauma of her first sexual encounter, however, regression occurred and remained where she was fixated psychologically. Pan supported his arguments by citing Xiaoqing's strange behavior after marriage. She is reported to have sat still for long periods of time and stood in the strong wind alone, watching. Both are signs of obsessive behavior.[23]

Pan attached his article "Theories of Sexual Development in Psychoanalysis" to his 1927 work *Analysis of Xiaoqing*, in which he explicated the differences between sexual fixation and regression. He emphasized that the consequences of the two are the same. When a woman is spoiled by her parents in early childhood and then encounters a boorish sexual partner in marriage, the end result may be fixation at the Oedipal stage, when she felt most gratified. If she is physically healthy, but experiences sexual trauma when she is not psychologically well prepared, regression is likely to occur, returning her to the psychological stage at which she was fixated.[24]

Pan went further by pointing out the ambiguity of Xiaoqing's case. He claimed that it was very rare in psychopathology to have a case of pure auto-love without some other forms of abnormal behavior.[25] This ambiguity led Pan to also suggest an Oedipus complex and homosexual inclination in Xiaoqing's case, which he termed "sub-streams" or side symptoms, although he ultimately diagnosed her with "shadow love."[26] In his psychosexual analysis of the case, he discussed Xiaoqing's homosexual inclination, transference problem, and paranoia. Pan first suspected a homosexual inclination in Xiaoqing's friendship with Lady Yang. They obviously had an intimate relationship and remained in close contact with each other. They called each other pet names and spent a lot of time together, just like lovers. Xiaoqing also revealed her homosexual tendency when she claimed in her writing that she adored the famous Song dynasty woman poet Zu Xiaoxiao, noting that she was not a heterosexual person and that there was no way she would ever miss a man.

Xiaoqing was also very close to her mother. Lady Yang, who was older than Xiaoqing, was like a mother to her; Xiaoqing addressed her as a mother in their correspondence. Pan's guess was that Lady Yang was Xiaoqing's objectified mother and lover; his psychoanalytical diagnosis was transference. According to Freud, transference occurs in heterosexual relationships, but if the libido is blocked and fixated, it is then transferred back to an earlier or even infantile psychological stage and ends in auto-love. Pan concluded that the complex was not limited to males, but extended to females who might take someone senior in age as the object of love.

Pan claimed that a person who has undergone regression tends to think highly of him- or herself, which fits into Freud's notion of "paranoia," which he elaborates upon in his description of the psychology of "delusions of grandeur" in the auto-love group. Pan again found proof of his supposition in Xiaoqing's poetry, which was filled with self-praise and her own name cited in parallel with historical figures. Xiaoqing was always skeptical; fearing that her husband's first wife would poison her, she rejected medication from her. Her physical symptoms thus worsened and developed along with her auto-love.

Freud's Concept of Auto-love and Its Application to Xiaoqing's Shadow Love

An open question is whether Pan's explication and application of Freud's theories are appropriate to the case of Feng Xiaoqing. Pan's basic reference was Freud's early work, *A General Introduction to*

Psychoanalysis, which he presented in Vienna between 1915 and 1917 in a series of lectures. He presented the concept of narcissistic love in Lecture 26, the theme of which was libido theory and narcissism. Freud highlighted the following related symptoms.[27]

> *Dementia praecox.* Freud considered *dementia praecox* a form of psychosis, as there is no libidinous occupation of objects in it, and the libido of the demented is diverted from its object, whereas in normal psychosexual development the ego engages in object choice. In this case, the libido is turned back upon the ego; this reflected turning back is the source of megalomania in *dementia praecox.* Freud saw megalomania as the immediate outcome of an exaggeration of the ego, which results from the drawing-in of a libidinous occupation with objects. Freud said he borrowed the term "libido narcissism" from one of the perversions described by Paul Naecke, although Pan claimed that it was Ellis (whose work Pan translated) who first adopted the term to discuss auto-love.[28]
>
> *Auto-love.* Freud said that auto-love happens to everyone during his or her early psychosexual development, followed by object love. He stated: "It is much more probable that this narcissism is the general and original condition, out of which the love for an object later develops . . ." He supposed that, whereas the central mass of the libido remains in the ego, and under normal conditions the ego-libido can be assumed to change into the object-libido, it can be taken up again by the ego without any difficulties.
>
> *Sexual fixation.* Freud assumed the libido to travel freely between auto-love and object love. However, when it failed to do so, mental illness occurred. Like *dementia praecox*, such illness was the result of the libido being forced away from the object and accumulated in the ego in the form of narcissistic libido. In this context, Freud mentioned fixation as a control factor resulting in this breach. This is the stage of primitive narcissism.
>
> *Secondary narcissism.* Megalomania occurs when libido travels back to the ego from the object. Freud said that secondary narcissism then occurs as a result of the recurrence of the original early infantile form.

In this stage, a beloved who should be the object choice is replaced by another based on familiar affinities, either someone of the same sex or a senior with whom the ego would like to identify as a role model.

Narcissistic object choice. Freud said that the choice of an object, which comes after the narcissistic stage, proceeds according to two types. The object choice of the first type is very similar in personality to the ego. Freud suggested that it was here that a disposition toward homosexuality might manifest itself. The second type is the dependent type, whose object choice is one who satisfies the earlier needs of the ego.

Narcissistic identification. This is the process by which the subject retrieves the libido from objects and replaces them with the ego. Failure of the objectification process may lead to self-blame for losing the object of love or sex. The idea is that it is the fault of the ego that has stopped caring about the object. Freud further suggested that the personal ego is treated in the same manner as the abandoned object who suffered all of the aggression. He used the term *ambivalence* to describe the state of love and hate that appears to the ego simultaneously.

Ego ideal. Freud said that an ego ideal is created during the ego development process of the narcissist, who uses it to evaluate the self and all of the ego's activities and that this idea is most likely to be senior. The logic is as follows. The ego wants to revisit the self-gratification it enjoyed in childhood, gratification that usually came from adults. The ego therefore identifies with the older people it encountered in childhood and regards them as ideal models. Freud said the purpose of the ego ideal is to re-establish the self-satisfaction that is bound up with the original infantile narcissism.

Pan's Reading and Appropriation of Freud's Theories

Pan believed that Freud's psychoanalysis suggested two stages of psychotherapy: the first is to diagnose the depression and the second to eliminate the resistance that caused it. The origin of the resistance is not the sub-conscious but the ego; now the ego needs to be healed and requires hints to get well. In the case of narcissism, the ego should at least have self-understanding or awareness of the key issues that caused the depression.[29] The notion of megalomania may shed light on Pan's definition of Xiaoqing's shadow love as a form of abnormal sexual psychology. Pan's understanding of auto-love and sexual regression was similar to Freud's, except that Freud emphasized fixation in his explanation of narcissism, whereas Pan claimed that fixation and regression exerted equal effects in Xiaoqing's case. Pan thought Xiaoqing's behavior demonstrated the megalomania suggested by Freud. Further, her homosexual tendency and ego ideal, as depicted by Pan, echo Freud's explanation of what happens at the stage of secondary narcissism.

Pan also noted that Xiaoqing was only half-conscious of her own shadow love symptoms and was in between auto-love and object choice. Another meaning of shadow love can be gleaned from Freud's work. Although he did not use the term in his *A General Introduction to Psychoanalysis*, he did say in Lecture 26 that "in dementia praecox the libido in its endeavor to return to the objects, i.e., to the images of the objects, really captures something, but only their shadows, the venial images belonging to them." This statement captures something of the true nature of Xiaoqing's symptoms, upon which Pan did not elaborate. Although he emphasized that shadow love is auto-love, he stated that the shadow reflects both the ego herself and the venial images of the object, as Freud described.

Freud suggested that hints be provided in psychotherapy to facilitate the patient's self-understanding. Pan was obviously aware of this suggestion and stated clearly that Xiaoqing had no desire to be healed. It seems that she had no motivation to get well, even though she had opportunities to extricate herself from her unfavorable situation and receive medication. Instead, she would go out in chilly weather to visit her own reflection in the water. She was obviously obsessed by this act and refused to listen to any hints about her mental illness. Pan's analysis also failed to delve deeper into Freud's idea of narcissistic identification, which refers to the ego's identification with the sexual object. That object may have caused pain or trauma to the subject, with the ego reverting its resentment to the self, ending up in melancholy and depression. A discussion of this concept could have shed additional light on Xiaoqing's self-destructive behavior and melancholy.

Finally, Pan did not elaborate upon Freud's notion of the ego ideal in Xiaoqing's case, although he did discuss megalomania. He suggested that Xiaoqing tended to idealize herself and thought very highly of herself, as evidenced in her poems, in which she likened herself to influential writers of the Han dynasty. She liked to dress up and admire herself in the mirror. In Freud's explication of the ego ideal, the ego tends to identify with those it depends on and to beautify the self to be more like them. This is a form of regression in Pan's understanding, although Freud did not use that term in his discussion of narcissism. Pan refers to Oedipus and a senior lover more often than the ego ideal, although he does use the term in his discussion of the marital lives of Chinese women living in the repressive conditions of feudal China.

Pan's Discourse on Women in Feudal China and Implications for Sex Education

It was Pan's concern over the living conditions of women in feudal China that provided him with the motivation to study Xiaoqing's case in depth. He stressed that the social situation of women in that era had received insufficient research attention, and expressed his intention to supplement scholarly understanding of it with psychoanalysis, which he introduced to China and concluded in three major points.[30]

First, he attributed Xiaoqing's mental illness to the repressive and gender-biased environment of feudal China. Second, he used statistics and surveys to suggest that Chinese women, particularly those in the intellectual class, were frequently physically weak and suffered from depression. Many of them died of tuberculosis, as Pan ascertained that Xiaoqing had (she is recorded as having died in a final paroxysm of blood and tears). Psychoanalysis relates sickness in women to their unhealthy sexual and psychosexual development; many in the feudal era died in severe melancholy and despair. Finally, he queried how these women could have mitigated their unhappiness in such a repressive society. Those investigated by Pan included women who were still single but past the marital age; those married to the "wrong" man; and widows whose husbands had died shortly after marriage. Pan found most of them to have suffered not only from mental illness, but also from tuberculosis and other respiratory diseases. The psychoanalytical reading is that they suffered from sexual repression, which resulted in mental imbalance and physical weakness; Pan quoted psychopathologists who saw a connection between tuberculosis and depression and other psychological disorders.

Yet historical documentations of the relationship between human emotions and illness was found in the classic *Huangdi neijing* 黃帝內經 as early as in the first century BC, which singled out anger (*nu* 怒), joy (*xi* 喜), pensiveness (*si* 思), worry (*you* 憂) and fear (*kong* 恐) as the five major human emotions. This is well discussed in Hsiu-fen Chen's study, "Emotional Therapy and Talking Cures in Late Imperial China," collected in Howard Chiang's volume.[31] Chen points out that, throughout the imperial period, the medical worldview assigned a manipulative effect on the physical body to the imbalance of these five emotional states, primarily through the movements of *qi* 氣 in the viscera. The various illnesses resulting from an irregular emotional condition; anger makes *qi* ascend; joy relaxes it; grief (*bei* 悲) dissipates it; fear makes it descend; cold contracts it; heat makes it leak out; fright (*jing* 驚) makes it chaotic; exhaustion consumes it; and pensiveness congeals it. The documentation also indicates that the cause of sickness was the various abnormal configurations of *qi* induced by the emotional imbalance. This reading may supplement Pan's Freudian version from a metaphysical perspective.[32]

Pan's study of Xiaoqing reveals his concern with sexual education in the China of his own day and with relations between the sexes. He made a number of suggestions in the study for ways to improve contemporary sex education.[33] First, he recommended that Chinese parents stop spoiling or overprotecting their children, to reduce regression and fixation. Second, he stated that China should promote women's education and enhance the range of social activities available to them. Women's indoor lifestyle in feudal China had reduced their opportunities for sexual gratification. Their restriction to interacting only with individuals of the same sex and being confined indoors may have promoted homosexuality, Pan believed. He suggested that a healthy and active social life was necessary for healthy sexual and psychosexual development and to "rectify" the inclination toward homosexuality, which he saw as unhealthy and abnormal.

Finally, Pan posited that the repressive Confucian society of feudal China had put women like Xiaoqing in jeopardy. Whether or not women were aware of their homosexual inclination, they were forced into heterosexual relationships, including marriage, leading to depression and related mental disorders. An unrealistic evaluation of oneself resulting from auto-love could easily lead to disappointment in a relationship, with women often thinking they were too good for the men they were with. Pan wanted to promote knowledge of the auto-love concept in China, in addition to psychoanalysis more broadly, in the belief that doing so would enhance self-awareness and improve relations between the sexes.[34] Pan found support for his arguments in an investigation of the mental descriptions and literary terms used in 234 pieces of writing produced by female writers in the Qing dynasty.[35] Almost all of them conveyed negative feelings and emotions and suggested abnormal behavior. The most common terms used were related to laziness, passivity, boredom, and frustration, and conveyed a sense of physical weakness, exhaustion, depression, and unhappiness. Pan concluded: "The reason for these female literati to be so down in mood and passive in activity is partly related to the physique of Chinese women, and yet it is their deficient sexual life and unhealthy sexual development that contribute to their detrimental mental state."[36]

Cases of auto-love and shadow love were also common in Europe. Havelock Ellis introduced the concept of psychological narcissism in 1898, pointing out that narcissistic symptoms were common among the women of his day.[37] If it is admitted that shadow love, a form of narcissism, is caused by fixation, regression, or both and related to social repression and a traumatic sexual experience, then it is easy to see the influences of social authoritarianism, patriarchal ideology, and physical subjugation on women's behavior and lifestyles in both Qing dynasty China and Victorian Europe. It was not until the turn of the twentieth century that people turned to psychoanalysis for reflection and understanding. Today, however, Freud's psychoanalytical discourse is itself condemned as a Victorian and patriarchal ideology. The notions of libido and narcissism have been deconstructed and analyzed, with their inherent sexual prejudices identified.

A Contemporary Reading of the Notion of Narcissism in Psychoanalysis as It Relates to Sex

Feminist psychologists have strongly criticized Freud's psychoanalysis for its authoritarian approach and patriarchal reading, which has shaped and constructed psychotherapy for women. They disagree with Freud's definition of female psychopathology, his descriptions of women, and his diagnoses and proposed therapies, and have criticized his essentialist reading of sex surrounding the ideas of masculinity, femininity, castration, and penis envy. Freud's depiction and analysis of narcissistic women have received particular attention and condemnation for their inherent sexual prejudice.[38]

Freud did elaborate upon his opinions concerning narcissism, for example, in *On Narcissism: An Introduction*, an extended essay he published in 1915, the same year he delivered the series of lectures that constitute *A General Introduction to Psychoanalysis*. Here I will need to quote an elaborated paragraph that is key to understand the concept of sexual object-choice:[39]

> Complete object-love of the attachment type is, properly speaking, characteristic of the male. It displays the marked sexual overvaluation which is doubtless derived from the child's original narcissism and thus corresponds to transference of that narcissism to the sexual object. This sexual overvaluation is the origin of the peculiar state of being in love, a state suggestive of a neurotic compulsion, which is thus traceable to an impoverishment of the ego as regards libido in favor of the love-object. A different course is followed in the type of female most frequently met with, which is probably the purest and truest one. With the onset of puberty, the maturing of the female sexual organs, which up till then have been in a condition of latency, seems to bring about an intensification of the original narcissism, and this is unfavorable to the development of a true object-choice with its accompanying sexual overvaluation. Women, especially if they grow up with good looks, develop a certain self-contentment which compensates them for the social restrictions that are imposed upon them in their choice of object. Strictly speaking, it is only themselves that such women love with intensity comparable to that of the man's love for them. Nor does their need lie in the direction of loving, but of being loved; and the man who fulfills this condition is the one who finds favor with them. The importance of this type of woman for the erotic life of mankind is to be rated very high . . . Such women have the greatest fascination for men, not only for aesthetic reasons, . . . [and] it seems very evident that another person's narcissism has a

> great attraction for those who have renounced part of their own narcissism and are in search of object-love. The great charm of narcissistic women has, however, its reverse side; a large part of the lover's dissatisfaction, of his doubts of the woman's love, of his complaints of her enigmatic nature, has its root in this incongruity between the types of object-choice . . . [In] narcissistic women, whose attitude towards men remains cool, there is a road which leads to complete object-love. In the child whom they bear, a part of their own body confronts them like an extraneous object . . . Before puberty they feel masculine and develop some way along masculine lines; after this trend has been cut short on their reaching female maturity, they still retain the capacity of longing for a masculine ideal—an ideal which is in fact a survival of the boyish nature that they themselves once possessed.

At least four main criticisms of the ideas that Freud propounded in the foregoing passage are possible from the feminist perspective. First, Freud suggests that the latency of the female sexual organs prior to puberty results in woman making different object-choices from man, leading to a narcissistic tendency. It sounds as if he is suggesting an inborn deficiency. He also suggests that women's physiological sexual structure brings about an intensification of the original narcissism, which is unfavorable to the development of a true object-choice and is accompanied by sexual over valuation. This idea seems deterministic in a sexual and biological way.

Second, Freud states that complete object-love of the attachment type is characteristic of the male and turns a child's original narcissism toward the sexual object. The further implication of the complete transfer of object-love is that the ego will comply with the reality principle, which refers to the norms or morality among his ego, object-love, and superego. Freud appears to be advocating the old patriarchal view that women need more education and control to strengthen their moral capacity, as they have a tendency toward egotism and narcissism because of their physiological sexual development, particularly in the latency period prior to puberty.

Third, if a narcissistic woman holds great attraction for men who have renounced part of their own narcissism and are in search of object-love, does this place her in a dangerous position? Freud suggested that a narcissistic woman whose attitude toward men remains cool often creates dissatisfaction in a male lover, who doubts her love and complains about her enigmatic nature. This suggestion offers an explanation for Xiaoqing's husband's sexual treatment of her.

Finally, Freud implied that the ego gains maturity when it completes the process of object-love, which should be heterosexual in nature. Homosexuality has a strong narcissistic flavor in Freud's view, meaning that the ego regresses or fixates and returns to auto-love, which should occur only at the infantile stage when the libido has not reached its mature sexual development. In Freud's writings, only mothers or women with a "masculine ideal" can complete the process of object-love. He believed that women develop along masculine lines before puberty. Once this trend is cut short on reaching sexual maturity, women retain the capacity to long for a masculine ideal—an ideal that is in fact the survival of the boyish nature that they themselves once possessed.[40] No feminist critique can agree with notions of a masculine ideal or an ideal man, or with the idea that men's object-love represents maturity and normal sexual psychology, whereas women should deny their narcissistic inclinations and follow a masculine ideal.

Conclusion

Pan Guangdan's case study of Feng Xiaoqing is based on his appropriation of Freud's psychoanalysis, his strong opinions about the repressive nature of Chinese feudal society, and the influence of the revolutionary and progressive thought sweeping China in the 1920s. Although Pan's work does not stand up to a contemporary feminist critique, he did succeed in pioneering research into the sexual psychology of Chinese women, highlighting revealing facts, statistics, surveys, and documentary evidence and illustrating the mental state, sexual repression, psychological depression, and general ill health of women in Feudal China, particularly members of the female literati. Pan's meticulous case study of Xiaoqing was the first of its kind in China; it paved the way for gender studies, women histories, and reflections on the psychosexual development of women in China, which is parallel to its physical impacts.[41]

12

FASHIONING BODY: HONG KONG CHINESE WOMEN, FASHION, AND IDENTITY ISSUES OF THE SIXTIES

This chapter not only shares observations and personal feelings that I had growing up in the "fashionable sixties" in Hong Kong, when fashion became a focus of female life in the small colony. It also serves the purpose of confirming the body construction related to social, economic, and political contexts and changes that Susan Brownell and Jeffrey Wasserstrom emphasize, for which readers should refer to Chapter 10. Fashion shapes and remakes bodies; body dressing and aestheticization produce an index of power, as suggested by Roland Barthes, in his analysis of the semiotics of fashion.[1]

The majority of Hong Kong women in the sixties came from Guangdong, a southern province of China (Figure 12.1); some were from the northern mainland regions. Most of them came to Hong Kong as refugees from the Second World War and from Communist China in 1949. Living standards in the early sixties in Hong Kong were still low; most of these women earned their living by working in factories or by doing factory work at home, where they could look after their families. At the same time, they devoted their time and energy to following foreign fashion by making their own clothes.

As in many Western countries, the decade was a restless era in Hong Kong during which tremendous political, economic, and cultural changes occurred. The dominance of fashion in women's lives, I believe, calls for more attention than the usual feminist questions concerning consumerism and the subordination of women, as fashion should also be regarded as a locus of struggle for identity. The process of searching for identity through fashion in the colonial city may be read as a response to the friction between East and West in both political and cultural dimensions.

1967: Before and After

According to the report of the 1961 census, the Hong Kong population was about 3,100,000; more than 1,300,000 were under the age of fifteen. During February 1962, thousands of political refugees arrived from China, enormously increasing the population and the labor force of the small colony. A brief account of significant social events of the sixties follows:

1963 Over 6,000 industrial enterprises established, with about 30,000 employees. The younger generation received better education.

1965 Rush on banks.

1966 Protests against fare increase on the Star Ferry, with thousands of people joining the demonstrations.

1967 Workers at a plastic products factory in Sun Po Kong went on strike, leading to anti-British government riots on a large scale.

First broadcast of free, non-subscription broadcasting of the Hong Kong Broadcast Company (TVB).

Over 200,000 students received secondary education.

1969 Heavy trading in stock market, new record set in the volume of buying and selling.

Wages increased, continuous inflation.

1970 Government approval of equal wages for equal work by male and female teachers, police, and nurses.

Women's incomes increased and their social status was elevated.

In the sixties, the image of women changed. Melancholic figures were replaced by strong, tough, and decisive females in Chinese movies, reflecting modification of women's identities. The domain of identity was discussed in newspapers and magazines; the phrase "Hong Kong people" appeared for the first time. A sense of belonging emerged, as the citizens of Hong Kong came out of the poverty of the fifties, experienced economic growth and improvement of living standards, and contributed to making Hong Kong a prosperous industrial city.

For these developments, 1967 was a key year, commonly regarded as a demarcation point in the history of Hong Kong. The political riots in the middle of the year meant that thousands of citizens lived in a chaotic situation, as Chinese Communist supporters fought violently with the Hong Kong British government. The Sino-British battle brought into question the identity of Hong Kong people, especially those who desperately hoped for stability in Hong Kong. After the riot, the government immediately organized various remedial activities to reinforce citizens' sense of belonging, focused on building a prosperous image for the city. These activities included the "Hong Kong Festival" and youth nights in which fashion shows were arranged to promote harmony and the concept of modernity in the colony.

Western modernization had a great impact on Hong Kong. From the growing import and export trade in the sixties came modern fashions, foreign goods, and culture that symbolized social progress, good taste, and elite style. People were excited about new ideas in industrial design and fashion. They tried to enjoy the modern present and forget the unhappy past in China. In the first "Hong Kong Fashion Festival," held in 1967 as part of the British government's attempt to rebuild a prosperous image, local garments were featured that were based on designs from Paris. The festival was a success. It laid the foundation for Hong Kong's fashion industry and defined the Hong Kong look for decades to come.[2]

The growth in the textile industry and in clothing exports was another factor in the flourishing of fashion in the sixties, when the

United States was the biggest clothing market. The number of persons employed and the number of garment factories increased three times during the sixties; the majority of workers in the industry were women, including those who worked at home with their own sewing machines.

Fashion and the Social Classes

For political and economic reasons, fashion shows became a form of mass entertainment, popular culture, and performing art. Both celebrities and ordinary people organized and participated in fashion activities. The popularity of fashionable garments in the sixties was promoted by other entertainment activities like go-go dance parties, bowling, and pop concerts. Both local and Hollywood movie stars were icons of fashion, for instance Audrey Hepburn, whose hairstyle was imitated by local young women. Underlying these fashionable looks was vigorous social mobility in response to the growth of capitalism and industrialization. It is interesting to see how fashion acted as a challenge to the upper classes by lower class people.

Women of the lower class used home sewing machines to make their own fashionable clothes based on magazines and paper patterns sold at newspaper stands. These were best-selling items, although the imitation of the sexy images in print materials did not immediately produce much liberation in sexuality or in the social roles of women. In the old Cantonese movies of the sixties, fashionable actresses still played conservative and victimized roles, holding submissive attitudes. No matter how modern they looked, they continued to portray values of chastity and loyalty to one man.

This was all especially exciting to working girls, who presented their challenges to the upper class via their homemade fashions. Their efforts prove Susan Kaiser's point, that working-class women challenged the elite control of fashion by remaking existing garments. These hearty, vivacious women enjoyed wearing bright colors and patterns, defying all laws of harmony and taste.[3] They followed the main style but added little details, as suggested by Roland Barthes: "a little nothing that changes everything, the details insure your personality."[4] The upper classes might have responded by using expensive materials, but the textile industry in return supplied their ordinary customers with fine, machine-made lace and imitation materials.

Development of Women's Clothing Language in the Sixties

Westernization and modernization challenged the cultural identity of Hong Kong people in a general way. Problems of identity were discussed in local Chinese newspapers in 1967 after the riot. Three models of "Hong Kong people" were analyzed: those who were inclined to conservative Chinese models; those who were individualistic; and those who simply followed foreign trends. Hong Kong women in the sixties attempted to integrate all of these models by eclectically combining traditional Chinese styles with current Western trends in fashion, while remaining rather more conservative in their ways of thinking. The result was the "compound look" of the period, which can be traced by surveying the development of the women's clothing language in Hong Kong.

Life before the sixties in Hong Kong is remembered as conservative and modest, when society was basically composed of upper and lower classes. Ordinary people dressed similarly to one another, while fashion was monopolized by upper-class celebrities and actresses. It was said that, by the sixties, fashion had ceased to exist in mainland China, while little was developed in Taiwan and other overseas Chinese communities, so that Hong Kong had no standard or language of modern Chinese fashion to follow.

Arriving in the fifties, the immigration of entrepreneurs from Shanghai to Hong Kong inspired the local garment industry. There was an upsurge of interest in the *qipao*.[5] Modeled by women celebrities and movie stars (Figure 12.2), the *qipao* developed in various styles and exerted its influence in the early sixties. *Qipao*s emphasized the maturity and the curvature of female bodies with silky, thin, and soft materials (Figure 12.3). It required slim bodies and, because of its close-fitting nature, controlled women's bodies and was uncomfortable.

In the early sixties, ordinary Hong Kong women wore shirts, skirts, and trousers of Western style in addition to simple *qipao*s. The styles were simple and the colors were basic. The look of casual dresses was similar to that of the *qipao*, in that they were tight on upper body and slim at the waist, although the lower part consisted of long, flared skirts. Popular patterns on fabrics were polka dots and checks. Scotch wool and flannel were fashionable materials in winter, dacron in summer, gradually replacing Chinese gauze and silk fabrics. Production techniques and capacity changed greatly at that time. Attaché bags, short and curly hair, and new moon-like eyebrows were also fashionable.[6] These brought a early mature look to young Hong Kong ladies, reminding us of fashionable Paris women in the fifties. Female models of the early sixties posed like sex symbols in the soft porn industry.

In the late sixties, the close-fitting style depicting female maturity was gradually replaced by a simple, girlish, and carefree look emphasizing youth. Women all looked like girls; the slim look was the standard of beauty. Skinny female figures were popular in all forms of media. Twiggy was the top model, with long eyelashes, big eyes, and thin legs dangling from a slender body. However, it should be noted that sensuality in women's fashion was still a major concern discussed in fashion magazines.

"Youth Storm" in Fashion History

Great similarities may be found between fashion development in the West in the sixties and that of Hong Kong. First, the "revolutionary sixties" in the West also ushered in big changes in fashion techniques and production. Second, after the two world wars, both societies experienced economic growth, social policy development, and moderation of the tax system. These had led to the upsurge of the middle class and a reduction in the polarization of social classes. In response to these changes was the democratic movement in fashion. People of different classes dressed similarly, which blurred the division of social classes. Third, while the youth population grew tremendously in the sixties in Hong Kong due to the influx of Chinese refugees in the fifties, the baby boom after the Second World War in the West contributed also to the large percentage of the populations under the age of twenty. Young people in both places had higher purchasing power than the elder generation and had become the target consumers of the fashion industry. Fashion was made for youngsters.

The Western political and cultural movements of youngsters in the sixties had produced special fashion languages that had a direct influence on fashion in the East. For instance, the spirit of the Beat Movement and the Flower Movement, as expressed by loose, carefree leather coats, rough jeans, and cotton T-shirts, were signs of anti-industrialization and anti-establishment feelings, and a yearning for liberation. People in these movements rejected close-fitting styles and artificial fabrics and enjoyed wearing "folk" dress. Ironically, these preferences were immediately absorbed by fashion designers like Yves St. Laurent, who produced new commercial clothing designs based on ideas initiated by the rebel youth.

One can read the fashion in the sixties as a sign of rebellion, when jeans signified rudeness, toughness, and freedom from care; mini-skirts were sexy, girlish, self- expressive, and liberated; bell-bottomed trousers signified the equalization of the sexes, or a form of asexuality; folk styles signified a return to nature and naiveté. As mentioned, fashion in Hong Kong in the late sixties followed closely that of Paris, as France had become the world's leading garment exporter. However, in addition to mini-skirts and bell-bottoms were Hong Kong-designed bead dresses and modified Chinese clothing. Hong Kong was also busy selling exotic images of Chinese femininity to Westerners.

As the teenage population of Hong Kong approached forty percent of the total population in the mid-sixties, it was obvious that the age factor dominated fashion, as was the case in the West. Despite a similar history of political unrest and economic crisis, the reasons why youngsters in Hong Kong did not develop cult movements like the Beat Movement and Flower Power might be related to both the traditional Chinese value of social harmony and British colonial government policies. However, sudden economic growth, internationalization, and modernization did bring great cultural challenges. The youth, especially those young Hong Kong women who benefited from more education and financial security, borrowed the language of clothing from others to speak for themselves.

Admittedly, Hong Kong women in the sixties still had an inferior status in every way. The majority of them were housewives, students, factory workers, and social and family dependents. However, they soon began to receive better education and job opportunities and to gain financial independence. Hong Kong women enjoyed more social activities and therefore demanded fashions with which to express their new identities. Even more important was the growing self-awareness discussed below.

Fashion in the Hong Kong Sixties: The New Woman Identity

It is said that fashion provides individuals with a symbolic mechanism for detaching from the past; it allows people to cope with the stresses of the present in an orderly way by helping to define what is appropriate in a world of uncertainties; and it prepares for the immediate future by providing a sense of anticipation or a clue to emerging issues and tastes.[7] We may say these functions met the needs of young Chinese women growing up in the era of Sino-British struggles and industrial growth. Involvement in fashion seems to have become a strategy for recreating the fragmented self.

Accompanying the rise of capitalism and industrialization was individualism. Fashion is always an enhancement of individuality; the interest in clothing of women during the sixties in Hong Kong could be said to have expressed a safe rebellion against the traditional imperative of women's conformity. It also provided consolation to individuals as it promoted self-esteem and the language of identity. It exploded out of enthusiasm, as the fashion codes of identity represented leisure, fun, youth and health, open-mindedness, playfulness, energy, independence, courage and, finally, subjectivity, no matter how controversial it could be.

As fashion shows became a popular form of mass entertainment, as mentioned above, fashion models were eagerly imitated by individuals. Women projected their self-images and fantasies onto those professional models that from time to time appeared fast, carefree, naughty, sharp, discriminating, balanced, easy-going, sophisticated, coquettish, serious, ingenuous, and so on. It is said that the multiplication of persons in a single being is always considered by fashion as an index of power.[8] This is one reason for the popularity of fashion in Hong Kong in the sixties, a time when women in the colony were finding their power.

It is always difficult to ignore feminist questions or criticisms of fashion that may be applied to the fashion phenomenon in Hong Kong, as pointed out by Kaiser and Wilson. The hedonistic mode of fashion is a disadvantage to women as a whole. Females do not necessarily tend to wear clothing items for the single purpose of appearing sexually attractive to men, but men tend to focus more on sensuality in their perceptions of women's appearances than do women.[9] The fluidity of identities in fashion promotes the thinning process of social meaning, standardizing the appearance and style of the female body and constituting the remainder of control of women inherited from tradition. Fashion also burns out the energy, spirit, and material power of women. Research shows that individuals who conform in terms of clothing are likely to have conforming personalities, to be restrained and submissive, to give in to social order, and to want to maintain harmonious relations. The obsession with popular fashion in the sixties was for the ordinary girl on the street, who equated clothes with the good life and also with breaking conventions and with democracy; yet democracy serves only to mask gross inequalities of wealth and opportunity.[10]

In addition, divisions and separations had occurred among women in Hong Kong in the sixties. Fashion was the sphere of young and unmarried women. Once a woman reached her thirties and if she married, her sphere was restricted to the family. She was not expected to be concerned about her appearance; she was likely to tuck up her hair to renounce her sexuality and to wear dull colors.[11] This was exactly what happened to my mother's generation.

Whether fashion is a way for women to speak for themselves or whether it is just another powerful form of oppression is a subject of endless feminist debate. The uncontroversial statement is that fashion is the battlefield for identity, which an individual perceives as representing or defining the self in a given social situation. This is socially constructed, either achieved or ascribed, and is a negotiation by which wearer and perceiver are able to understand the wearer's identity through a process of communication. This interplay works between individuality and conformity, identification and differentiation. In the light of the above analysis, fashion in the late sixties in Hong Kong was obviously a form of open resistance to the traditional Chinese control of female bodies. Its popularity represented the active negotiation of a new gender and cultural identity by Hong Kong women living in the colony.

Conclusion

Homi Bhabha has asserted that, in the post-colonial period, women can utilize their own peripheral position to challenge ideologies in the center.[12] Fashion facilitated this challenge in the sixties in Hong Kong as it threatened feudal Chinese constraints on women by liberating women's bodies via fashionable dress. It deviated from the idea of a backward Communist China by embracing modern Western designs. Moreover, it subverted submissive attitudes toward the British government by choosing rebellious ways of dress and gesture. Hong Kong women's fashion in the sixties was a silent revolution; the struggle for new identities which it involved was not passive or "imported," but an active construction initiated by the women themselves.

Fifty years later, the fashion designer Vivienne Tam from Hong Kong again makes use of silk and Chinese fabrics for the global market. Chapter 5 details the story of Tam's embroidery and the ways she survives in the global world of fashion. In her design, beading and sequins are used for trimming; this style, which dominated women's fashion in the sixties, has now become the favourite of Tam's clients. In her memoir, Tam mentioned her visits to the flea market in the sixties that she did not only see fashion from all periods, but also supplies from all over the world. There were so many fabrics and notions to choose from, resulting in all kinds of mixed, cross-cultural, and innovative fashion possibilities.[13] Chapter 5 concludes that Tam's East-meets-West design appropriated exotic, traditional and mysterious Oriental elements with a new and modern edge (Figure 12.4, Appendix), which is also gendered in the sense that the Orient starts by playing the feminine role of an Other passively gazed at by the masculine West. Now the Orient gazes back, bringing out a new femininity in traditional women's embroidery work and creating a successful market niche.

Vivienne Tam's words confirm this chapter's conclusion that fashion and gender are always in the making; this is the reason why the East-meets-West Hong Kong fashion in the sixties flourished: "Things blend with one another to create a hybrid of qualities and essences. The composite elements retain their original natures, yet by coalescing they gain a richness and variety previously impossible."[14]

13

SEX AND EMOTION: THE REPRESENTATION OF CHINESE FEMALE SEX WORKERS IN RECENT DISCOURSES AND THE COSMOPOLITAN CONTEXT

The craze for Ang Lee's movie *Lust, Caution* stirred up discussions about sexuality that had been quite missing in Chinese cinema. The work received mixed and contradictory reviews from both Chinese and international critics. Chinese critics were more positive than the latter; they understood the terror that China experienced at the Japanese invasion during the Second World War. Other common concerns about the film included female sexuality and the realistic depiction of the intense sex scenes. The reception of the work created an interesting phenomenon across Chinese cities and Taiwan, focusing on the discourses on sex and love represented in this project, originally inspired by writer Eileen Chang's short novel.

The seven minutes of sexual scenes in the film made a difference in the responses of viewers. There were *Lust, Caution* tours organized for mainland viewers to come to Hong Kong just to watch the full version. The sexual depiction of the female character was obviously the central core of the work. Ang Lee's choice of treatment and adaptation could have been the result of two idioms quoted in Eileen Chang's original novel. Chang cited the idiom proposed by a Chinese scholar, "the road to a woman's heart is through her vagina," a response to the foreign idiom "the road to a man's heart is through his stomach."[1] The young, shy Wong Chia Chi 王佳芝 , though unconvincing, is portrayed as a patriot who leads the daring assassination attempt on Yee, a high-ranking Kuomintang official with overt ties to the collaborational government headed by Wang Jingwei 汪精衛 in Shanghai during 1942, when China was under Japanese occupation. This brave act seems to have been motivated by her admiration for the student revolutionary leader Kuang Yu Min, rather than by her ambition to eliminate a national traitor. Yet after sharing intense sexual relations with Yee, Wong confesses her emotional motivation to him, reinforced by his gift of a Cartier diamond ring. She finally thwarts the plan and meets a tragic end, playing out the female version of the traditional curse that a man dismantles a country because of his lust for a woman. The further implication here is that confusion of love and sex will lead to disaster for both sexes.

The title of the film and the novel, *Lust, Caution*, reads like a warning to the woman in the story rather than to the leading man. A traitor is not supposed to be able to love; he should have no feeling for another person. All a traitor should be interested in is the fulfillment of basic instincts. The body-mind dichotomy parallels that of sex and love, which dominates the representation of the national traitor. This duality is also of relevance to the female character, who contributes her body as a tool and adopts sex as an instrument for assassination. While the woman is not ready for sexual affinity and pleasure, the portrait of her "fall" and sexual indulgence fascinated Chinese viewers to a great extent. The situation becomes more upsetting and dangerous as she develops feelings for the traitor.

I should note that most Western critics reacted very cautiously to the sexual treatment in the film. Dana Stevens of *Slate* claimed that *Lust, Caution* harbored no illusions about the transformative potential of either revolutionary violence or sexual passion. Mike LaSalle of the *San Francisco Chronicle* commented that Ang Lee's *Lust, Caution* was an immersion into another time, place, and mentality, but not reality. Roger Ebert of the *Chicago Sun-Times* said that the film made less sense than sensibility. Jack Mathews of *New York Daily News* said, even more directly, "I didn't feel the love between the flowering idealist and the ruthless killer. If I did, I would have given the movie four stars. Everything else is wonderful." Perhaps the comments of *Village Voice's* Robert Wilonsky said it best, that Ang Lee's foray into forbidden love in this work was as monotonous and disaffecting as *Brokeback Mountain* was gripping and immediate. The common take that most American critics shared was that it was one of the most cautious readings of lust ever portrayed on film. Lau Tin Chi, a Hong Kong radio host, doubted somehow: "some viewers tried to determine if the sex is indeed simulated, because Leung thrusts with conviction. The sex must be emotionally satisfying to the point of having a transcending effect on both lovers."[2]

The Western reception found the mixture of indifference, caution, lust and passion unconvincing, and also incredible and unnecessary; as Anthony Lane of *The New Yorker* comments, "running two hours and forty minutes, [the film] never finds the same balance: by the time he [Leung, who plays the traitor] gets to the lust, it is too late to throw caution to the winds." This is to say that the duality or the exclusivity of sex and love should be a comfort in the context of the film, and that it should be applied at least to certain human relationships.

Feminist Challenges to the Duality of Sex (Body) and Love (Mind)

As explicated in Chapter 1, Western feminist philosophers and biologists have been trying to destabilize the notion of "biological sex." Judith Butler's famous argument is that the body is only posited or signified as prior to signification.[3] The positing process also constitutes and conditions the "materiality" of the body. What enables this positing is a problematic gendered matrix that fixes the "irreducible" materiality into a bunch of taken-for-granted discourses on sex and sexuality. These discourses can be conducted in several ways. First, as Irigaray argues, inasmuch as a distinction between form and matter is offered within phallo-centrism, there is an exclusion of the "female." Within the male-female (form-matter) binary, the female is not an intelligible term but a further materiality.[4] Second, the return to biological essentialism is strongly contested, since one can argue that "physical experiences" do not make someone a woman, but rather the specific social regulatory ideals by which female bodies are trained and formed.

Consideration of the categories of economy, politics, heterosexuality, philosophy, and subject and object relations is necessary. Economically, Judith Butler points out, the female must be the subordinate term in a binary opposition of masculine-female for that economy to operate.[5] The worse social operation is to treat a woman's speech and her behavior as hysterical (rooted in the Greek word *hystera*, meaning uterus), thereby confining women to the biological. Philosophically, Moira Gatens argues that traditional philosophical conceptions of corporeality are counterproductive to the attempt to construct an autonomous conception of women's bodies. In our culture, every woman is normatively defined as the opposite and complement of man.[6] The proper function of a woman's body is to receive, take, accept, welcome, include, and even comprehend. "She" has no proper shape and is not a body. The receptacle principle, which applies universally, is then associated with the female.[7]

The consequent social implications to both women and corporeality are thus often passive and negative, and function conceptually to be of service to reason, civilization, and progress.[8] Gatens further points out that this dualist notion of the body involves an implicit alignment between women and irrationality.[9] As discussed in the first chapter of this book, feminist scholars can identify lines of investigation of the body in contemporary thought that may be regarded as legacies of the Cartesian view, which treat the body as primarily an object and the mind as a neutral judging subject. The conventional reading is that the mind is equivalent to the masculine, and the body to the feminine, excluding women as possible subjects of knowledge and morality. Women's bodies are weaker, more prone to (hormonal) irregularities, intrusions, and contingencies.[10]

The body has remained a conceptual blind spot in both mainstream Western philosophical thought and contemporary feminist theories. The human subject has long been regarded as composed by several related binaries: mind and body, sense and sensibility, outside and inside, self and other, depth and surface, reality and appearance, transcendence and immanence, psychology and physiology, form and matter, and so on. This binary thinking hierarchizes and ranks two polarized terms, so that one becomes privileged and the other is suppressed, subordinated, and negated. The situation is more complicated when the body is associated with the "female." It has even been proposed that it is in the West and in our time that the female body has been constructed not only as a lack or absence, but also as a formlessness that engulfs all form, a disorder that threatens all order.[11]

So what happened to the female character in *Lust, Caution*, who assumed her own body as a sexual object? How did she transform her role from spy or assassin to that of lover? What made her change from a bodily object to a subject who finally dismantled the ambitious plot and project? The answer implied was sex and lust in the first degree. The theme reinforced the patriarchal myth that in women, sex and love are one, while in men they may be separate domains.

Feminist scholars query Simone de Beauvoir's famous postulation that "one is not born, but rather becomes a woman." Judith Butler sees this statement as apparently implying that biological sex is not an immutable essence. For if genders are in some sense chosen, then what happens to the ways in which we are, as it were, already culturally interpreted? When the body is conceived as a cultural locus of gender meanings, it becomes unclear what aspects of this body are natural or free of cultural imprint. Indeed, according to Butler, we will be unable to find a body that antecedes its cultural interpretation, and gender is the acculturation of the corporeal. In Butler's reading, one may surpass the body, but this does not mean that one definitively gets beyond the body. This is because the body is not static, but is a mode of intentionality, a directional force and mode of desire. She says: "As a condition of access to the world, the body is a being comported beyond itself, referring to the world and thereby revealing its own ontological status as a referential reality."[12]

This condition is itself a corporeal experience; the body is experienced as a mode of becoming. Butler stresses that though we "become" our genders in Beauvoir's view, gender is not traceable to a definable origin because it is itself an originating activity incessantly taking place.[13] This is a subtle and strategic project, for becoming a gender is a mindful process in a cultural reality laden with sanctions, taboos, and prescriptions. Butler elaborates that this is a choice to assume a certain kind of body, to live or wear one's body in a certain way in a world of already established corporeal styles.[14]

This reminds readers of her famous gender performance theory. The subject goes through a painful process when it experiences moments of gender dislocation. Butler says if human existence is always gendered existence, then to stray outside established gender is in some sense to put one's very existence into question. One would have to confront the burden of choice intrinsic to living as a man or a woman or some other gender identities, and this is a freedom made burdensome through social constraints.[15] Butler based her famous critique on the dichotomy of the notions of "sex" and "gender," saying that if a person accepts the body as a cultural situation, then the notion of a natural body and a natural "sex" would seem increasingly suspect. And if one's body is a situation and a field of cultural possibilities both received and reinterpreted, then both gender and sex seems to be thoroughly cultural affairs.

Butler adds that a woman who exists on the metaphysical order of being is not something already accomplished, self-identical, static, but someone on the metaphysical order of becoming who invents possibility into her experience, including the possibility of never becoming a substantive, self-identical "woman."[16] The interest here is then to explore how some contemporary Chinese women who utilize their sexual bodies in an instrumental way go through the cultural possibilities and social situations; and the ways these bodies are living through, being received, represented, and reinterpreted. The sex and love relations of sex workers will be examined.

Discourses on Sex and Love in a Traditional Manual for Chinese Sex Workers

The Chinese scholar, Liu Fu 劉復, found a book that recorded stories and notes on female prostitution in the late Ming in 1926. As Harriet Zurndorfer suggests, the late Ming was the period when cities flourished as never before. In her words, urban prosperity stimulated the promotion of relative freedom in the pleasure districts, which attracted a wide range of prostitution clients, from literati and students who were seeking relief from study and the civil service examinations to merchants requiring lavish entertainment.[17] This explains why "pleasurable" places flourished. I use the term prostitutes here in the way that the term was used in the late Ming social context. Since the title page was torn, Liu named the book after the first sentence "world affairs were as ambiguous as dreams in springtime," and entitled it *Hunrupian* 渾如篇 (Chapters of ambiguity).[18] People found in it manuals or service guidelines for Ming female prostitutes, manifesting the professionalism and work ethic of the industry in the period, as well as its sex and love relations.

One of the guidelines for refusing sex service revealed choices of customers. It was said that the sex workers should refuse service to sex customers who were indifferent:[19]

If you do not feel for each other, it is better to stop the relation at the right moment. After he is willing to come up to you, you will soon know if he will continue. It is like that you have devoted your heart to the moon, but the moon does not shine on it. If he is indifferent to your service, he is also indifferent to all your other areas . . . your eagerness will go nowhere.

姊妹有三不接：一不接寡情，寡情休要接，終久會閃人，未合情如蜜，纔好便抽身，哄人上翠樓，捐梯沒下程，將心托明月，明月不照臨，一處情兒寡，處處定無情，冷眼望山高，熱心空志誠。

The above quotation implies that the relation between worker and client should be a caring one, and that feeling and emotional involvement are important. It would make no sense to provide sex services to someone who had no feeling for his partner.

The following eight states depict the feeling, or *qing*, of the Ming prostitutes on their side:[20]

Interested: The prostitute sees that the client is handsome and intelligent. She does not say a word but wants anxiously that she can sleep with him, enjoy having sex with him, and feel gratified in her heart and body. Though this is not happening yet, she is interested in having a commitment with him.

有意：妓者見子弟風流出眾，俊逸超羣，口中不言，心內自省，怎能㲉衾枕齊肩，何日裏帶綰同心，楚雨巫雲，雖未曾施，盟山誓海，已屬有意。

Missing Each Other: The prostitute is emotionally involved with her client. Once they are separated, her heart is heavy and she cannot sleep through long, lonely nights. She fears that his feeling for her will diminish due to the separation, and that she will be sad from not being with him anymore. She hates the fact that they are so far apart and that they can hardly correspond with each other. And her smartness and submissiveness has also made him miss her.

掛意：妓者與子弟兩情正濃，一旦分袂，此心耿耿，長夜不寐，怕的別離心變，愁的後會無期，恨雲山阻隔，怪鴻鴈音稀，只因乖巧聰明，惹得他牽腸掛意。

Compliments: The prostitute has separated from the client and they are living far apart. They miss each other and take their chances in correspondence. When they meet mutual friends or guests, they will send each other love notes and messages. They now hold hands and remind each other: "Don't forget to send me compliments whenever you can."

致意：妓者與子弟天各一方，人居兩地，滿腔心事，倩誰稍寄，即討青鸞繫扎，怎得黃犬傳詩，若遇賓朋與知己，細數離思千萬縷，執手漫叮囑，多多煩致意。

Concerns: The prostitute and the client share great passion. They care about each other in every step and moment. Their encounter is brief but stronger than a marital one. She smiles when she greets him with her cabin door open. She stands in tears when she misses him. She cares so much for his loving concerns.

著意：妓者與子弟到情熱處，不比平常，步步認真，絲絲留意，雖口露水之交，更勝結縭之義，見了他笑臉相迎，携了香閨，別了他瞻望弗及，佇泣如雨，為什麼著緊相關，都出自一念著意。

Seriousness: The prostitute and the client are serious with each other. They are genuinely in love and are not pretending. They talk about the future and express themselves in frank and truthful ways. There are no plots, no false hopes, no lies, and no dishonesties.

實意：妓者與子弟情濃意浹，處以本心，不假色笑，不虛奉承，說將來家常談話，做出來老實真情，圈套機謀，未見萌於念慮，貼法騙語，安忍播諸口唇，諄諄實意，自始至終。

Doubtless: The prostitute and the client are so much in love that they become one. They talk about anything, including their plans for elopement. They trust each other and grant each other access to their own wealth and properties. They don't have doubts about their feeling for each other.

私意：妓者與子弟相忘形骸，不論你我，以致私奔暗約，鼠竊狗偷，胸中隱諱，無不傾吐，身邊蓄積，盡托收貯，並無疑忌之心，乃見私厚之意。

Good Will: The prostitute sees that the client is smart and handsome and she strongly falls for him. She cares about him and loves him. She is very excited to meet him and is completely glad to see him. She cares if he is feeling cold or hungry, and she has all kinds of good will for him. Her feeling is really good though it is not about marriage.

好意：妓者見子弟才高貌美，稱心滿意，百樣疼腔，千般愛意，聞著聲兒驚跳，覷著影兒歡喜，愁他冷，怕他飢，恨不得含他肚裡，世上願盟設盡，人間美事無遺，這段恩情，只少嫁娶，果然是一腔好意。

Sickness: The prostitute and the client are very much in love and they are serious with each other. But since their way to marriage is blocked, the woman feels sad and depressed. She gets thinner and loses her appetite. She entertains her other clients with no engagement. She sits alone and sighs a lot. She does not comb or tidy up; she does not eat or drink and has become forgetful, just because of him.

病意：妓者與子弟美好切骨，勢阻佳期，愁怯怯，紅顏瘦損，悶沉沉，白晝瘖寐，見了賓朋，故意強笑，別了姊妹，獨坐長吁，鬟容不思整理，茶飯不知滋味，提起東來忘了西，這病兒全然為你。

The above texts are depictions without judgment or comment. The states depict some real scenes of prostitution where genuine love and passion do exist and are regarded as natural and possible situations. But there exists also the defense mechanism that careful prostitutes do adopt and conduct in cautious ways, not only physically but also psychologically and emotionally. Here are the two scenes noted in the *Hunrupian*:[21]

Yuan Fun (緣份): "You do not need to be very special or wealthy to get my heart and attention. For it is just a matter of chance (*yuan fun*) for our encounter. Once we started our love, this is a tough engagement. It will end when our *yuan fun* is fulfilled. Till then, you will just be the same as before."

姊妹暫好有二：一緣分：人品苦不出眾，寶鈔未必豐厚，只因緣分湊巧，一旦情意相投，這綢繆，真個厚，料情難罷手，只恐緣滿與分足，你又依舊依舊。

> *Smartness*: "You are so handsome and charming that I immediately fell for you at first sight; it happened even prior to my service. Definitely there are people who are smart as well, and so this feeling will not last. When I meet another smart friend, my dear, you may fall behind again."
>
> **標致：**相貌生得清雅，人物委實風流，一見就和你厚，未有先與你偷，若論好，多個頭，只恐不長久，再遇標致一朋友，你又靠後靠後。

The mixture of the situations quoted above demonstrates the variety of feeling and relations that prostitutes may hold toward their clients. They are considered to be honest, normal, and natural. There are cautions on some forms of relations, which is understandable for the safety and the well-being of the prostitutes.

The above discussion was echoed in pre-1949 tabloid magazines, featuring stories of prostitution in old Shanghai. A typical plot recounts the liaison of a courtesan with a provincial governor under Qing rule. She accumulates a sum via her sex labor and keeps what he has saved to buy her out of the brothel to purchase him an official post. Finally, she dies alone, all of a sudden, leaving him valuable jewelry and the inspiration to rise in officialdom. His success is due to a loyal and loving courtesan.[22] Numerous versions of this courtesan and customer relationship are portrayed in literary and visual representations, which confirm the moral and professional codes inherited by Confucian-influenced courtesans.

Harriet Zurndorfer is very correct in pointing out that, during the course of late Ming, courtesans became a kind of "cultural ideal." There were popular stories of how they became symbols of morality, as a response to Confucian's *lixue* 理學, which emerged from the moral discussion of the Southern Song and emphasized the moral perfection of the individual.[23] The emotion discussed in this chapter, which was implied throughout the *Hunrupian*, refers to the notion of *qing* 情 . *Qing* in the Confucian sense means more than the feeling, emotion, sentiment, sensitivity, or passion that Zurndorfer mentions, which she also contrasts with *li* 理 (moral reasoning). Zurndorfer writes that *li* "represented stale didacticism, rigid dogmatism, and artificial regulation," while *qing* "signified the plain expression of fresh, natural, romantic and unsophisticated emotions."[24]

Representations on Sex and Emotion among Sex Workers in Hong Kong Cinema

Stanley Kwan's famous movie, *Rouge* 胭脂扣, demonstrates some of the states depicted in the *Hunrupian*. The main character, Ru Fa 如花, played by Anita Mui, works in a popular brothel in Sheung Wan, Hong Kong. She is emotionally very much involved with her client, a rich boy played by Leslie Cheung. They even agree to commit suicide together when their road to marriage is blocked, butas soon as Ru Fa's suicide is successful, her client changes his mind, confirming the social gap between them and attitudes toward prostitutes at the turn of the century. Ru Fa then becomes a wandering ghost looking for her lover in the midst of the Sheung Wan district. The romantic story was adapted to illustrate the practical nature of relations between a contemporary couple, reinforcing the long tradition of love and loyalty legends among Chinese female sex workers.

In the film story, the legacy of late Ming courtesans remains. Zurndorfer observes:

> During the late Ming the "cult of *qing*" became immensely popular, and a means for men and women to explore the interplay of ethics and culture. The courtesan became a focal point of this examination. The sensuous side of her existence came to be perceived as the embodiment of *qing*, variously expressed as freedom and independence of spirit, courage and heroic action, detachment and understanding, true feeling and magnanimous spirit. . . . The connection between the marginality and dubious social station of the late Ming courtesan and her elevation as the symbol of refinement, high culture, freedom, and the possibility of action was observed . . .[25]

In her observation, courtesans appear as models of loyalty, virtue, and courage, often more so than the male characters. We see all these in the film *Rouge*.

Film representations of sex workers in love have been diminishing since the 2000s, replaced by scenes of unsentimental exchange in the growing sex commerce of the postcolonial city, when sex workers flooded in from the north mainland. The influx has been threatening the industry and acted as a catalyst of change, including of the sexual and emotional relationship between workers and clients. Competition is keen and sex workers have clarified their labor aims and objectives. Their working guidelines, if there are any, are the naked truth of monetary returns and strictly business, with no romantic or emotional nonsense.

The film *Gam gai* 金雞 (Golden Chicken), made in 2002, for example, presented the life of a Hong Kong sex worker in an amusing way. The main character, Kam (played by Sandra Ng), began as an underaged "fish-ball girl" and becomes a popular showgirl who wins over clients with her impersonations of famous movie comedians like Jackie Chan. This character does everything for money, yet she has an unrequited love for a mysterious gangster, Yeh (Wu Kwan), and a long-time friendship with a former client, Professor Chan (Tony Leung). There is also an unplanned pregnancy, which leads to an opportunistic romance with Richard (Felix Wong), a wealthy businessman client. The film's portrayal of a sex worker's genuine relations with clients are convincing, but do not lead to any substantial or fruitful endings. Old prejudices and practical concerns overruled romance. Kam faced tough competition in the sex industry until the end.

Other films on the subject produced in the 2000s in Hong Kong have totally denied romantic values. Fruit Chan's movie *Durian, Durian* 榴槤飄飄 , made in 2000, portrays sex workers coming from the mainland in the form of a docu-drama. Ah Yan (Qin Hailu), the main character, who comes from northeast China, returns to the northeast to invest what she has earned from her sex work after her three-month Hong Kong visa expires. The character is represented in a realistic way, and her relations with her clients are very light-hearted, with no emotional involvement, but easy lies. There is no tragic sense, love, illusions, or false hopes, but direct material returns and purposes. The sex worker achieves what she wants via the sex trade and she fulfills her wishes back home. The indifferent story treatment and camera movements filters out the emotional elements, except the one between Ah Yan and a little girl, who mails her the symbolic, smelly durian fruit. These representations depicted sex commerce in a most effective film language.

A featured world premiere at the 31st Hong Kong International Film Festival (2007), *Whispers and Moans* 性工作者十日談, directed by Herman Yau, is another sex-worker film that places doubts on emotional involvements in the sex trade. The film is based on a book of interviews with real-life Hong Kong sex workers and gives the subject a stronger dramatic treatment. With mainland sex workers attracting more customers and the hostess club in danger of closing down, the career working girls find hope only in the strict sex business. Again, illusions of love affairs with clients are denied and distorted and do not become an issue or agenda in the film. The Hong Kong female sex workers keep their love for lovers other than their clients while the mainland workers keep their hearts for their hometowns. While the Hong Kong female sex workers were still struggling to get rid of their sadness and emotions, the mainland ones were represented in the film as tough and professional.

Instrumental Representations and the Cosmopolitanism of Sex Commerce

The integration of the Chinese economy with global markets has had multiple effects on Chinese social life. Considered in the market or consumer context, desire and pleasure are integral parts of material and social production, as is the productions of more desire and pleasure. As Arif Dirlik has suggested, the market economy and the promotion of consumption serve as distractions from politics; production and culture have mingled with one another through commodification and consumption.[26]

Lisa Rofel further claims that "cosmopolitanism" serves as one of the key nodes through which sexual, material, and affective desires are expressed.[27] Cross-country sex commerce, in this sense, is a self-conscious transcendence of locality, accomplished through the formation of a consumer or a service provider identity.[28] Cosmopolitanism is domesticated through a series of structural dichotomies and structured forgettings that reinvent the past.[29] In the case of sex trade, the old Western structural dichotomies of the body and the mind, male and female, sex and love, and so on, are revived in the figures of Chinese female sex workers, who are represented as selling their bodies without carrying their souls in the busy traffic. The representations can also be read as acting against cosmopolitanism as a totalizing force—that is, the place of no place—by locating the specificities of identities formed through attachments to a place, and treating people as representations.[30]

Under the topic of this chapter, it is the case that Mainland Chinese female sex workers are represented differently from those of Hong Kong in Hong Kong cinema. This fulfills the related imaginations, including the popular imaginations that Hong Kong people, while materialistic, are more "humane" in general terms than Mainland Chinese. While Chinese leaders like to speak of "using capitalism to develop socialism," female sex workers coming from the north in *Whispers and Moans* claim that they want to "contribute" to China through their sex services. These scenes are received with laughter, but the women characters do seem to have greater freedom in pursuing purposeful goals, and they act as bodily subjects.

Prostitution is defined as the exchange of sex and sexual services for money or other material benefits; as a social institution, its definition is to allow certain powers of command over one person's body to be exercised by another.[31] There exists a major divide between feminists defining prostitution as sexual domination and the essence of women's oppression and those who maintain that women freely opt to do sex work. The representations mentioned in this chapter demonstrate the willingness and the allowance conducted by the women sex workers themselves in China, including their own direction and the duality formulation of their bodies and their mind, their sex and emotion. They are also discourses through which new forms of Chinese female sexual subjects are produced, formed, imagined, and enriched in the cosmopolitan cultural and consumption contexts. It is an illustration of Foucault's statement that "every representation must be immediately endowed with life in the living body of desire, every desire must be expressed in the pure light of a representative discourse," be it in the form of submission or liberation.[32]

Gail Hershatter provides a thorough reflection on the many facets of the recent discourses of prostitution in the new China.[33] Scholars justify the history of prostitution with the particularities of Chinese social development and literary tradition, in which courtesan stories have become a genre. On the other hand, for political correctness, they also state that prostitutes form a corrosive, malignant tumor on society; their service is an act that degrades women and is a sign of paradise lost or poverty in a male-centered society.[34] Hershatter is correct to observe that as Chinese rural people have moved to cities in recent decades, the stimulation of the international market and rapid changes in some Chinese cities have led to changes in sexual concepts and values. In retelling history to justify the present, Hershatter concludes that prostitutes were multiply deployed as figures in Republican China: as historical figures of the nation's cultural heritage; as prominent subjects in the male literary reservoir; as exemplars of traditional female virtue; and with their bodies as sites of nostalgia and popular entertainment.[35] The bodily representation, together with its mannerism, of the prostitution subjects illustrate our discussion in the beginning paragraphs of this chapter, that the body is not static, but is a mode of intentionality, a directional force, and mode of desire. One sees from various contemporary representations of prostitution in China Hershatter's realistic statement that the meanings of prostitution will continue to be recreated and negotiated in China, as elsewhere.[36]

Appendix

IMAGES

Figure 5.1
Rank Badge,
Qing dynasty
(1644–1911),
late 18th–early
19th century, silk,
12 3/4 x 12 1/2 in.
The Metropolitan
Museum of Art.

Figure 5.2
Woman's Birthday or Informal Ceremonial Robe,
Qing dynasty
(1644–1911), late
19th–early 20th
century, silk,
53 x 53 in.
The Metropolitan
Museum of Art.

Figure 5.3 "Painting of a Chinese lady embroidering," from the collection of the Shao Xiaocheng Chinese Embroidery Institute in Beijing, in *Chinese Embroidery—An Illustrated Stitch Guide*, by Shao Xiaocheng (Shanghai Press; Better Link Press, 2014).

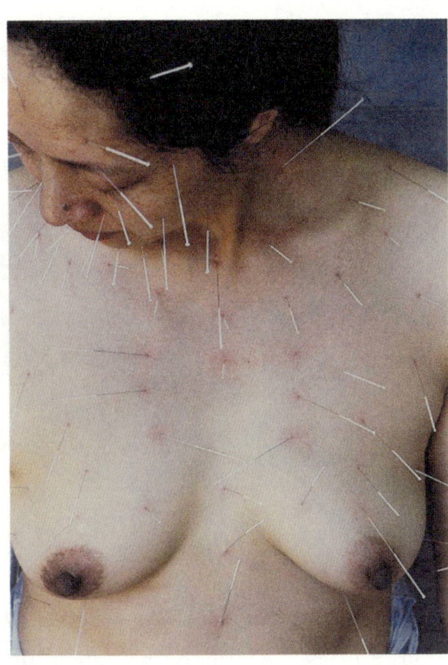

Figure 7.1
He Cheng Yao.
99 needles, 2002.

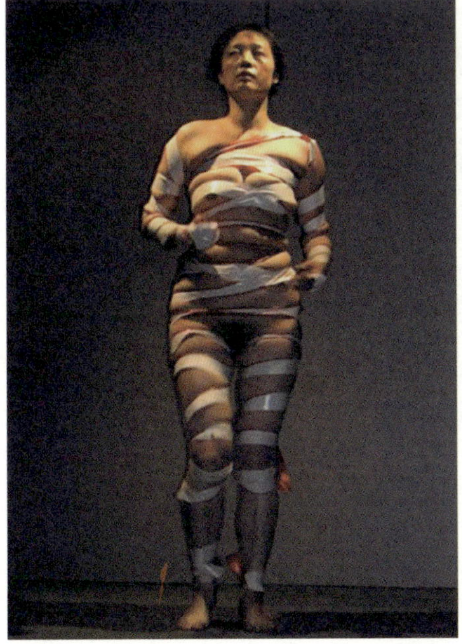

Figure 7.2
He Cheng Yao.
Public Broadcast Exercise, 2004.

Figure 8.1 Geyuan. Image by the author, 2014.

Figure 8.2 Bamboo at Geyuan. Image by the author, 2014.

Figure 8.3 Rock formations at Geyuan. Image by the author, 2014.

Figure 8.4 *Penjing* at Geyuan. Image by the author, 2014.

Figure 8.5 Rock pond at Geyuan. Image by the author, 2014.

Figure 9.1 Xi Shi, a traditional recognized *meiren*, depicted and imagined in the album *Gathering Gems of Beauty* (畫麗珠萃秀), authored by He Dazi 赫達資, Qing Dynasty (1644–1911), from The Collection of National Palace Museum, Taipei, Taiwan.

Figure 10.1
Advertisement with two women in cheongsam dresses, 1920's Shanghai. Textile Research Centre, Leiden, The Netherlands.

Figure 10.2
A woman working in China in the 1950s. www.womenofchina.cn

Figure 10.3 *Go among the workers, peasants and soldiers* (1970). International Institute of Social History.

Figure 10.4 A training class for the Beijing 2008 Olympic Games medal ceremonies hostesses in Beijing, January 9, 2008. Imaginechina/Corbis.

Figure 10.5 Dancer at the Beijing 2008 Olympic Games Opening Ceremony, 8 August, 2008. Tim Hipps, FMWRC Public Affairs.

Figure 10.6 Dancers at the Beijing 2008 Olympic Games Opening Ceremony, 8 August, 2008. Tim Hipps, FMWRC Public Affairs.

Figure 11.1
Cover image of Pan Guangdan's book *Feng Xiaoqing: A Case Study of "Shadow Love."*

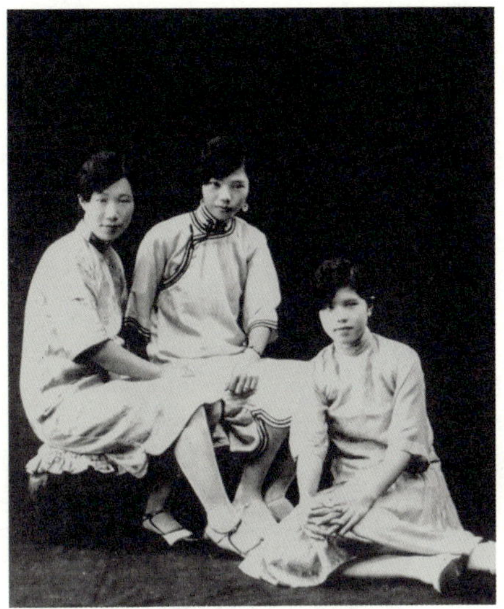

Figure 12.1
Hong Kong girls in cheongsam, late 1920s. Collection of the Hong Kong Museum of History.

Figure 12.2
Photograph of Zhou Xuan, Chinese actress, 1930s. C. H. Wong Photo Studio, Shanghai, China. Wikipedia Commons.

Figure 12.3 Hong Kong Cheongsam Fashion, 1960s. Collection of the Hong Kong Museum of History.

Figure 12.4 Embroidered dress from the Vivienne Tam Spring 2015 Ready-to-wear collection. Ovidiu Hrubaru/Shutterstock.com.

LIST OF PERMISSIONS

ARTICLES

Grateful acknowledgement is made for permission to reproduce the following previously published articles: “Contemporary Feminist Body Theories and Mencius' Ideas of Body and Mind,” *The Journal of Chinese Philosophy* 27, no. 2 (2000): pp. 155–169; “Chinese Philosophy and the Suggestion of a New Aesthetics,” *Journal of Chinese Philosophy* 23 (1996), pp. 453–466; “Reclaiming the Body: Francis Bacon's Fugitive Bodies and Confucian Aesthetics on Bodily Expression,” *Contemporary Aesthetics* 2 (2004), pp. 621–631; “Female Bodily Aesthetics and Their Early Revelations in the Book of Songs,” in *Overt and Covert Treasures: Essays on the Sources for Chinese Women's History*, edited by Clara Ho (Hong Kong: Chinese University of Hong Kong, 2012), 113–130; “Expression Extreme and History Trauma in Female Bodily Art in China: The Case of He Cheng Yao,” in *Strategic Strategies in Contemporary Chinese Art*, edited by Mary Bittner Wiseman and Liu Yuedi (Leiden: Brill Academic Publishing, March 2011), pp 171–191; “Female Bodily Aesthetics, Politics, and Feminine Ideals of Beauty in China,” in Peggy Zeglin Brand (ed.), *Beauty Matters* (Bloomington: Indiana University Press, 2000), pp. 169–196; “Beauty and the State: Female Bodies as State Apparatus and Recent Beauty Discourses in China,” published in *Beauty Unlimited*, edited by Peggy Zeglin Brand (Bloomington: Indiana University Press, 2013), pp. 368–384; “Feminist Aesthetics in Body: Hong Kong Chinese Women, Fashion & Identity in the Sixties,” *Anthropos* 28, nos. 3–4 (1996), pp. 55–61; and “Sex and Emotion: Change of the Related

Discourses among Some Chinese Female Sex Workers and their Representations in the Cosmopolitan Context," *The International Journal of the Humanities* 9, no. 8 (2012), pp. 217–229.

IMAGES

Grateful acknowledgement is made for permission to reprint the following images: *Rank Badge with Tiger*, Qing dynasty (1644–1911), late 18th–early 19th century, silk, 12 3/4 x 12 1/2 in., The Metropolitan Museum of Art, www.metmuseum.org; *Woman's Birthday or Informal Ceremonial Robe*, Qing dynasty (1644–1911), late 19th–early 20th century, silk, 53 x 53 in. The Metropolitan Museum of Art, www.metmuseum.org; "Painting of a Chinese lady embroidering," from the collection of Shao Xiaocheng Chinese Embroidery Institute in Beijing, *Chinese Embroidery—An Illustrated Stitch Guide*, by Shao Xiaocheng (Shanghai Press; Better Link Press, 2014); *99 Needles*, He Chengyao, body art performance (2002); *Public Broadcast Exercise*, He Chengyao, body art performance (2004); Gathering Gems of Beauty《畫麗珠萃秀 冊 吳西施》, He Dazi 赫達資, Qing Dynasty (1644–1911), The Collection of National Palace Museum; "China train hostesses for Olympic gold ceremonies," Beijing, (Imaginechina/Corbis, 2008); "2008 Summer Olympics—Opening Ceremony—Beijing, China," (CC 2.0, U.S. Army Photos by Tim Hipps/FMWRC Public Affairs, 8 August 2008), https://www.flickr.com/photos/familymwr/4927973743/in/album-72157624812644826/, https://www.flickr.com/photos/familymwr/4928598762/in/album-72157624812644826/; "A woman working in China in the 1950s," www.womenofchina.cn, http://www.womenofchina.cn/womenofchina/html1/culture/costumes/13/9818-8.htm; *Go among the workers, peasants and soldiers*, (CC 2.0, International Institute of Social History, 1970), https://www.flickr.com/photos/iisg/4753981811/; "A Shanghai advertisement for Victoria soap," 1920s, TRC Leiden, http://www.trc-leiden.nl/index.php?option=com_content&viewsarticle=&id=186&lang=en; "Photograph of Zhou Xuan, Chinese actress," (CC 2.0, public domain, C. H. Wong Photo Studio, Shanghai, China), https://commons.wikimedia.org/wiki/File:Zhou_Xuan_by_C.H.Wong_Photo_Studio.jpg; "Hong Kong girls in cheongsam," late 1920s. Collection of the Hong Kong Mseum of History; Hong Kong Cheongsam Fashion, 1960s. Collection of the Hong Kong Museum of History; and Vivienne Tam Spring 2015 Ready-to-wear collection shown at the Mercedes-Benz Fashion Week Spring 2015 on September 7, 2015, New York, NY. Ovidiu Hrubaru/ Shutterstock.com.

NOTES

Introduction

1. Roland Barthes, *The Fashion System* (New York: Hill and Wang, 1983), pp. 254–256.

1 Contemporary Feminist Body Theories and Mencius' Ideas of Body and Mind

This chapter is developed from my previously published article under the same title in *The Journal of Chinese Philosophy* 27, no. 2 (2000): 155–169.

1. Judith Butler, *Bodies That Matter* (New York: Routledge, 1993), p. 30.
2. Ibid., p. 29.
3. Ibid., p. 39.
4. Moira Gatens, *Imaginary Bodies: Ethics, Power and Corporeality* (London: Routledge, 1996), pp. 21–35.
5. Jane Arthurs and Jean Grimshaw (eds.), *Women's Bodies: Discipline and Transgression* (London: Cassell, 1999), p. 59.
6. Ibid., p. 52.
7. Thomas Laqueur, *Making Sex: Body and Gender from the Greeks to Freud* (Cambridge, MA: Harvard University Press), p. 88.
8. Butler, *Bodies That Matter*, p. 36.

9. C. Pateman, *The Sexual Contract* (Cambridge: Polity Press, 1988), Chapter 4.
10. Gatens, *Imaginary Bodies*, pp. 25, 37, and 49.
11. Iris Young, *Throwing Like a Girl: And Other Essays in Feminist Philosophy and Social Theory* (Indianapolis: Indiana University Press, 1990), pp. 143–148.
12. Liz Frost, "Doing Looks: Women, Appearance and Mental Health," in Arthurs and Grimshaw (eds.), *Women's Bodies: Discipline and Transgression*, p. 119.
13. Butler, *Bodies That Matter*, pp. 40–53.
14. Gatens, *Imaginary Bodies*, pp. 49–50.
15. See G. Lloyd, *The Man of Reason* (London: Methuen, 1984).
16. Elizabeth Grosz, *Volatile Bodies: Toward a Corporeal Feminism* (Indianapolis: Indiana University Press, 1994), pp. 6–7.
17. Ibid., p. 8.
18. Ibid., p.14.
19. Gatens, *Imaginary Bodies*, p. 55.
20. Ibid., p. 57.
21. Ibid.
22. Ibid., p. 203.
23. Ibid., p. 21.
24. Ibid., p. 22.
25. Ibid., p. 23.
26. Christine Battersby, *The Phenomenal Woman: Feminist Metaphysics and the Patterns of Identity* (Cambridge: Polity Press, 1988), p. 102.
27. Translation from Wing-Tsit Chan, *A Source Book in Chinese Philosophy* (Princeton: Princeton University Press, 1963).
28. Ibid., p. 66.
30. Ibid., pp. 272–273.
31. Ibid., p. 243.
32. Ibid., pp. 482–483.
33. Ibid., pp. 386–387.
34. Ibid., pp. 344–346.
35. See "The Great Appendix" in *I-Ching*, translated by C. F. Baynes (New Jersey: Princeton University Press,1950).
36. Cheng Chung-ying, *New Dimensions of Confucian and Neo-Confucian Philosophy* (Albany: State University of New York Press, 1991), pp. 188–195.
37. Ibid., pp. 98–105.
38. Ibid., p. 105.

2 Chinese Philosophy and the Suggestion of a Matriarchal Aesthetics

This chapter is a revision of my previous article, "Chinese Philosophy and the Suggestion of a New Aesthetics," published in *Journal of Chinese Philosophy* 23 (1996), pp. 453–466.

1. Hilde Hein and Carolyn Korsmeyer (eds.), *Aesthetics in Feminist Perspective* (Bloomington: Indiana University Press, 1993), p. 179.
2. Immanuel Kant, *Critique of Judgment*, translated by Werner S. Pluhar (Indianapolis: Hackett, 1987), p. 210.
3. See Jane Kneller, "Discipline and Silence," in Hein and Korsmeyer (eds.), *Aesthetics in Feminist Perspective*, p. 181.
4. Kant, *Critique of Judgment*, p. 241.
5. Hein and Korsmeyer (eds.), *Aesthetics in Feminist Perspective*, p. 184.
6. See Timothy Gould, "Intensity and Its Audiences: Toward a Feminist Perspective on the Kantian Sublime," in *Feminism and Tradition in Aesthetics*, edited by Peggy Zeglin Brand and Carolyn Korsmeyer (University Park: Pennsylvania State University Press, 1995), p. 70.
7. Immanuel Kant, *Observations on the Feeling of the Beautiful and Sublime*, translated by J. T. Goldthwait (Berkeley: University of California Press, 1960 [1764]).
8. Ibid., p. 81.
9. See Christine Battersby, "Stages on Kant's Way: Aesthetics, Morality, and the Gendered Sublime," in Brand and Korsmeyer (eds.), *Feminism and Tradition in Aesthetics*, p. 104.
10. Joseph Margolis, *Pragmatism Without Foundations* (New York: Basil Blackwell, 1986), p. 303.
11. See Joanne B. Waugh, "Analytic Aesthetics and Feminist Aesthetics: Neither/Nor?" in Brand and Korsmeyer (eds.), *Feminism and Tradition in Aesthetics*, pp. 411–413.
12. See Heide Göttner-Abendroth, "Nine Principles of a Matriarchal Aesthetic," in *Feminist Aesthetics*, edited by Gisela Ecker, translated by Harriet Anderson (Boston: Beacon Press, 1985), pp. 81–94.
13. Chan Wing-tsit, *A Source Book in Chinese Philosophy* (Princeton: Princeton University Press, 1963), p. 207.
14. Mou Zongsan 牟宗三, *Intellectual Intuition and Chinese Philosophy* 智的直覺與中國哲學 (Taipei: Commercial Press, 1974), pp. 208–211.

15. Ibid., p. 184.
16. Tang Junyi 唐君毅, *Lun Zhongguoren wen jingshen* 論中國人文精神 [Spiritual values of Chinese culture] (Taipei: Cheng Chung Book Stores, 1987), p. 18.

3 Reclaiming the Body: Francis Bacon's Fugitive Bodies and Confucian Aesthetics on Bodily Expression

This chapter is a revised version of my article, "Reclaiming the Body: Francis Bacon's Fugitive Bodies and Confucian Aesthetics on Bodily Expression," *Contemporary Aesthetics* 2 (2004), pp. 621–631.

1. Andrew Brighton, *Francis Bacon* (London: Tate Gallery Publishing, 2001), p. 8.
2. Ibid., p. 9.
3. See http://www.tate.org.uk/art/artworks/bacon-three-studies-for-figures-at-the-base-of-a-crucifixion-n06171 for the figure. Retrieved on Feb. 21, 2016.
4. Brighton, *Francis Bacon*, p. 16.
5. Nick Millet, "The Fugitive Body: Bacon's Fistula," in *The Body*, edited by Andrew Benjamin (London: Academy Editions, 1993), pp. 40–51.
6. Ernst van Alphen, *Francis Bacon and the Loss of Self* (London: Reaktion Books, 1992), p. 114.
7. Ibid., pp. 115–116.
8. Ibid., pp. 117–118.
9. Leo Bersani, "Is the Rectum a Grave?" *October* 43 (Winter 1987), 197–223.
10. Van Alphen, *Francis Bacon and the Loss of Self*, p. 160.
11. Brighton, *Francis Bacon*, p. 15.
12. Elizabeth Grosz, "Psychoanalysis and the Body," in *Feminist Theory and the Body: A Reader*, edited by Janet Price and Margrit Shildrick (Edinburgh: Edinburgh University Press, 1999), p. 267.
13. Ibid., pp. 267–270.
14. Friedrich Wilhelm Nietzsche, *Thus Spoke Zarathustra: A Book For Everyone And No One*, translated with a new introduction by R. J. Hollingdale (Harmondsworth: Penguin Books, 1969), p. 62.
15. Friedrich Wilhelm Nietzsche, *The Gay Science with a Prelude in Rhymes and Appendix of Songs*, translated with commentary by Walter Kaufmann (New York: Vintage Books, 1974), pp. 176–177.
16. Friedrich Wilhelm Nietzsche, *Twilight of The Idols and The Anti-Christ,* translated with an introduction and commentary by R. J. Hollingdale

(Harmondsworth: Penguin Books, 1968), p. 73.
17. Ibid., p. 101.
18. Van Alphen, *Francis Bacon and the Loss of Self*, p. 118.
19. Barbara Brook, *Feminist Perspectives on the Body* (New York: Pearson Education, 1999), pp. 116–117.
20. Denise Riley, "Bodies, Identities, Feminisms," in Price and Shildrick (eds.), *Feminist Theory and the Body: A Reader*, pp. 221–223.
21. Moira Gatens, "Power, Bodies and Difference," in Price and Shildrick (eds.), *Feminist Theory and the Body: A Reader*, p. 228.
22. Michael Sullivan, *The Arts of China* (Berkeley: University of California Press, 1984), p. 131.
23. Richard M. Barnhart, "Li Kung-lin's Use of Past Styles," in *Artists and Traditions: Uses of the Past in Chinese Culture*, edited by Christian R. Murck (Princeton: Princeton University Art Museum, 1976), pp. 51–71.
24. Sullivan, *The Arts of China*, pp. 90–91.
25. See http://big5.xinhuanet.com/gate/big5/news.xinhuanet.com/shuhua/2013-08/05/c_125119351.htm for the whole painting. Retrieved on Feb. 21, 2016.
26. See http://www.britishmuseum.org/research/collection_online/collection_object_details/collection_image_gallery.aspx?partid=1&assetid=102650001&objectid=234466 for the scroll. Retrieved on Feb. 21, 2016.
27. Sullivan, *The Arts of China*, pp. 91–92.
28. James R. Ware (trans.), *The Sayings of Mencius* (Taipei: Confucius Publishing, 1970), p. 52.
29. Ibid., p. 42.
30. Ibid., p. 188.
31. Ibid., p. 190.
32. Ibid., p. 210.
33. Ibid., p. 234.
34. See Gatens, "Power, Bodies and Difference," pp. 230–231.
35. Judith Butler, *Bodies That Matter* (New York: Routledge, 1993), p. 235.
36. Ibid., p. 238.

4 Discourses on Female Bodily Aesthetics and Their Early Revelations in *The Book of Songs*

This chapter is developed from my published article, "Female Bodily Aesthetics and Their Early Revelations in the Book of Songs," in *Overt and*

Covert Treasures: Essays on the Sources for Chinese Women's History, edited by Clara Ho (Hong Kong: The Chinese University of Hong Kong, 2012), pp. 113–130.

1. Stephen Owen's foreword in *The Book of Songs: The Ancient Chinese Classic of Poetry*, translated by Arthur Waley, with additional translations by Joseph R. Allen (New York: Grove Press, 1996), pp. vii–xxv.
2. Ibid., p. xvi. As Owen observes, "the living do homage to the ancestors and the ancestors watch over the living; the present acts with past examples in mind; men and women speak to one another in love or anger; the common people praise or blame their rulers, and the best rulers act in the interest of the common people."
3. Ibid., p. 343. This should include Sima Qian, who described the editorial process of the *Songs* in *Shi ji*.
4. Haun Saussy, *The Problem of A Chinese Aesthetic* (Stanford: Stanford University Press, 1993), p. 49.
5. Arthur Waley, "Postface: A Literary History of the *Shi jing*," in Waley (trans.), *The Book of Songs*, pp. 336–343. Waley said the songs suggested "the range of possibilities and the accompanying sediments of primary and secondary orality that would be found therein: from the festival round dance with its 'heave-ho' refrains and the antithetical courting songs with their formulas of romance, to the solemn dramas of the ancestral temple with their concern for models and prescribed rituals." Critics said that at the level closest in time to Confucius (551–479 BC), most references were to music and musical performance, especially the propriety thereof, instead of to the words themselves.
6. Ibid., p. 344.
7. Ibid., p. 354. See also Saussy's translation of Zhu Xi's preface: "How did this come about? Most historians of the subject point to the philosopher and erudite Zhu Xi (1130–1200), whose edition of the *Odes* often distances itself, on grounds of verisimilitude, from the moralizing maneuvers of the ancient Prefaces. As Zhu Xi tells it, 'When I began to write my *Annotations to the Odes*, I used the Little Prefaces as my guides to the literal meaning, and where their glosses would work, I twisted the sense in their favor. Afterwards, I felt uneasy, and when I redid the annotations, I kept the Little Prefaces but took issue with them here and there. Still, the ports' meaning came through. When you've discarded all the old explanations, then the meaning

of the *Odes* comes alive again.' "

8. Ibid., pp. 346–350.
9. James Legge, *The Chinese Classics*, Vol. 4. (London: Hong Kong University Press, 1960), p. 34.
10. Ibid., p. 374.
11. Waley, (trans.), *The Book of Songs*, p. 48 and Legge, *The Chinese Classics*, Vol. 4, p. 94.
12. Ibid., p. 214.
13. Waley, *The Chinese Classics*, Vol. 4, p. 205.
14. Ibid., p. 93.
15. Ibid., p. 283.
16. Ibid., p. 10.
17. Ibid., p. 69.
18. Ibid., p. 65.
19. Ibid., p. 72.
20. Ibid., p. 30.
21. Ibid., p. 14.
22. Ibid., p. 76.
23. Ibid., p. 101.
24. Ibid., p. 65.
25. Ibid., p. 68.
26. Ibid., p. 33.
27. Ibid., p. 17.
28. Ibid., p. 46.
29. Ibid., pp. 120–121.
30. Ibid., pp. 210–211.
31. Ibid., pp. 313–317.
32. Ibid., pp. 214–215.
33. Eva K. W. Man, "Female Bodily Aesthetics, Politics, and Feminine Ideals of Beauty in China," in *Beauty Matters*, edited by Peggy Zeglin Brand (Bloomington: Indiana University Press, April, 2000), p. 183.
34. Ibid., pp. 184–185. See Wu's translation of *Tanji congshu* (first published by Zhuo Wang and Chao Zhang in 1695, republished in Shanghai: Guji chubanshe, 1993, pp. 141–142) in *Writing Women in Late Imperial China*, edited by Ellen Widmer and Kang-i Sun Chang (Stanford: Stanford University Press, 1997), pp. 438–439.
35. Man, "Female Bodily Aesthetics, Politics, and Feminine Ideals of Beauty in

China," p. 186.

36. The Great Preface defined *feng* in this way: "Thus when the affairs of one state are embodied in the experience of a person, this is called a *feng* [air]. But when they speak of the affairs of the entire empire or the customs (*feng*) of the four quarters, this is called a *ya* [ode]."
37. See Legge, *The Chinese Classics*, Vol. 4, pp. 37–39.

5 Reflections on Traditional Chinese Women's Embroidery: The Subject of Bodily Expression, Gender Identity, and Fashion

1. E. W. Barber, *Women's Work: The First 20,000 Years* (New York: W. W. Norton & Company, 1995), pp. 29–32.
2. Nancy Z. Berliner, *Chinese Folk Art: The Small Skills of Carving Insects* (Boston: Little, Brown and Company, 1986), pp. 153–154.
3. Ibid., p. 156.
4. Ibid.
5. Ibid., p. 158.
6. Ibid., p. 159.
7. Wang Yarong, *Chinese Folk Embroidery* (London: Thames and Hudson, 1987), p. 14.
8. Ibid., pp. 14–16.
9. Ibid., p. 19.
10. Ibid.
11. Berliner, *Chinese Folk Art*, p. 153.
12. Ibid., p. 160.
13. Ibid., p. 164.
14. Ibid., p. 165.
15. Ibid.
16. Francesca Bray, *Technology and Gender: Fabrics of Power in Late Imperial China* (Berkeley: University of California Press, 1997), pp. 265–269.
17. Marsha Weidner, "Women in the History of Chinese Painting," in *Views From Jade Terrace: Chinese Women Artists 1300–1912*, edited by Marsha Weidner (Indianapolis: Indianapolis Museum of Art and Rizzoli, 1988), p. 21.
18. Grace Fong, "Female Hands: Embroidery as a Knowledge Field in Women's Everyday Life in Late Imperial and Early Republican China," paper presented at the International Symposium on "Daily Life, Knowledge, and Chinese Modernities," Institute of Modern History, Academia Sinica, Taipei,

Republic of China, November 21–23, 2002.

19. Ibid., p. 29.
20. Ibid., p. 30.
21. Ibid., p. 37.
22. Ibid., p. 35.
23. Ibid., p. 14, note 16.
24. Ibid., p. 40.
25. See "Equal Rights and Important Role in Economic Sphere," *White Papers of the Government: Human Rights in China*, November 1991, http://english.peopledaily.com.cn/whitepaper/8(3).html.
26. Berliner, *Chinese Folk Art*, pp. 85–88.
27. Vivienne Tam and Martha Huang, *China Chic* (New York: Harper Collins, 2000), p. 128.
28. Christopher Michaud, "New York Fashion Week Finds Designers Reflective," http://www.hurriyetdailynews.com/new-york-fashion-week-finds-designers-reflective.aspx?pageID=438&n=new-york-fashion-week-finds-designers-reflective-2000-02-11. Retrieved on Oct. 31, 2015.
29. http://www.newspapers.com/newspage/61399583/. Retrieved on Oct. 31, 2015.
30. Tam and Huang, *China Chic*, pp. 30–34.

6 Kissing in Chinese Culture

1. Herant A. Katchadourian and Donald T. Lunde, *Fundamentals of Human Sexuality*, 3rd ed. (New York: Holt, Rinehart and Winston, 1975), pp. 312–313.
2. Douglas Wile, *Art of the Bedchamber: The Chinese Sexual Yoga Classics Including Women's Solo Meditation Texts* (Albany: State University of New York Press, 1992), pp. 108–109.
3. Ibid., p. 116.
4. Ibid., pp. 104–105.
5. Ibid., p. 138.
6. Ibid., pp. 142–143.
7. Ruan Fangfu, *Sex in China: Studies in Sexology in Chinese Culture* (New York: Plenum Press, 1991), pp. 22–23.
8. Ibid., p. 57.
9. Ruan, *Sex in China*, pp. 165–167.
10. Ibid., p. 180.

7. Extreme Expression and History Trauma in Women's Body Art in China: The Case of He Chengyao

This chapter is developed from my published article, "Expression Extreme and History Trauma in Female Bodily Art in China: The Case of He Cheng Yao," in *Strategic Strategies in Contemporary Chinese Art*, edited by Mary Bittner Wiseman and Liu Yuedi (Leiden: Brill Academic Publishing, March 2011), pp. 171–191.

1. As in Jones's words, "works that involve the artist's enactment of her or his body in all of its sexual, racial, and other particularities and overtly solicit spectatorial desires unhinge the very deep structures and assumptions embedded in the formalist model of art evaluation." Amelia Jones, *Body Art/Performing the Subject* (Minneapolis: University of Minnesota Press, 1998), p. 5.
2. Ibid., p.13.
3. Andrea Pagnes, "Body Issues in Performance Art: Between Theory and Praxis," http://www.artandeducation.net/paper/body-issues-in-performance-art-between-theory-and-praxis/. Retrieved on Oct. 15, 2015.
4. Ibid.
5. Ibid., p. 14.
6. Ibid., p. 24.
7. Ibid., p. 24.
8. Rofel argues here that "'socialism with Chinese characteristics' is how the Chinese government comes to grips with tethering economic reform to neoliberal capitalism." See Lisa Rofel, *Desiring China: Experiments in Neoliberalism, Sexuality, and Public Culture* (Durham, NC: Duke University Press, 2007), p. 111.
9. Rofel writes, "It serves as one of the key nodes through which sexual, material, and affective desires bind citizen-subjects to state and transnational neoliberal policies." Ibid.
10. Ibid.
11. Ibid., p. 112.
12. Ibid., p. 113.
13. Ibid., p. 118.
14. Patricia Druck and Inka Schube (eds.), *Social Creatures. How Body Becomes Art* (Hannover: Sprengel Museum, 2004), p. 14.
15. Ibid., p. 15.

16. Moira Gatens, *Imaginary Bodies: Ethics, Power and Corporeality* (London: Routledge, 1996), pp. 25, 37, and 49.
17. Iris Young, *Throwing Like a Girl: And Other Essays in Feminist Philosophy and Social Theory* (Indianapolis: Indiana University Press, 1990), pp. 143–148.
18. Jones, *Body Art/Performing the Subject*, p. 5.
19. Thomas J. Berghuis, *Performance Art in China* (Hong Kong: Timezone 8, 2006), p. 10.
20. Joseph Beuys, Gerhard Steidl, and Klaus Staeck, *Honey is Flowing in All Directions* (Heidelberg: Edition Staeck, 1997).
21. He, Chengyao 何成瑤. *Mother and I* 媽媽和我. Body performance art presented in August 2001 in Chongqing, China.
22. *Spellbound Aura: The New Vision of Chinese Photography*. Taipei: Contemporary Art Foundation, 2004, pp. 78–81.
23. He, Chengyao 何成瑤. *Lift the Cover from Your Head* 掀起你的蓋頭來. *Cruel/Loving Bodies* 酷／愛身體 . Shanghai: Shanghai Duolun Museum of Modern Art. 2006, pp. 26–28.
24. *Spellbound Aura: The New Vision of Chinese Photography*. Taipei: Contemporary Art Foundation, 2004, pp. 78–81.
25. He, Chengyao 何成瑤. *The Possibility of Hair* 頭髮的可能性, Body Performance Art, Manchester Chinese Center, 2006.
26. Gao Minglu 高名潞 ,*Qiang: Zhongguo dangdai yishu de lishi yu bianjie* 牆：中國當代藝術的歷史與邊界 [The wall: Reshaping contemporary Chinese art] (Beijing: Zhongguo Renmindaxue chubanshe, 2006), pp. 256–272.
27. He, Chengyao 何成瑤 . *Illusion* 幻影 , Body Performance Art, Beijing Art Archive Gallery, 2002.
28. Gao Minglu, *Qiang*, pp. 256–272.
29. As quoted at the beginning of this article, Jones describes how body art "opens out subjectivity as performative, contingent, and always particularized rather than universal, implicating the interpreter within the meanings and cultural values ascribed to the work of art." (See note 1). On feminist aesthetics, see: Eva Kit Wah Man, "Some Reflections on the Notion of Feminist Aesthetics," paper presented at the Fourteenth Congress of the International Association of Empirical Aesthetics, held in Prague, August 1996, p. 5.
30. Mi Xie'er 米歇爾 , Liu Beicheng 劉北成 , and Yang Yuanyi 楊遠嬰 . Trans. *Fu Ke: Fengdian yu wenming* [Foucault's *Madness and Civilization*] (Beijing: Sanlian shudian, 2003).
31. Retrieved from http://www.art-here.net/html/av/4697_1.html.

32. Susan Brownell and Jeffrey Wasserstrom (eds.), *Chinese Femininities/ Chinese Masculinities* Los Angeles: University of California Press, 2002), p. 442.
33. Berger, John. "From Ways of Seeing." In *The Feminism and Visual Culture Reader*, edited by Amelia Jones, (New York: Routledge, 2003) p. 39.
34. Kenneth Clark, *The Nude: A Study in Ideal Form. Princeton* (Princeton: Princeton University Press, 1956), pp. 3–6.
35. François Jullien, *The Impossible Nude: Chinese Art and Western Aesthetics* (Chicago: University of Chicago Press, 2007), p. 4.
36. Ibid., p. 13.
37. He, Chengyao 何成瑤 . "Lift the Cover from Your Head" 掀起你的蓋頭來 . *Cruel/Loving Bodies* 酷 / 愛身體 . Shanghai: Shanghai Duolun Museum of Modern Art. 2006, pp. 26–28.
38. See *Yishu, Journal of Contemporary Chinese Art*, www.yishujournal.com/story.aspx?uid=2008032112014162
39. Retrieved from http://www.art-here.net/html/av/4697_1.html.
40. He Chengyao was a featured artist in *Global Feminisms* at the Brooklyn Museum, curated by Maura Reilly and Linda Nochlin in 2007.
41. See the catalogue of the exhibition edited and written by the curator, Maura Reilly, published for and by the Brooklyn Museum on the exhibited event "Global Feminisms: New Directions in Contemporary Art," 2007.
42. Renee Martyna, "Whither Global Feminism?" p. 12. Retrieved from http://www.carleton.ca/e-merge/docs_vol3/articles/Whither_Global_Feminism.pdf.
43. See He's artist statement, ibid.

8 Notes on a Chinese Garden: Comparative Responses to Arnold Berleant's Environmental Aesthetics

1. Arnold Berleant, *Aesthetics Beyond the Arts: New and Recent Essays* (Aldershot: Ashgate Publishing, 2012), pp. 131–147.
2. Tang Junyi 唐君毅 , *Zhongguo wenhua zhi jingshen jiazhi* 中國文化之精神價值 [The spirit of Chinese culture] (Taipei: Zheng Zhong Publishing, 1979).
3. Arnold Berleant, *Rethinking Aesthetics* (Aldershot: Ashgate Publishing, 2004)
4. Ibid., p. 35.
5. Ibid., p. 18.
6. Ibid., p. 33.

7. Michael Sullivan, *The Arts of China* (Los Angeles: University of California Press, 1984), p. 131.
8. See http://www.ceiba.cc.ntu.edu.tw/fineart/database/chap18/18-03-06x.jpg and http://www.guoxue.com/nl/syxy/007.jpg for details.
9. Berleant, *Rethinking Aesthetics*, p. 106.
10. Chan Wing-tsit, *A Source Book in Chinese Philosophy*, p. 207.
11. Tang, *Zhongguo wenhua zhi jingshen jiazhi*, p. 187.
12. Berleant, *Rethinking Aesthetics*, p. 109.
13. Ibid., pp. 91–92.
14. Ibid., pp. 95–98.
15. Ibid., p. 92.
16. Ibid., pp. 95–98.
17. Ibid., pp. 107–109.
18. Berleant, *Aesthetics Beyond the Arts: New and Recent Essays.*
19. Ibid., p. 68.
20. Ibid., p. 69.
21. Ibid., p. 70.
22. Ibid., p. 77.
23. Ibid., p. 132.
24. http://en.wikipedia.org/wiki/Geyuan_Garden, retrieved 13 September 2014.
25. Berleant, *Aesthetics Beyond the Arts: New and Recent Essays*, p. 141.
26. "Introduction to the history of Geyuan Garden", http://www.ge-garden.net. Retrieved 13 September 2014.
27. Ibid., pp. 132–142.
28. Tang, *Zhongguo wenhua zhi jingshen jiazhi* , p. 303.
29. Ibid., p. 304.
30. Ibid., p. 305.
31. Ibid., p. 316.
32. Ibid.
33. Berleant, *Aesthetics Beyond the Arts: New and Recent Essays*, p. 136.
34. Ibid.
35. James Cahill, lecture on Chinese garden at the Society for Asian Art in San Francisco, Feb. 1990. His lecture notes were posted online after he passed away in 2014. http://jamescahill.info/the-writings-of-james-cahill/cahill-lectures-and-papers/228-clp-13-1990-gardens-in-chinese-painting-society-for-asian-art-sf, retrieved on Oct 12, 2015.
36. Maggie Keswick, *The Chinese Garden: History, Art and Architecture* (Cambridge, MA: Harvard University Press, 2003), p. 217.

9. Female Bodily Aesthetics, Politics, and Feminine Ideals of Beauty in Chinese Traditions

This chapter is a revised version of my previously published article, "Female Bodily Aesthetics, Politics, and Feminine Ideals of Beauty in China," in Peggy Zeglin Brand (ed.), *Beauty Matters* (Bloomington: Indiana University Press, 2000), pp. 169–196.

1. Moira Gatens, *Imaginary Bodies*, pp. 8–9.
2. Christine Battersby, *The Phenomenal Woman: Feminist Metaphysics and the Patterns of Identity* (Cambridge: Polity Press, 1998), pp. 19–20.
3. Brownell and Wasserstrom (eds.), *Chinese Femininities/ Chinese Masculinities* (Los Angeles: University of California Press, 2002), p. 6.
4. Ibid., p. 15.
5. Ibid., p. 25.
6. Douglas Wile, *Art of the Bedchamber: The Chinese Sexual Yoga Classics Including Women's Solo Meditation Texts* (Albany: State University of New York Press, 1992), p. 46.
7. Chinese source from *Yu-fang Chih-yao* (Essentials of the Jade Chamber") in Te-hui Yeh, *Shuang-mei ching-an ts'ung-shu* [Shadow of the double plum tree collection] (Changsha, 1903), trans. in Wile, *Art of the Bedchamber*, p. 100.
8. Ibid., p. 106.
9. Ibid., p. 106 n. 61.
10. Ibid., p. 106.
11. Hsi-hsien Teng, *Tzu-chin kuang-yao ta-hsien hsiu-chen yen-I* [Exposition of cultivating the essence by the great immortal of the purple gold splendor], in R. H. Van Gulik, *Erotic Colour Prints of the Ming Period*, trans. in Wile, p. 137.
12. Chinese source from *Sunü miao lun* (The wondrous discourse of Sunü), trans. in Wile, *Art of the Bedchamber*, p. 128.
13. Wing-Tsit Chan (trans.), *A Source Book in Chinese Philosophy*, p. 56.
14. Paul S. Ropp, "Ambiguous Images of Courtesan Culture in Late Imperial China," in Widmer and Chang, *Writing Women in Late Imperial China*, p. 17.
15. Susan Naquin and Evelyn Rawski, *Chinese Society in the Eighteenth Century* (New Haven: Yale University Press, 1987), p. 80.
16. Naquin and Rawski, *Chinese Society in the Eighteenth Century*, p. 110.
17. Ibid., p. 109.

18. Ropp, "Ambiguous Images of Courtesan Culture in Late Imperial China," p. 43.
19. Ibid., pp. 18–19.
20. Robert Hans van Gulik, *Sexual Life in Ancient China*, trans. by Li Xiaochen and Guo Xiaohui (Shanghai: Shanghai People's Press, 1990), p. 287.
21. Dorothy Ko, *Every Step a Lotus: Shoes for Bound Feet* (Berkeley: University of California Press, 2001), p. 52.
22. Ibid., p. 54.
23. Ko writes, "the materials and tools needed were not specialized gadgets but everyday items already in use in the women's rooms. These include such sewing implements as scissors, needles, and thread—the former for trimming the toenails and the latter for sealing the binders tight. The binding cloth would have been woven afresh. For adult women the average size of the cloth is about 10 cm wide by 4 meters long (4 inches by 13 feet), but the length varies. Women wove the cloth and stored it in a roll, like fresh bandages, ready to be torn off at the desired length." Ibid., p. 54.
24. Shu Nu Wang 王書奴 , *Zhongguo chang ji shi* 中國娼妓史 [History of Chinese prostitutes] (Shanghai: Shenghuo Press,1935), pp. 312–314.
25. Ropp, "Ambiguous Images of Courtesan Culture in Late Imperial China," pp. 22–23.
26. Harriet Zurndorfer, "Prostitutes and Courtesans in the Confucian Moral Universe of Late Ming China (1550–1644)," *International Review of Social History* 56 (2011), p. 202.
27. Wu Hung, "Beyond Stereotypes: The Twelve Beauties in Qing Court Art and the Dreams of the Red Chamber" in Widmer and Chang (eds.), *Writing Women in Late Imperial China*, pp. 306–365.
28. Ibid., p. 326.
29. See Wu's analysis of Wei Yong's (fl. 1643–1654) literary work "Delight in Adornment," in ibid., pp. 325-6.
30. See Wu's translation of *Tanji congshu* (first published by Zhuo Wang and Chao Zhang in 1695, republished in Shanghai: Guji chubanshe, 1993), pp. 141–142, in Widmer and Chang (eds.), *Writing Women in Late Imperial China*, pp. 338–339.
31. Ibid., p. 350.
32. Ibid., p. 363.
33. See Beverly Bossler, *Courtesans, Concubines, and the Cult of Female Fidelity: Gender and Social Change in China, 1000–1400* (Cambridge, MA: Harvard University Asia Center, 2012).

34. Widmer and Chang (eds.), *Writing Women in Late Imperial China*, pp. 19–29.
35. Ibid., p. 29.
36. The Chinese name of the poem is "Tan wugeng," written by Guangsheng Hua in the early nineteenth century, in Ropp, "Ambiguous Images of Courtesan Culture in Late Imperial China," pp. 39–40.
37. Battersby, *The Phenomenal Woman*, pp. 20–21.
38. Susan R. Suleiman(ed.), *The Female Body in Western Culture: Contemporary Perspectives* (Cambridge, MA: Harvard University Press, 1986), p. 7.
39. Naomi Wolf, *The Beauty Myth: How Images of Beauty Are Used Against Women* (New York: Anchor Books, 1992), pp. 13–14.
40. Ibid., pp. 59–60.
41. Ibid., p. 60.
42. Excerpt cited from Bao Mingxin, *Shizhuang biaoyan yishu* 時裝表演藝術 [Fashion show artistry] (Shanghai: China Textile University Press, 1997), p. 29.
43. Susan Kaiser, *The Social Psychology of Clothing* (New York: Macmillan, 1990), p. 488.
44. As Naomi Wolf pointed out, whereas modern women are growing, moving, and expressing their individuality, "beauty" is by definition inert, timeless, and generic. Wolf, *The Beauty Myth*, pp. 16–17.
45. Battersby, *The Phenomenal Woman*, p. 23.

10 Beauty and the State: Literati Fantasy, Iron Girls, and the Olympics Hoopla

This article is a revised version of my article, "Beauty and the State: Female Bodies as State Apparatus and Recent Beauty Discourses in China," published in *Beauty Unlimited*, edited by Peggy Zeglin Brand (Bloomington: Indiana University Press, 2013), pp. 368–384.

1. Gordon B. Forbes, Linda L. Collinsworth, Rebecca L. Jobe, et al. "Sexism, Hostility toward Women, and Endorsement of Beauty Ideals and Practices: Are Beauty Ideals Associated with Oppressive Beliefs?" *Sex Roles* 56 (2007), pp. 265–266. Retrieved from http://dx.doi.org/10.1007/s11199-006-9161-5.
2. Forbes et al., "Sexism, Hostility toward Women, and Endorsement of Beauty Ideals and Practices," p. 273.
3. Guo Haiwen, "The Cultural Explanation on Evolution of Chinese Women's

Beauty in the 20th Century," *Chinese Women College Journal* 1 (2008), pp. 107–111.

4. Susan Brownell and Jeffrey Wasserstrom (ed.), *Chinese Femininities/ Chinese Masculinities* (Los Angeles: University of California Press, 2002), p. 438.
5. Ibid., p. 441.
6. Gao Yunxiang, "Nationalist and Feminist Discourses on *Jianmei* (Robust Beauty) during China's 'National Crisis' in the 1930s," in *Translating Feminisms in China*, edited by Dorothy Ko and Wang Zheng (Malden, MA: Blackwell, 2007), pp. 104–130.
7. Ibid., p. 104.
8. Ibid., pp. 106–108.
9. Ibid., p. 108.
10. Ibid., p. 111.
11. Ibid., p. 115.
12. Gao quotes Article 4, issued by the national government on the movement, which states, "all customs that hinder the regular physical growth of young men and young women should be strictly prohibited by the countries, municipalities, villages and hamlet; and their programmes should be fixed by the Department of Education and the Training Commissioner's Department." Although this clause was primarily directed at the prevalent rural customs of breast-binding and foot-binding, it was instrumentalized in quite a few other ways. Ibid., pp. 117–118.
13. Ibid., p. 118.
14. Jin Yihong. "Rethinking the 'Iron Girls': Gender and Labour during the Chinese Cultural Revolution," in Ko and Wang (eds.), *Translating Feminisms in China* (Malden, MA: Blackwell, 2007), pp. 188–214.
15. Ibid., p. 194.
16. Both "The White-Haired Girl" (*Bai Maonü,* 1965) and "The Red Detachment of Women" (*Hongse Niangzi Jun*, 1964) were in the standard national ballet repertoire after the founding of the PRC in 1949. Both successfully promoted the socialist agenda of class struggles and political correctness. "The White-Haired Girl" was premiered by the Shanghai Dance Academy in 1965; the eight-act ballet is an adaptation of the Chinese opera of the name that premiered in 1945. It tells of a peasant girl, Xi'er, whose father is beaten to death by the despotic local landlord because he is unable to pay his debts. She is taken by force to work in the landlord's home and finally escapes into the mountain forest. Her fiancé joins the Eighth Route Army and returns three years later to liberate the village and rescue the girl. By then, Xi'er has endured such suffering that her long black hair turns white.

"The Red Detachment of Women" was produced by the Central Ballet of China in 1964. The six-act ballet deals with a Communist-led company of women on Hainan Island during the civil war in the early 1930s. It shows the liberation of a peasant slave girl, who becomes a member of the Communist Party and finally the leader of the company.

17. Rofel, *Desiring China*, p. 111.
18. Ibid., p. 118.
19. Ibid., p. 121.
20. Ibid., p. 111.
21. See Jean Baudrillard, *The Consumer Society: Myths and Structures* (London: Thousand Oaks, 1998).
22. Min Xu and Qian Xiao-feng, "Weight-reducing Advertising and Morbid Slim Culture—On Mass Media's Cultural Control of Women's Bodies," *Collection of Women's Studies* 3: 46 (May 2002), pp. 22–29. The journal is published in China by Hangzhou.
23. Ibid.
24. Rofel, *Desiring* China, p. 57.
25. Ibid., p. 111.
26. Ibid., p. 111.
27. Brownell and Wasserstrom, *Chinese Femininities/Chinese Masculinities*, p. 443.
28. Ibid., p. 8.
29. Ibid., p. 33.
30. Harriet Evans, "Past, Perfect or Imperfect: Changing Images of the Ideal Wife" in Brownell and Wasserstrom (eds.), *Chinese Femininities/Chinese Masculinities*, pp. 335–360.

11 Psychoanalysis and Women's Physiology and Psychopathology in Feudal China: A Case Study by Pan Guangdan

1. Gatens, *Imaginary Bodies: Ethics, Power and Corporeality*, pp. 21–35.
2. Genevieve Lloyd, *The Man of Reason: "Male" and "Female" in Western Philosophy* (London: Methuen, 1984) is an example.
3. Though historical precedents are now reviewed and well discussed, like Howard Chiang (ed.), *Psychiatry and Chinese History* (London: Pickering & Chatto, 2014), which explores historical precedents of medical knowledge about human psychology in late imperial China. The discussion was held

long before Sigmund Freud's discussion of dreams in the twentieth century. One of the evidences turn to a 1636 compendium, *Meng lin xuan jie* 夢林玄解, published in the late Ming dynasty. The volume is regarded as an encyclopedia of dream-related knowledge that predated the introduction of Western psychoanalysis in early twentieth-century China. (See Chiang, *Psychiatry and Chinese History*, p. 2, and Brigid Vance, "Exorcising Dreams and Nightmares in Late Ming China," in the same volume, pp. 17–36).

4. Havelock Ellis, *Psychology of Sex*, trans. Guangdan Pan (Beijing: Joint Publishing, 1987), p. 179.
5. Pan Guangdan. *The Secret of Feng Xiaoqing's Psychopathology, with Commentaries by Xiang Zhen and Shi Bo* (Beijing: Culture and Art Publishing Co., 1990), p. 1.
6. Ibid., publication note.
7. Ibid.
8. Ibid., translator's note, p. 1.
9. Ibid., pp. 114–116.
10. Ibid., publication note.
11. Ellis, *Psychology of Sex*, pp. 2–3.
12. Pan, *The Secret of Feng Xiaoqing's Psychopathology*, p. 1.
13. Ibid., pp. 20–27.
14. Ibid., pp. 20–21.
15. Ibid., p. 42.
16. Ibid., p. 26.
17. Ibid., pp. 29–33.
18. Ibid., p. 31.
19. Ibid., p. 32.
20. Ibid., pp. 33–39.
21. Ibid., pp. 40–43.
22. Ibid., p. 36.
23. Ibid., p. 15.
24. Ibid., p. 16.
25. Ibid., pp. 26, 43–47.
26. Ibid., p. 27.
27. Sigmund Freud, *A General Introduction to Psychoanalysis*, trans. Joan Riviere (New York: Boni & Liveright, 1924), pp. 418–437.
28. Pan, *The Secret of Feng Xiaoqing's Psychopathology*, p. 27.
29. Freud, *A General Introduction to Psychoanalysis*, pp. 352–354.
30. Pan, *The Secret of Feng Xiaoqing's Psychopathology*, pp. 48–50.

31. Hsiu-fen Chen, "Emotional Therapy and Talking Cures in Late Imperial China," in Chiang (ed.), *Psychiatry and Chinese History*, pp. 37–54.
32. Ibid., and see also Chiang's introduction in Chiang, *Psychiatry and Chinese History*, p. 3.
33. Ibid., p. 50.
34. Ibid.
35. Ibid., p. 65.
36. Ibid., pp. 62–67.
37. Havelock Ellis, *Psychology of Sex*. New York/ Toronto: The New American Library, 1933, p. 102.
38. See Mary Crawford and Rhoda Unger, *Women and Gender: A Feminist Psychology*, 3rd ed. (Boston: McGraw-Hill Companies, 2000).
39. Sigmund Freud, *On Narcissism: An Introduction*, trans. James Strachey (London: Hogarth Press, 1962), pp. 88–89.
40. Ibid., p. 90.
41. Li, Qiao. "The Shadow Love of Feng Xiaoqing and Ancient Enquiry in Psychology," in *Zhong he wei yu: Pan Guangdan bai nian dan chen ji nian* 中和位育：潘光旦百年誕辰紀念 [Equilibrium and harmony, order and cultivation: Commemorating the hundred-year anniversary of Pan Guangdan's birth], edited by Pan Naimu (Beijing: Zhongguo Renmindaxue chubanshe, 1999), p. 423.

12 Fashioning Body: Hong Kong Chinese Women, Fashion, and Identity Issues of the Sixties

This chapter is developed from my previous article, "Feminist Aesthetics in Body: Hong Kong Chinese Women, Fashion & Identity in the Sixties," *Anthropos* 28, nos. 3–4 (1996), pp. 55–61.

1. Roland Barthes, *The Fashion System* (New York: Hill and Wang, 1983), p. 243.
2. Matthew Turner, Irene Ngan, and Lydia Ngai (eds.), *Hong Kong Sixties: Designing Identity* (Hong Kong: Hong Kong Arts Centre Press, 1994), p. 5.
3. Kaiser, *The Social Psychology of Clothing*, p. 437.
4. Barthes, *The Fashion System*, p. 243.
5. Naomi Szeto, *Dress in Hong Kong* (Hong Kong: Urban Council, 1992), p. 31.
6. Wu Hao and Committee on Exhibition of Hong Kong Fashion History, *Hong Kong Fashion History* (Hong Kong: Committee on Exhibition of Hong

Kong Fashion History, 1992), p. 36.

7. Kaiser, *The Social Psychology of Clothing*, p. 488.
8. Barthes, *The Fashion System*, pp. 254–256.
9. Kaiser, *The Social Psychology of Clothing*, p. 335.
10. Elizabeth Wilson, *Adorned in Dreams* (Berkeley: University of California Press, 1985), p. 176.
11. Kaiser, *The Social Psychology of Clothing*, p. 430.
12. Homi K. Bhabha, "The World and The Home," *Social Text* 31–32 (1993), pp. 141–153.
13. Vivienne Tam and Martha Huang, *China Chic* (New York: ReganBooks, 2000), p. 262.
14. Ibid., p. 256.

13 Sex and Emotion: The Representation of Chinese Female Sex Workers in Recent Discourses and the Cosmopolitan Context

This chapter is developed from my recently published work, "Sex and Emotion: Change of the Related Discourses among Some Chinese Female Sex Workers and their Representations in the Cosmopolitan Context," *The International Journal of the Humanities* 9, no. 8 (2012), pp. 217–229.

1. Eileen Chang, *Lust, Caution and Other Stories*, translated by Julia Lovell (London: Penguin, 2007).
2. Lau Tin Chi, host of the RTHK radio programme *Free as the Wind*, made the comment shortly after the film was released in Hong Kong.
3. Butler, *Bodies That Matter*, p. 30.
4. Ibid., p. 39.
5. Ibid., p. 8.
6. Gatens, *Imaginary Bodies: Ethics, Power and Corporeality*, pp. 25, 37, and 49.
7. Butler, *Bodies That Matter*, pp. 40–53.
8. Gatens, *Imaginary Bodies: Ethics, Power and Corporeality*, pp. 49–50.
9. See Lloyd, *The Man of Reason*.
10. Elizabeth Grosz, *Volatile Bodies: Toward a Corporeal Feminism* (Indianapolis: Indiana University Press, 1994), p. 14.
11. Gatens, *Imaginary Bodies: Ethics, Power and Corporeality*, p. 203.
12. Ibid., pp. 49–50.
13. Grosz, *Volatile Bodies: Toward a Corporeal Feminism*, pp. 6–7.
14. Ibid., p. 8.

15. Ibid., p. 14.
16. Gatens, *Imaginary Bodies: Ethics, Power and Corporeality*, p. 22.
17. Zurndorfer, "Prostitutes and Courtesans in the Confucian Moral Universe of Late Ming China (1550–1644)," *International Review of Social History* 56 (2011), p. 199.
18. Shen Wenyu, *Hunrupian* (Beijing: Beixin Publishing, 1927).
19. Ibid., p. 23.
20. Ibid., pp. 35–38.
21. Ibid., pp. 47–8.
22. See records in Gail Hershatter, *Dangerous Pleasures: Prostitution and Modernity in Twentieth Century Shanghai*. L.A.: University of California Press, 1997, p. 396.
23. Harriet Zurndorfer, p. 208.
24. Ibid., p. 208.
25. Ibid., p. 209.
26. Arif Dirlik and Zhang Xudong. "Introduction: Postmodernism and China", *Boundary 2* (1997); 24; 3; Academic Research Library, p. 12.
27. Lisa Rofel. *Desiring China: Experiments in Neoliberalism, Sexuality, and Public Culture*. Durham and London: Duke University Press, 2007, p. 111.
28. Ibid.
29. Ibid., p. 112.
30. Ibid., pp. 114–5.
31. Joyce Outshoorn. "Introduction: Prostitution, women's movements and democratic politics" in Joyce Outshoorn (ed.) *The Politics of Prostitution: Women's Movements, Democratic States and the Globalization of Sex Commerce*. UK: Cambridge University Press, 2004, p. 3.
32. Michel Foucault. *The Order of Things*, U.K.: Tavistock, 1970, p. 209.
33. See note xxii, chapter 15 in Hershatter's work on history, memory, and nostalgia of Chinese prostitution.
34. Hershatter, p. 395.
35. Ibid., p. 398.
36. Ibid.

BIBLIOGRAPHY

Alphen, Ernst van. *Francis Bacon and the Loss of Self*. London: Reaktion Books, 1992.

Andrews, Julia. *Painters and Politics in the People's Republic of China, 1949–1979*. Berkeley: University of California Press, 1994.

Arthurs, Jane and Jean Grimshaw. Eds. *Women's Bodies: Discipline and Transgression*. London: Cassell, 1999.

Bao Mingxin, *Shizhuang biaoyan yishu* 時裝表演藝術 [Fashion show artistry]. Shanghai: China Textile University Press, 1997.

Barber, E. W. *Women's Work: The First 20,000 Years*. New York: W. W. Norton & Company, 1995.

Barnhart, Richard M. "Li Kung-lin's Use of Past Styles." In *Artists and Traditions: Uses of the Past in Chinese Culture*, edited by Christian R. Murck. Princeton: Princeton University Art Museum, 1976, pp. 51–71.

Barthes, Roland. *The Fashion System*. New York: Hill and Wang, 1983.

Battersby, Christine. *The Phenomenal Woman: Feminist Metaphysics and the Patterns of Identity*. Cambridge: Polity Press, 1988.

———. "Stages on Kant's Way: Aesthetics, Morality, and the Gendered Sublime." In Brand and Korsmeyer, eds., *Feminism and Tradition in Aesthetics*, pp. 88–114.

Baudrillard, Jean. *The Consumer Society: Myths and Structures.* Thousand Oaks: Sage, 1998.

Berghuis, Thomas J. *Performance Art in China.* Hong Kong: Timezone 8, 2006.

Berleant, Arnold. *Aesthetics Beyond the Arts: New and Recent Essays.* Aldershot: Ashgate Publishing, 2012.

———. *Rethinking Aesthetics.* Aldershot: Ashgate Publishing, 2004.

Berliner, Nancy Z. *Chinese Folk Art: The Small Skills of Carving Insects.* Boston: Little, Brown and Company, 1986.

Bersani, Leo. "Is the Rectum a Grave?" *October 43* (1987), pp. 197–223.

Beuys, Joseph, Gerhard Steidl, and Klaus Staeck. *Honey is Flowing in All Directions.* Heidelberg: Edition Staeck, 1997.

Bhabha, Homi K. "The World and The Home." *Social Text* 31–32 (1993), pp. 141–153.

Blue, Adrienne. *On Kissing: Travels in an Intimate Landscape.* New York: Kodansha International, 1997.

Bossler, Beverly J. *Courtesans, Concubines, and the Cult of Female Fidelity.* Cambridge, MA: Harvard University Asia Center, 2013.

Brand, Peggy Zeglin, and Carolyn Korsmeyer. Eds. *Feminism and Tradition in Aesthetics.* University Park: Pennsylvania State University Press, 1995.

Bray, Francesca. *Technology and Gender: Fabrics of Power in Late Imperial China.* Berkeley: University of California Press, 1997.

Brighton, Andrew. *Francis Bacon.* London: Tate Gallery Publishing, 2001.

Brook, Barbara. *Feminist Perspectives on the Body.* New York: Pearson Education, 1999.

Brownell, Susan, and Wasserstrom, Jeffrey. Eds. *Chinese Femininities/ Chinese Masculinities.* Los Angeles: University of California Press, 2002.

Butler, Judith. *Bodies That Matter.* New York: Routledge, 1993.

Cahill, James. *Compelling Image: Nature and Style in Seventeenth-century Chinese Painting.* Cambridge, MA: Harvard University Press, 1982.

Chan, Wing-Tsit. *A Source Book in Chinese Philosophy.* Princeton: Princeton University Press, 1963.

Chang, Eileen. *Lust, Caution and Other Stories.* Translated by Julia Lovell. London: Penguin, 2007.

Chen, Hsiu-fen. "Emotional Therapy and Talking Cures in Late Imperial China." In Chiang, ed., *Psychiatry and Chinese History*, pp. 37–54.

Cheng, Chung-ying. *New Dimensions of Confucian and Neo-Confucian Philosophy.* Albany: State University of New York Press, 1991.

Chiang, Howard. Ed. *Psychiatry and Chinese History.* London: Pickering & Chatto, 2014.

Clark, Kenneth. *The Nude: A Study in Ideal Form.* Princeton: Princeton University Press, 1956.

Crawford, Mary, and Rhoda Unger. *Women and Gender: A Feminist Psychology.* 3rd ed. Boston, MA: McGraw-Hill, 2000.

Dirlik, Arif, and Zhang Xudong. *Postmodernism and China.* Durham, NC: Duke University Press, 2000.

Druck, Patricia, and Inka Schube. Eds. *Social Creatures. How Body Becomes Art.* Hannover: Sprengel Museum, 2004.

Ellis, Havelock. *Psychology of Sex.* New York: The New American Library, 1933.

———. *Psychology of Sex*, trans. Guangdan Pan. Beijing: Joint Publishing, 1987.

Evans, Harriet. "Past, Perfect or Imperfect: Changing Images of the Ideal Wife." In Brownell and Wasserstrom, eds., *Chinese Femininities/ Chinese Masculinities*, pp. 335–360.

Fong, Grace. "Female Hands: Embroidery as a Knowledge Field in Women's Everyday Life in Late Imperial and Early Republican China." Paper presented at the International Symposium on *Daily Life, Knowledge, and Chinese Modernities*, Institute of Modern History, Academia Sinica, Taipei, Republic of China, November 21–23, 2002.

Forbes, Gordon B., Linda L. Collinsworth, Rebecca L. Jobe et al. "Sexism, Hostility toward Women, and Endorsement of Beauty Ideals and Practices: Are Beauty Ideals Associated with Oppressive Beliefs?" *Sex Roles* 56 (2007), pp. 265–266. http://dx.doi.org/10.1007/s11199-006-9161-5.

Foucault, Michel. *The Order of Things.* London: Tavistock, 1970.

Freud, Sigmund. *A General Introduction to Psychoanalysis.* Translated by Joan Riviere. New York: Boni & Liveright, 1924.

———. *On Narcissism: An Introduction*. Translated by James Strachey. London: Hogarth Press, 1962.

Frost, Liz. "Doing Looks: Women, Appearance and Mental Health." In Arthurs and Grimshaw, eds., *Women's Bodies: Discipline and Transgression*, pp. 117–135.

Furth, Charlotte. *A Flourishing Yin: Gender in China's Medical History 960–1665*. Berkeley: University of California Press, 1999.

Gao Minglu 高名潞 . *Qiang: Zhongguo dangdai yishu de lishi yu bianjie* 牆：中國當代藝術的歷史與邊界 [The wall: Reshaping contemporary Chinese art]. Beijing: Zhongguo Renmindaxue chubanshe, 2006, pp. 256–272.

Gao, Yunxiang. "Nationalist and Feminist Discourses on *Jianmei* (Robust Beauty) during China's 'National Crisis' in the 1930s." In *Translating Feminisms in China*, edited by Dorothy Ko and Wang Zheng. Malden, MA: Blackwell, 2007, pp. 104–130.

Gatens, Moira. *Imaginary Bodies: Ethics, Power and Corporeality*. London: Routledge, 1996.

———. "Power, Bodies and Difference." In Price and Shildrick, eds., *Feminist Theory and the Body: A Reader*, pp. 227–234.

Göttner-Abendroth, Heide. "Nine Principles of a Matriarchal Aesthetic." In *Feminist Aesthetics*, edited by Gisela Ecker, translated by Harriet Anderson. Boston: Beacon Press, 1985, pp. 81–94.

Grosz, Elizabeth. "Psychoanalysis and the Body." In Price and Shildrick, eds., *Feminist Theory and the Body: A Reader*, pp. 267–271.

———. *Volatile Bodies: Toward a Corporeal Feminism*. Indianapolis: Indiana University Press, 1994.

Gould, Timothy. "Intensity and Its Audiences: Toward a Feminist Perspective on the Kantian Sublime." In Brand and Korsmeyer, eds., *Feminism and Tradition in Aesthetics*, pp. 66–87.

Gulik, Robert Hans van. *Sexual Life in Ancient China*. Translated by Li Xiaochen and Guo Xiaohui. Shanghai: Shanghai People's Press, 1990.

Guo, Haiwen. "The Cultural Explanation on Evolution of Chinese Women's Beauty in the 20th Century." *Chinese Women College Journal* 1 (2008), pp. 107–111.

He, Chengyao 何成瑤 . "Lift the Cover from Your Head" 掀起你的蓋頭來. *Cruel/ Loving Bodies* 酷 / 愛身體 . Shanghai: Shanghai Duolun Museum of Modern Art. 2006, pp. 26–28.

He Liu, Lydia, Rebecca E. Karl, and Dorothy Ko. *The Birth of Chinese Feminism: Essential Texts in Transnational Theory.* New York: Columbia University Press, 2013.

Hein, Hilde, and Carolyn Korsmeyer. Eds. *Aesthetics in Feminist Perspective.* Bloomington: Indiana University Press, 1993.

Hershatter, Gail. *Dangerous Pleasures: Prostitution and Modernity in Twentieth Century Shanghai.* Los Angeles: University of California Press, 1997.

Hershatter, Gail, Christina Gilmartin, Lisa Rofel, and Tyrene White. *Engendering China: Women, Culture, and the State.* Cambridge, MA: Harvard University Press, 1994.

Holloway, Kenneth W. *Guodian: The Newly Discovered Seeds of Chinese Religious and Political Philosophy.* Oxford: Oxford University Press, 2009.

Hung, Wu. "Beyond Stereotypes: The Twelve Beauties in Qing Court Art and the *Dream of the Red Chamber.*" In Widmer and Chang, *Writing Women in Late Imperial China*, pp. 306–365.

Jin, Yihong. "Rethinking the 'Iron Girls': Gender and Labour during the Chinese Cultural Revolution." In *Translating Feminisms in China*, edited by Dorothy Ko and Zheng Wang, trans. Kimberley Manning and Lianyun Chu. Oxford: Blackwell, 2007, pp. 188–214.

Jones, Amelia. *Body Art/ Performing the Subject.* Minneapolis: University of Minnesota Press, 1998.

Jullien, François. *The Impossible Nude: Chinese Art and Western Aesthetics.* Chicago: University of Chicago Press, 2007.

Kaiser, Susan. *The Social Psychology of Clothing.* New York: Macmillan, 1990.

Kant, Immanuel. *Critique of Judgment*, translated by Werner S. Pluhar. Indianapolis: Hackett, 1987.

———. *Observations on the Feeling of the Beautiful and Sublime*, translated by J. T. Goldthwait. Berkeley: University of California Press, 1960. Originally published 1764.

Katchadourian, Herant A., and Donald T. Lunde. *Fundamentals of Human Sexuality.* 3rd ed. New York: Holt, Rinehart and Winston, 1975.

Keswick, Maggie. *The Chinese Garden: History, Art and Architecture.* Cambridge, MA: Harvard University Press, 2003.

Kneller, Jane. "Discipline and Silence: Women and Imagination in Kant's Theory of Taste." In Hein and Korsmeyer, eds., *Aesthetics in Feminist Perspective*, pp. 179–192.

Ko, Dorothy. *Cinderella's Sisters: A Revisionist History of Footbinding.* Berkeley: University of California Press, 2005.

———. *Every Step a Lotus: Shoes for Bound Feet.* Berkeley: University of California Press, 2001.

———. *Teachers of the Inner Chambers: Women and Culture in Seventeenth-Century China.* Stanford: Stanford University Press, 1994.

Ko, Dorothy, JaHyun Kim Haboush, and Joan R Piggott. Eds. *Women and Confucian Cultures in Premodern China, Korea, and Japan.* Berkeley: University of California Press, 2003.

Ko, Dorothy, and Zheng Wang. Eds. *Translating Feminisms in China: A Special Issue of Gender and History.* Malden, MA: Blackwell, 2007.

Kohn, Livia. *Zhuangzi: Text and Context.* St. Petersburg, FL: Three Pines Press, 2014.

Kuriyama, Shigehisa. *The Expressiveness of the Body and the Divergence of Greek and Chinese Medicine.* New York: Zone Books, 1999.

Laqueur, Thomas. *Making Sex: Body and Gender from the Greeks to Freud.* Cambridge, MA: Harvard University Press.

Legge, James. *The Chinese Classics*, Vol. 4. London: Hong Kong University Press, 1960.

Li, Qiao. "The Shadow Love of Feng Xiaoqing and Ancient Enquiry in Psychology." In *Zhong he wei yu: Pan Guangdan bai nian dan chen ji nian* 中和位育：潘光旦百年誕辰紀念 [Equilibrium and harmony, order and cultivation: Commemorating the hundred-year anniversary of Pan Guangdan's birth]. Edited by Pan Naimu. Beijing: Zhongguo Renmindaxue chubanshe, 1999.

Lloyd, Genevieve. *The Man of Reason: "Male" and "Female" in Western Philosophy.* London: Methuen, 1984.

Man, Eva K. W. "Beauty and the State: Female Bodies as State Apparatus and Recent Beauty Discourses in China." In *Beauty Unlimited*, edited by Peggy Zeglin Brand. Bloomington: Indiana University Press, 2013, pp. 368–384.

———. "Chinese Philosophy and the Suggestion of a New Aesthetics." *Journal of Chinese Philosophy* 23 (1996), pp. 453–466.

———. "Expression Extreme and History Trauma in Female Bodily Art in China: The Case of He Cheng Yao." In *Subversive Strategies in Contemporary Chinese Art*, edited by Mary Bittner Wiseman and Liu Yuedi. Leiden: Brill Academic Publishing, 2011, pp. 171–191.

———. "Female Bodily Aesthetics and Their Early Revelations in the Book of Songs." In *Overt and Covert Treasures: Essays on the Sources for Chinese Women's History*, edited by Clara Ho. Hong Kong: Chinese University of Hong Kong, 2012, pp. 113–130.

———. "Female Bodily Aesthetics, Politics, and Feminine Ideals of Beauty in China." In *Beauty Matters*, edited by Peggy Zeglin Brand. Bloomington: Indiana University Press, 2000, pp. 169–196.

———. "Reclaiming the Body: Francis Bacon's Fugitive Bodies and Confucian Aesthetics on Bodily Expression." *Contemporary Aesthetics* 2 (2004), pp. 621–631.

———. "Sex and Emotion: Change of the Related Discourses among Some Chinese Female Sex Workers and their Representations in the Cosmopolitan Context." *The International Journal of the Humanities* 9, no. 8 (2012), pp. 217–229.

———. "Some Reflections on the Notion of Feminist Aesthetics." Paper presented at the Fourteenth Congress of the International Association of Empirical Aesthetics, held in Prague, August 1996.

Mann, Susan, and Yu-Yin Cheng. Eds. *Under Confucian Eyes: Writings on Gender in Chinese History.* Berkeley: University of California Press, 2001.

Margolis, Joseph. *Pragmatism Without Foundations.* New York: Basil Blackwell, 1986.

Martyna, Renee. "Whither Global Feminism?" Carleton University, 2007. http://www.carleton.ca/e-merge/docs_vol3/articles/Whither_Global_Feminism.pdf.

Mi Xie'er 米歇爾, Liu Beicheng 劉北成, and Yang Yuanyi 楊遠嬰. Trans. *Fu Ke: Fengdian yu wenming* [Foucault's *Madness and Civilization*]. Beijing: Sanlian shudian, 2003.

Millet, Nick. "The Fugitive Body: Bacon's Fistula." In *The Body*, edited by Andrew Benjamin. London: Academy Editions, 1993, pp. 40–51.

Mou Zongsan 牟宗三. *Intellectual Intuition and Chinese Philosophy* 智的直覺與中國哲學. Taipei: Commercial Press, 1974.

Naquin, Susan, and Evelyn Rawski. *Chinese Society in the Eighteenth Century.* New Haven: Yale University Press, 1987.

Nietzsche, Friedrich Wilhelm. *The Gay Science with a Prelude in Rhymes and Appendix of Songs*, translated with commentary by Walter Kaufmann. New York: Vintage Books, 1974.

———. *Thus Spoke Zarathustra: A Book For Everyone And No One*, translated with a new introduction by R. J. Hollingdale. Harmondsworth: Penguin Books, 1969.

———. *Twilight of The Idols and The Anti-Christ,* translated with an introduction and commentary by R. J. Hollingdale. Harmondsworth: Penguin Books, 1968.

Outshoorn, Joyce. "Introduction: Prostitution, Women's Movements and Democratic Politics." In *The Politics of Prostitution: Women's Movements, Democratic States and the Globalization of Sex Commerce*, edited by Joyce Outshoorn. Cambridge: Cambridge University Press, 2004, pp. 1–20.

Owen, Stephen. "Foreword." In *The Book of Songs: The Ancient Chinese Classic of Poetry*, translated by Arthur Waley, with additional translations by Joseph R. Allen. New York: Grove Press, 1996.

Pagnes, Andrea. "Body Issues in Performance Art: Between Theory and Praxis." http://www.artandeducation.net/paper/body-issues-in-performance-art-between-theory-and-praxis. Retrieved on Oct. 15, 2015.

Pan, Guangdan. *The Secret of Feng Xiaoqing's Psychopathology, with Commentaries by Xiang Zhen and Shi Bo.* Beijing: Culture and Art Publishing,1990.

Pateman, Carole. *The Sexual Contract.* Cambridge: Polity Press, 1988.

Price, Janet, and Margrit Shildrick. Eds. *Feminist Theory and the Body: A Reader.* New York: Routledge, 1999.

Riley, Denise. "Bodies, Identities, Feminisms." In Price and Shildrick, eds., *Feminist Theory and the Body: A Reader*, pp. 220–226.

Rofel, Lisa. *Desiring China: Experiments in Neoliberalism, Sexuality, and Public Culture*. Durham, NC: Duke University Press, 2007.

Ropp, Paul S. "Ambiguous Images of Courtesan Culture in Late Imperial China." In *Writing Women in Late Imperial China*, edited by Ellen Widmer and Kang-i Sun Chang. Stanford: Stanford University Press, 1997, pp. 17–45.

Ruan, Fangfu. *Sex in China: Studies in Sexology in Chinese Culture*. New York: Plenum Press, 1991.

Saussy, Haun. *The Problem of A Chinese Aesthetic*. Stanford: Stanford University Press, 1993.

Shen, Wenyu. *Hunrupian*. Beijing: Beixin Publishing, 1927.

Steele, Valerie, and John S. Major. *China Chic: East Meets West*. New Haven: Yale University Press, 1999.

Suleiman, Susan R. Ed. *The Female Body in Western Culture: Contemporary Perspectives*. Cambridge, MA: Harvard University Press, 1986.

Sullivan, Michael. *The Arts of China*. Berkeley: University of California Press, 1984.

Szeto, Naomi. *Dress in Hong Kong*. Hong Kong: Urban Council, 1992.

Tam, Vivienne, and Martha Huang. *China Chic*. New York: ReganBooks, 2000.

Tang Junyi 唐君毅. *Zhongguo wenhua zhi jingshen jiazhi* 中國文化之精神價值 [The spirit of Chinese culture]. Taipei: Zheng Zhong Publishing, 1979.

———. *Lun Zhongguoren wen jingshen* 論中國人文精神 [Spiritual values of Chinese culture]. Taipei: Cheng Chung Bookstores, 1987.

Theiss, Janet. *Disgraceful Matters: The Politics of Chastity in Eighteenth-Century China*. Berkeley: University of California Press, 2005.

Turner, Matthew, Irene Ngan, and Lydia Ngai. Eds. *Hong Kong Sixties: Designing Identity*. Hong Kong: Hong Kong Arts Centre Press, 1994.

Vitiello, Giovanni. *The Libertine's Friend: Homosexuality and Masculinity in Late Imperial China*. Chicago: University of Chicago Press, 2011.

Wang, Robin R. *Yinyang: The Way of Heaven and Earth in Chinese Thought and Culture.* Cambridge: Cambridge University Press, 2012.

Wang, Shunu. *Zhongguo changji shi* [History of Chinese prostitutes]. Shanghai: Shenghuo Press, 1935.

Wang Yarong. *Chinese Folk Embroidery.* London: Thames and Hudson, 1987.

Ware, James R. *The Sayings of Mencius.* Taipei: Confucius Publishing, 1970.

Waugh, Joanne B. "Analytic Aesthetics and Feminist Aesthetics: Neither/Nor?" In Brand and Korsmeyer, eds., *Feminism and Tradition in Aesthetics*, pp. 399–415.

Weidner, Marsha Smith. "Women in the History of Chinese Painting." In *Views From Jade Terrace: Chinese Women Artists 1300–1912*, edited by Marsha Smith Weidner. Indianapolis: Indianapolis Museum of Art, 1988, pp. 13–30.

Widmer, Ellen, and Kang-I Sun Chang. *Writing Women in Late Imperial China.* Stanford: Stanford University Press, 1997.

Wile, Douglas. *Art of the Bedchamber: The Chinese Sexual Yoga Classics Including Women's Solo Meditation Texts.* Albany: State University of New York Press, 1992.

Wilhelm, Richard, and Cary F. Baynes. Trans. *I-Ching, or Book of Changes.* Princeton: Princeton University Press,1950.

Wilson, Elizabeth. *Adorned in Dreams: Fashion and Modernity.* Berkeley: University of California Press, 1985.

Wolf, Naomi. *The Beauty Myth: How Images of Beauty Are Used Against Women.* New York: Anchor Books, 1992.

Wu, Hao, and Committee on Exhibition of Hong Kong Fashion History. *Hong Kong Fashion History.* Hong Kong: Committee on Exhibition of Hong Kong Fashion History, 1992.

Wu, Kuang-ming. *On Chinese Body Thinking: A Cultural Hermeneutic.* Leiden: Brill, 1997.

Xu Min and Qian Xiao-feng. "Weight-reducing Advertising and Morbid Slim Culture—On Mass Media's Cultural Control of Women's Bodies." *Collection of Women's Studies* 3: 46 (May 2002), pp. 22–29.

Young, Iris. *Throwing Like a Girl and Other Essays in Feminist Philosophy and Social Theory.* Indianapolis: Indiana University Press, 1990.

Zito, Angela, and Tani Barlow. Eds., *Body, Subject, and Power in China*. Chicago: University of Chicago Press, 1994.

Zhu Qi, Yao Juichung, and Fumio Nanjo. *Spellbound Aura: The New Vision of Chinese Photography*. Taipei: Contemporary Art Foundation, 2004.

Zurndorfer, Harriet. "Prostitutes and Courtesans in the Confucian Moral Universe of Late Ming China (1550–1644)." *International Review of Social History* 56 (2011), pp. 197–216.

INDEX